S0-BBR-223

Brown and Rosanne!
Great to be with
you.

Yours, McKinley

LIVING WITH MUSLIMS
An American Family Of Seven—
34 Years With Muslims In Their Land

JIM MCKINLEY

CHICAGO SPECTRUM PRESS
LOUISVILLE, KENTUCKY 40207

Copyright © 2007 by James F. McKinley, Jr.

 CHICAGO SPECTRUM PRESS
4824 BROWNSBORO CENTER
LOUISVILLE, KENTUCKY 40207
502-899-1919

All rights reserved. Except for appropriate use in critical reviews or works of
scholarship, the reproduction or use of this work in any form or by any electronic,
mechanical, or other means now known or hereafter invented, including photo-
copying and recording, and in any information storage and retrieval system, is
forbidden without written permission of the author.

Printed in the U.S.A.

10 9 8 7 6 5 4 3 2 1

ISBN: 1-58374-172-0
        978-1-58374-172-6

With great help from
Mary Clifford
and
Vicki Bierman

LOCATION OF BANGLADESH

CONTENTS

FOREWORD 7
DEDICATION 9
  A Special Thanks.. 10
PREFACE 13
INTRODUCTION 25

CHAPTER ONE
One Year of Language Study in Dhaka............................ 43
CHAPTER TWO
Three Years in Comilla 50
CHAPTER THREE
Learning to Live with Feni Muslims 61
CHAPTER FOUR
Difficult Days in Feni... 71
CHAPTER FIVE
A Wedding, a West Pakistani, and Our Muslim Visitors................. 86
CHAPTER SIX
What to Do? At Least 300,000 People Had Died 95
CHAPTER SEVEN
War Begins — Maybe Three Million People Will Die 111
CHAPTER EIGHT
Traveling over 100 Miles in Thirty-Six Hours 126
CHAPTER NINE
Dhaka — A Place of Security! 138
CHAPTER TEN
Traveling in War-Torn Land.. 154
CHAPTER ELEVEN
Assurance in the Midst of Chaos 164
CHAPTER TWELVE
Travel to Pabna and the Feni Tough Captain 173
CHAPTER THIRTEEN
A New Muslim Friend 185
CHAPTER FOURTEEN
Two Young Men and a Muslim Village 194
CHAPTER FIFTEEN
A Pleasant but Partly Difficult Trip
to the Tidal Wave Disaster Area....................................... 204

CHAPTER SIXTEEN
Final Days of War for Independence in Bangladesh 210
CHAPTER SEVENTEEN
Unwelcomed in Feni, Our Home 226
CHAPTER EIGHTEEN
Struggling in the New Country 234
CHAPTER NINETEEN
Tragedy to My Family and to Others 248
CHAPTER TWENTY
Meeting the Bangladeshi President 260
CHAPTER TWENTY-ONE
Driving in Bangladesh 270
CHAPTER TWENTY- TWO
Peace-Time Difficult Days
A Messy Situation but Good Results 279
CHAPTER TWENTY-THREE
The Good and the Bad 285

AFTERWORD
    Part One 300
    Part Two
        To Muslim People Across The World I Kindly Write
        The Following 305
    Part Three
        To The Western World 308
    Part Four
        So, Where Does All Of This Leave Us? 311

BOOKS ON ISLAM OR ABOUT ISLAM 313

FOREWORD

How does one even begin to describe Jim McKinley? Let me make the attempt: missionary par excellence; lover of the human race; a zealot for bringing people to Jesus; humble, but not obsequiously so; unrivaled energy; fearless; and a man whom I have been privileged to call a friend for forty-five years.

Few American missionaries have incarnated their life in a Muslim culture for over three decades. What a challenge to watch Jim at close range for twenty of those years. I was repeatedly awed as I observed this human dynamo in action. It would be my considered opinion that Jim never refused a request for assistance from anyone. His selflessness is the stuff of legends in Bangladesh.

During the 1971 Bangladesh civil war I walked with him for twenty miles in searing April heat. What I saw was a man with a mission. No obstacle could restrain him from his goal of reaching his beloved missionary colleagues. We observed scores of burning houses along the road. Bengalis told us of slaughtered families and beautiful young girls who had been raped. Jim's passion and compassion filtered through the Stygian darkness of man's brutality as a full moon pierces the blackness of night.

Because of various circumstances, Jim's colleagues had evacuated Dhaka at the commencement of the War of Independence. They had left house keys and mission valuables in my possession for temporary safekeeping. When Jim, Betty and their four children were finally able to reach Dhaka, they were physically and emotionally exhausted. Jim appeared at our front door to request keys to the now-empty mission homes. "Jim," I said, "will you be leaving soon for the States?" With a pained but determined look flashing across his sunburned face, he forcefully blurted out, "Not unless we are compelled to." And remain the family did, for the complete nine months of the genocide.

Read this book and capture the heart of a man who with his family walked (and at times ran) through the crucible of pain, perplexity, and fatigue. There is no missionary on Earth that I admire more than Jim McKinley.

> To God be the glory.
> Phil Parshall
> SIM
> Charlotte, NC

DEDICATION

Thousands of the kindest of people have prayed for my immediate family through the years and many of those surely are worthy of having this book, *Living With Muslims*, dedicated to them but I also am sure that those good people expect me to dedicate it to my family.

As sincerely as possible, I dedicate *Living With Muslims* to Betty, Cherie, Kathy, Keith, Wade and Jill. Without them there surely would not be any such book. So, to them, my Big Six, I dedicate *Living With Muslims.*

Today, January 24, 2006, is Betty's birthday and her physical therapist has just departed our residence here in Louisville, Kentucky. Two weeks ago, Betty had a knee replacement and certainly I am her primary care-taker but others do help. If the two of us hang around until August 20, 2006, we will celebrate fifty-two years of married life together. You will read about **thirty-four years** of our togetherness in this book.

For sure, the spouses of our children and the eleven grandchildren are very much a part of who Betty and I are, so I must express my gratitude to them for their loving kindness and full support. You will notice that Cherie, as a baby, was with Betty and me when we took that forty-two day journey out to East Pakistan in 1958. For whatever it may be worth, also remember that Cherie, Kathy, Keith and Wade made their journeys back to the United States long before Betty's and my final journey back to the USA. However, can you believe it? Jill, our youngest, graduated from high school in Penang,

Malaysia, only a few weeks before our final return journey back to the "Land that we love," so "one went out with us and one returned with us" thirty-four years later. Therefore, to Betty and our five children, I dedicate this book.

A SPECIAL THANKS

Back in 1978, I wrote some of the stories found in this book but they, though with the same truth as now written, were not sold in bookstores and other business places. And later three more were written and not sold in bookstores either.

The first three books were sold by Highview Baptist Church here in Louisville, Kentucky. So, I thank former Pastor Bill Hancock, Associate Pastor Norman Coe and current Pastor Kevin Ezell for all of their personal help and surely I thank Highview Baptist Church.

Then, more recently, Campbellsville Baptist Church has helped and is helping with the fourth book and I thank former Pastor James Jones and current Pastor Skip Alexander for all of their help as well as thanks to Campbellsville Baptist Church.

Obviously, because of the dedication of this book which you have or will read, you will see that I am deeply thankful to my total family.

And then also, I think it only proper that I express thanks, in a special way, to three of the Southern Baptist couples who served in East Pakistan/Bangladesh at approximately the time Betty and I served. Those families are, Tom and Gloria Thurman, R. T. and Fran Buckley, and James and Guinevere Young. You will read about these three families in this book. As Betty and I now are retired, so are these three former colleague families. It will be many years before the next Southern Baptist missionary will retire after serving a career in Bangladesh. And I must thank every missionary of Southern Baptists in East Pakistan/Bangladesh, who served a long time or even a short time, for their help to me. I say that without hesitation.

There are others to whom I say thanks. One of those mentioned in this book is Phil Parshall and his family. Our paths crossed many times and those crossings were helpful to me.

Through the years, I was closely linked to New Zealand and Australian Baptists. I mention Ray Schaffer (now deceased) of the Australians and Bob Alcorn and Stuart Avery (now deceased) of the New Zealanders. On many occasions, I certainly was deeply involved with these three and their colleagues.

Though we were associated with him for only a short time, I will always be deeply thankful to Leslie Wenger (now deceased) of the British Baptists for his kindness to my family when we much needed extra kindness. I well remember on Sunday morning after we, as a family, made the two-day trip from our home in Feni to Dhaka, how helpful Mr. Wenger, as, we called him, was to us.

And as I stood a long distance away with friend, Mark Tucker, we watched as Mr. Wenger walked up to the soldiers at the Dhaka airport. Mr. Wenger was wearing a much worn jacket and the soldiers stripped him of that jacket and made a ugly search of his body as if he were a suspect and that date was 1971 or during the Bangladesh liberation movement. As Mr. Wenger entered the airport terminal he turned and waved to us. These were Pakistani soldiers and of course, Muslims. Mr. Wenger had come to the then East Pakistan only a few years earlier. In Srirampur, India, where Mr. Wenger had been serving, he had been involved in a heated argument with Hindu radicals. They pushed him so that he stumbled on a Hindu grave and was accused of desecrating that grave and he had to leave India. I cried as Mark Tucker and I watched that kind Christian gentleman enter the terminal.

I strongly believe all Christians should openly acknowledge that in Jesus the Messiah, the Savior and the Lord, we are brothers and sisters. I was asked to lead several Bible studies for a group of European Lutheran missionaries. I loved the time with them and always departed their meetings when they had times for their mission business. But I had noted in their program that at the close of these sessions, they were to observe the Lord's Supper. So, just before I gave the final Bible study, I told the leader I would depart before they observed that holy occasion. His answer was, "But we want you to lead us in observing the Lord's Supper." Thanks to these Lutheran brothers and sisters for that kindness to me.

Among missionary friends I must also say a "thank you" to Calvin Olson and Ron Peck of the Assemblies of God. They were my friends as were many of their colleagues.

Though there are many others about whom or to whom I should say thanks, I must mention four administrators of the International Mission Board of Southern Baptists. Those four were the 'regional directors' under whom I served during those almost thirty-four years. They are Dr. Winston Crawley, Dr. J. D. Hughey, Dr. Bill Wakefield and Dr. Jerry Rankin.

Lest I be corrected by someone, before I write it, let me say that each of those four had to be most tolerant of me through the years. At least I felt I gave them added difficulties though they were my bosses. They had to be kind, gracious persons to keep me somewhat in a position of a servant missionary. Thanks to these four well-trained, gracious gentlemen for letting me serve out my career under them.

Through my years as an international missionary, it was never necessary for me to ask for financial support from anyone. That was the responsibility of the International Mission Board who depended on the churches of the Southern Baptist Convention. Those churches and that Board did their job very well.

As much as is humanly possible to express that thanks, "Thanks millions especially to those churches."

PREFACE

For about one year, I had been struggling with the title of a book that I hoped to write. As time flew by, I contemplated using the title *Living Among Muslims*. However, I was never satisfied with that title.

Then, one night in our home following dinner, the subject of my attempting to write seemed to become an interest of one of our dinner guests. One family with children departed earlier so that left Betty and me with a couple whose children were not present in our home that evening.

With two men and two women remaining, we had two animated subjects going. I wanted the gentleman with whom I was participating in conversation to help me with the subject for the book I was even then attempting to write. So I told him about the possibility of the two titles with one being *Living Among Muslims* and the other one *Living With Muslims*. My friend did not hesitate to give me his opinion. He said something like this: "From what I know about your family, when you served for thirty-four years overseas, you as a family certainly did live with Muslims."

My opinion was that I should carefully consider what that friend had said. So, within a few days I was writing the title *Living With Muslims*. Beyond my friend's help, I began thinking of some experiences which might give me more assurance with that title. One experience was when airplanes of the Pakistani Air Force struck the little town where my family was living. After those planes made several attacks, I ran downtown to the main streets of Feni, East Pakistan. What I witnessed was horrible to view. The date was April

6, 1971. The people of East Pakistan had rebelled against the control of the national government of Pakistan. Pakistan then made its military attack on the people the night of March 25, 1971. Though we as a family continued living as we had for the past more than seven years, we knew that sooner or later some kind of attack was to happen in Feni.

I did all I could to help by carrying bodies to the little hospital. I knew that with only one doctor for most of those people sufficient help was impossible. But on several occasions that late afternoon I heard local people say to me, "Sir, we are glad you are with us."

Thinking of that experience reminded me that the title *Living With Muslims* was okay. But thinking back to those difficult days I remembered thinking of what might happen to us and others of our little town of about twenty-five thousand people. Some of my thinking, of course, was about my family and what might happen to us. We were six in number. Betty and I were among the fortunate parents. We had two sons and two daughters. The two daughters were older and in many respects acted like second parents to those two little boys. The older of the two boys was less than one year old when we had first moved to Feni in 1964. The other son had been born in January, 1966.

This was our home. We were Christian missionaries and people near and far knew that. We deeply believed in being faithful to our God whom we believed had revealed Himself perfectly through Jesus the Christ. The people of that area of East Pakistan had indicated that they had deep positive feelings toward us even though their religion was different than ours. Our children played with their children. We ate together on many occasions. Now, in 1971, while waiting for what was to happen next, our differences seemed to mostly disappear.

Then, those planes of the Pakistani Air Force struck again. As earlier, many died in the streets. Many, badly wounded, would die later and others would be crippled for the rest of their days.

To indicate how little I understood about war, I told our children that when the Pakistani soldiers came into Feni, I would walk out our front gate and show myself as a foreigner. Months later I learned that when the soldiers entered our town everyone in their sight was shot.

What we were going to do was the question which continually hounded me as a husband and a father of four children. One beautiful offer came to us. A young man whom I did not even know very well came to me and said, "Sir, you must leave this town. The soldiers will come and that could be very bad." This kind gentleman added, "Our family lives some distance from the main roads and we have decided that we want you to come with your family and live in our house for whatever time you like. We will move out and into the house of other greater family members so you will have our house just for your family."

A Muslim family made such a beautiful offer to us as Christian missionaries. I thought long about that kind offer, but I knew we had to get totally out of this area. Later, I told the gentleman that we were going to attempt to make the long journey to the capital city of Dhaka. We declined his gracious offer but after many years, I still well remember what he said to help us and his greater family's kind consideration.

So, I conclude, without doubt, that we did live with Muslims in spirit and in deed and hopefully what you read will confirm that we lived with Muslims.

As I now write I want this book to be informal. I want it to be somewhat as if I were talking with you as the reader. I understand that you can't literally talk back to me but try to feel what I am saying and that will certainly suffice for me and hopefully will cause the book to be more meaningful to you.

When a patriotic American thinks of Muslims today, we most often think of September 11, 2001. The Muslims who attacked our country on that day most certainly had long thought of us as "infidels" and "polytheists." To them we were surely thought of as those who believe in three gods. That day will long be remembered by most Americans. Some will have hatred against those who attacked us and whose leaders continue to cause young men and even occasionally young women to think badly against all Americans and then they act within those beliefs. As I think of those young men and those who sponsored and trained them, I can only pray that the God of Love, the Creator God, the Eternal God and the God who has perfectly revealed Himself as One who loves and gave Himself through Jesus the Christ, wants to give His human creation life's best.

For many Christians, bad feelings are found and deeply settled in their minds. For others of us we find our primary role to be that of praying for all people and living as best we can through God's Spirit so that we can kindly and graciously make Him known to all people. We believe deeply that all people can find a new kind of life through what God has done and does for us.

Often, as my family lives in the United States of America, I hear various descriptions given of Muslim people. Well, I can say that if they as Muslims have any resemblances to Christians, when it comes to variety, then they are not all alike in belief or in behavior. Be prepared to find that I will tell about people who called themselves Muslims, but they acted, often, not with the bad behavior or deeds. While most were good to us as a missionary family, others attempted bad things against us.

But as I write I will always remember, though at times it may not be clear enough, that the God whom I know can change not only beliefs, but behavior.

I will sometimes use fictitious names. But I will not inform you whether or not I am using real names or fictitious ones. The reason for this is that I want to always protect others. So, if there is blame to be given I readily accept that blame. However, to do that, I do not live in fear but I also say that I do not, in any way, want to appear that I am above fear. I usually say that I have often been afraid but that I do not live in fear. But I will add that I try to ignore harmful or possibly harmful blame for anything written. The big thing is I am glad you are reading this book and I hope it will help you as you relate to Muslim people who are now found in probably all countries of the massive world in which we live.

Now I do need to add that I have not usually been a careful student of Islam. However, since September 11, 2001, I have tried to read much on Islam. My books on Islam, as I understand them, are from one direction to the farthest in the opposite direction in religious thinking. Then, I try to read just as many books which are probably considered "middle of the road."

Also, I want to say that I read the Quran in English. Then, at times when I have questions that do not seem clear as I read, I am happy to turn to my special Quran which has one line in Arabic, a second line in Arabic transliteration into Bangla (the language of Bangladesh) and then the final line of the three is in Bangla. If I have any difficulty with the Bangla, after a little work with a Bengali dictionary, I can usually fully understand that translation.

Though I have friends among missionaries and former missionaries who have a good understanding of Islam, I usually do not trouble them by asking for help. I simply work on the subject until it at least begins to become clear to me and when that happens, even though I am moving along in age, I remember quite well. Hence, I give considerable time in now attempting to understand Islam.

Probably the reason I try to learn about Islam this late in life is that so many people seem to be scholars overnight, meaning pretending to be scholars. Sometimes, those people write books as if they were scholars without much study. If I did make any claim to being an Islamic scholar, I probably would write about that religion to clear up many matters which seem to be so unclear to so many. But since I am not in that role, I am especially anxious to read what my friends write.

Now, when you complete your reading of the many stories in this book, you may wonder why I did not attempt to do more writing about witnessing to Muslims. The reason I did not write about that is there are others who are capable of doing that and who will be fair in that writing.

The above paragraph leads me to write the following. I do not hesitate to say that during most of my years of living with Muslims, I did with every opportunity give a positive clear witness to the One who is my personal Lord Jesus the Christ. I loved my life of living for Him in a country which was primarily made up of Muslim people. I deeply believe that any believer in Jesus never wastes a positive witness. Results sometimes are slow but I learned long ago that everything done or thought or said for the glory of the Living God is never wasted. Sometimes, we may not see those results and others miss those results probably more often than we miss them.

This leads to another very personal statement and that is, I always considered myself to be a faithful international Christian missionary. Though like most of you who read what I am writing, I had my share of failures. I declare that my life's first goal was to be faithful to the organization that sponsored my family and me as international missionaries. Then, I always felt my deepest responsibility to be faithful to the believers in Jesus the Christ of the country where I served, and I wanted to be faithful to other international missionary colleagues who served with that same local organization. Finally, in particular I found myself attempting to be faithful to all other international missionaries of Christian groups who served in East Pakistan/Bangladesh.

I know the above paragraph was a massive goal but it is my deep feeling that any person who does not attempt those goals of faithfulness has no claim or rightful claim to be an international missionary. It means you love, have respect for, and constantly make every effort to be a person of the Living God in belief and in deeds of action. This also means we should never seek fame by being abusive. We will take insults and threats and do our best with those.

Sometimes it takes loads of courage to react to seeming abuse to you as a person. I will probably say more about this in one of the regular chapters of this book, but I think it might be helpful to say a part of it now.

Soon after arriving in Feni, East Pakistan in 1964, I discovered that I had been given a name by several groups of young men. It happened like this the first time I heard this ungraciously spoken name. I was walking by myself in an area of the town when suddenly, without any introduction, I heard in the local language, "Hey, red monkey." I primarily thought, "These young men have been set up by radical Muslims." With this in mind I simply kept on walking toward my destination.

However, as time passed, this situation did not trouble me. I could manage those titles but here I am more than forty years later referring to that situation. If I had not been the father of three children at that time, I might have reacted differently. Anyone who has spent much time with children knows that sometimes bad thoughts turn into words so I continued to tolerate this situation.

As an international missionary, I could have made a mess of our presence in Feni. But in such situations, giving time to the One who can solve all problems if He so chooses in such situations, surely helped me. Let me say, I was and am glad I belong to Him.

But now let us look briefly at how this particular place in God's world became the nation of Bangladesh. Though it is small in size, it is probably the world's ninth largest country in population.

If we just think of the twentieth century, things have moved rapidly for this area of the world. During World War II, India was still under the British. But soon after the end of the war, plans were activated for the British to leave India. But it was soon understood that the Muslims of India were insisting that they have something to say about what would happen at the time of self-government for India.

In this process, many Muslim leaders were determined that the primary Muslim areas of India would become a separate nation from the Hindu part of that nation. By 1947 many decisions had been made by the British, the Hindus of India and the Muslims of India.

When the day of independence finally came, the primary Hindu parts of India were to become Hindustan or the place of the Hindus. Two sections of that former nation were to become Pakistan or the place of the pure or Muslims. But those two parts were located, one in the eastern area of India and that would be called East Pakistan and the other section of Pakistan was to be West Pakistan located on the western side of India. There were about one thousand miles of Hindustan or India separating those two parts of Pakistan. Though there were several areas where final decisions were most difficult to make and one in particular, that of Kashmir, lingers even until today as one of the world's troublesome areas due to both India and Pakistan making their claims. I only say that those of us who truly care about this great section of God's world should faithfully pray that somehow a lasting peace can come between India and Pakistan with geographical areas being finalized.

So, when my family arrived in East Pakistan on November 25, 1958, the country was only eleven years old. But their early days were not easy ones. Millions of Hindus, especially from East Pakistan, moved into India and millions of Muslims moved from India into the two parts of Pakistan. Deaths were common in all areas of this mass movement. Many were natural deaths probably due to added stress in addition to early illnesses. But many deaths were caused by violence.

But our early days or months or even years led us to thinking that Pakistan was a viable nation. Later years were to prove we had been wrong but that again only indicated how little many of us as international missionaries know about national and international politics.

When we first arrived in East Pakistan, the provincial capital was Dhaka (then spelled Dacca) with a population of 560,000. In 2005, the population of that city may have reached 12,000,000. In 1958, the population of East Pakistan was, as reported by some sources, 51,000,000. The size of that area of God's world was about that of the state of Arkansas or Iowa.

The history of this part of the world is most interesting. For example, present day Bangladesh may have a population of 140,000,000 making it among the top ten nations of the world in population and present day Pakistan has even more people.

But looking back to 1947, it is good to remember that present day Bangladesh was called East Bengal and the area on two sides of today's Bangladesh was West Bengal. East Bengal was primarily Muslim while West Bengal was primarily Hindu. It is also good to recall that even in 1947, after the creation of these two nations, India had perhaps the world's third largest group of Muslims in the countries of the world and East Pakistan had the world's third largest group of Hindus. So, any time, when there was trouble involving Muslims in India or Hindus in Pakistan, that difficulty reached all parts of those two nations.

But in this preface, I think it is also good for me to give a personal opinion of that 2005 situation as I understand it. These three nations, India, Pakistan and Bangladesh, seem to do much better in their treatment of the massive religious minorities of these three countries. Also, it should be mentioned that for Christians, a much smaller minority religious group, there may be more persecution against them today than there is persecution involving the mistreatment of Muslims or Hindus. Of course, I am concerned about this situation.

But looking more closely at Bangladesh, that land or place of the Bangla or Bengali people, today we see this vast nation continuing in her struggle for democracy. It seems to me that she should be proud of her role as a viable nation especially as it involves democracy for her people.

Also, over the years the Hindu percentage of the Bangladesh population seems to be decreasing. The *1990 Statistical Yearbook* of Bangladesh states the Hindu population of 1951 to be 22.0 percent but in 1981 their percentage was 12.1 percent. The same source gives the Bangladesh Muslim population in 1951 to have been 76.9 percent while in 1981 it had increased to 86.6 percent.

Though I will not directly quote any one source, today's religious population percentage is something like 87.0 percent Muslim and Hindu percentage 11.0. That leaves something like 2.0 for all others including Christians and Buddhists.

Therefore, we are talking about a primarily Muslim people. Hence, I feel the title given for this book may be, at least, somewhat correct. I will give a few examples of how Muslims gave help to many Hindus during the time of the Bangladesh liberation from Pakistan.

During our thirty-four years in East Pakistan/Bangladesh, I must say that I never met an international missionary who I thought was involved in local politics. Of course, we are trained not to interfere by the organizations which send us, but it is also right to say that when there is persecution of any group of people, we have a deep quiet concern.

I do not hesitate to say that through the years I knew most of the USA ambassadors to Bangladesh. But I did not share matters, which I understood to be happening locally, with any of them. I will add that during the independence movement in Bangladesh, when I returned from trips back to Feni, which was still our home, often there would be a person from the USA consulate waiting to ask me about my trip. I will also relate later one experience where I made my personal position on what was happening in East Pakistan well known to those involved with the USA government. If an international missionary doesn't have a deep kind feeling toward the people with whom and among whom you serve, then my opinion is that you should return to your home country or maybe move on to another country for your ministry in the name of Almighty God.

This doesn't indicate that in any way you love your home country less. In fact, it may mean you love your mother country more because you have a passport from that country and you know that officially, you are not obligated in any way to share anything you know with your country's officials. This is what I call the application of democracy as it relates to religion.

On one occasion, and I am pleased to relate this, an ambassador asked me if I would plan a trip for him to an area I knew very well. But when I asked him if I could plan for him to spend the nights of this trip with a colleague of mine, he kindly replied, "No, I am expected to stay in a Bangladesh Government rest house." I planned his trip with this in mind.

Then, on behalf of my country, I was asked by our embassy to give the dedication prayer at the time of the opening of a new embassy building. I was most pleased to do so. For the first time in my life I wrote the prayer as I talked to/with the God whom I served. That day, the President of Bangladesh and many cabinet ministers and secretaries were present, as well as a known Muslim imam gave a prayer in Arabic; hence I have no idea what he said.

An assistant secretary of state from Washington was present as were many government persons from other nations. I was nervous and recall everything as if this had only happened yesterday; when I stood to pray, if I had stepped back a short distance, I would have stepped on the feet of the Bangladeshi President. I admit that I concluded the prayer by saying, "I make this prayer in the name of the One who makes it possible for me to pray to You as Almighty God." I do remember well that one of those present, a Polish dignitary, thanked me for my prayer. Thanks also came from several cabinet secretaries of the Bangladesh government, who were all Muslims, and from one of the highest ranking USA embassy people. This person later asked me for a copy of the prayer. However, I do not know what I did with that copy. I conclude, in most countries of the world, as an international missionary, people from all walks of life where you serve expect you to be faithful to your home country. But they do not expect you to be an agent of your country nor theirs.

However, I do believe we were cautious about what we said about the national borders of India and Pakistan. When we traveled the old road going south or north of Feni, I often pointed out to our little daughters that the border of India was only a short distance from the road on which we were traveling. In fact, just about five miles from south of Feni, the border of India was probably no more than five hundred feet from the road. We knew that our passports and visas were not marked for us to ever cross this border, or go nearer to it than the road.

In 1961, Betty, Cherie, Kathy and I went to Darjeeling, India for a short vacation. Of course, we had a visa from the Indian government. Our travel took us to Calcutta and then we flew to a small town, just north of East Pakistan. From there we went by taxi to Darjeeling. Money left us too quickly and at that time we had no credit cards, so one morning the four of us went to an Indian bank. In just a few minutes we departed that bank with cash from a check on a USA bank. That was quite a feat back then but I think the presence of a young family removed any doubt about us which might have meant dishonesty.

While in Darjeeling, we met an Indian couple who invited us to visit them in Assam, India. This was almost unbelievable for we were sure that India would not give us a visa for visiting that area. But we easily received a visa in Dhaka from the Indian consulate. That visit in April of 1962 gave us the opportunity of seeing areas of India which most foreigners would never see. We were delighted to have time with that gracious couple.

Even now, many years later, when thinking about the opportunity to move so easily between these two countries at that time, seems almost impossible. But in July of 1962, we were in Calcutta, India on our way back to the United States. Again, we had no difficulty in getting a visa for overnight stay in India. But that was our last visit to India until we were on our way from Bangladesh to the United States for our third return since leaving the USA in 1958. But note that much had happened in those ten years. East Pakistan no longer existed. That area was the new nation of Bangladesh. I will write much about that change and the relationships between these three countries, India, Pakistan and Bangladesh, remembering that these were one country in the first half of 1947.

Also, as I write the twenty three chapters following the "Introduction," which follows this preface, I will mostly share experiences, some of which I wrote earlier. I will do my best to be honest in those stories but they will be about our relationships with Muslim people. It has always been a joy of mine to remember most of those kinds of experiences.

Also remember that I will write an "Afterword," in which I will intend to make many statements in light of September 11, 2001, and the open attack on the United States of America by a group of Muslims.

Hopefully this Preface will help you see and feel the life of an American family over a period of about thirty-four years in a Muslim country. Then, the "Introduction" will tell how we got to that part of God's world and then the stories of our relationships with Muslims will follow.

INTRODUCTION

This introduction will bring the reader to the time of our first arrival in East Pakistan on November 25, 1958 and it will give you a glimpse of our family of seven whom you will later meet in the stories of this book.

Betty, my wife, was born in Louisville, Kentucky. Betty remained in Louisville until she went to Campbellsville Junior College in January, 1950. As most of you as readers will know, Louisville is on the south side of the Ohio River. The opposite side or north side of the Ohio River is Indiana.

I was born on a farm in Clinton County, Kentucky, and the county seat town is Albany. Clinton County is bordered on the south by Tennessee. I grew up on that farm near the Clinton-Wayne County line. Often, especially to purchase farm equipment, we traveled to Monticello, the county seat of Wayne County. So, through the years I felt I was a part of both counties.

Though we retired from the Foreign Mission Board (now International Mission Board) in 1992 and live in Louisville, one of my great joys is to return often to Clinton County to at least visit with a few relatives and friends whom I still remember well. I also like to say that Betty "grew" up in Louisville and I "growed" up in Clinton County.

I graduated from Clinton County High School in May, 1946. In August of that same year, before my seventeenth birthday, I became a student at the University of Kentucky. That was also the time of the return of many students who had been in the military during World War II. One of the men, who became a friend, was from Hazard,

Kentucky. He had been shell shocked and I never saw him again after I dropped out of the University to farm my father's Clinton County farm. Through the years I have often thought of that friend whom I admired so much for his courage. He often broke out in sweat but wiped that sweat away and kept going. I was sixteen when I first met him and he was probably twenty-four years of age.

Betty graduated from Shawnee High School in Louisville in 1949. We met at Campbellsville Junior College in January, 1950. We completed the four semesters at Campbellsville in December, 1951.

In January, 1952, I went to Wayland College in Plainview, Texas to complete my college education. That Texas Baptist College was about twelve hundred miles away from "my old Kentucky home," and through the years I have often been asked why I went so far away to complete my college education. Remember that in 1952 much was happening in the southern part of the United States in race relations.

About the middle of 1951 a black female teacher in northwestern Texas made an application to Wayland College for admission and the college president, after getting a majority vote from the trustees, stood with her and she was admitted as a student. Also, at that time there were many internationals from several countries of the world who were Wayland students. I heard about all of this in early October, 1951, when the president of Wayland spoke to a state meeting of Baptist students in Kentucky. That meeting was held on the campus of the University of Kentucky. While attending that meeting I made my decision to become a student at Wayland.

During the years I was in Texas, Betty worked at a day-time job and attended night classes at University of Louisville. From early January, 1951, until we were married August 20, 1954, we were together on only thirty-one different days. Our children, through the years, have often teased us by saying we were not in love; otherwise we could not have been together so infrequently. But that was the point—we were in love and could wait for our wedding day.

During our days at Campbellsville Junior College, Betty and I were fortunate indeed to have made friends for life with several faculty members and students. My experience at Wayland was no less. Today, Betty and I count many of the students who became our friends at Campbellsville and Wayland as most important in living out our lives for our Lord God. You might ask how Betty would claim students at Wayland as her friends.

Betty's friendship with three Wayland girls deepened greatly when she visited me there. These three girls were Edna, Carolyn, and Carolyn. These three were my friends. One of the Carolyns often teased me about my Kentucky girl, but when she met Betty that teasing ceased. Several times, I went home with the other Carolyn who lived on a Texas farm with her parents' family. No one could have a deeper friendship than the one between Edna and me.

Only a few years ago, Betty and I were returning from San Diego where we had visited with my only brother, Wade, and his family. Our plans included visiting Edna and her husband who lived in New Mexico as we made our way home to Louisville. We knew Edna was not well, but we didn't know that she would hardly recognize us. She was home with her gracious husband, Jay.

Jay had been a student in New Mexico when I was at Wayland and often, when he came to visit Edna at Wayland, I would have a little time with him. He was my friend. Several times after our retirement, Jay and Edna visited one of their daughters who was a medical doctor in nearby Ohio. What a privilege it was for us to have them in our home here in Louisville on two of their return trips to New Mexico. Not long after our visit with Jay and Edna in New Mexico, we learned of Edna's death. We had lost a friend, but Jay's loss was far greater than ours.

The two Carolyns were just as much my friends and Betty's friends as were Edna and Jay. One of the Carolyns is married to Phil and the other is married to Bob. Bob and Phil have been my friends since we first met in early 1952 and the years have not separated us. In fact, we were together in November, 2004.

My first Wayland roommate was Franklin Chen. At the time we were together, Franklin's grandfather was the Methodist pastor of President General Chiang Kai Shek in Taiwan. That was 1952, when I first went to Texas.

My second roommate at Wayland was Bill Nakahira. Bill's home was Wahiwa, Hawaii. Bill graduated from Wayland in May, 1953, and looking back it is almost too much to remember. After Bill's graduation, we traveled on the same flight from Texas to Hawaii. You see I had just been appointed by Texas Baptist students to be a summer-missionary to that beautiful land of Hawaii. But that was not the last time we were together. I will mention only one of those times. Betty and I, with four of our children, were making our way across the Pacific on our return journey to East Pakistan, so we stopped in Honolulu for a few days.

I doubt that I can find the photo today, but I remember so well, Bill, in his swimming suit as were all the others, down on the floor in our hotel room. Our two boys were light skinned and with that powerful beach sun, they were more than pink, they were red.

More than thirty-five years later one of those sons of ours was making a trip across the Pacific and made the same stop in Honolulu for a rest. He and his wife had four young children and they had a perfect host in my beloved friend, Bill. Life moves on.

I had spent two wonderful years at Campbellsville Junior College, and my five semesters at Wayland were much the same. When I was a young boy back in Kentucky, I remember that our church and several Baptist churches in our area had a special lunch several times with a black Baptist Church. We jokingly called that time together "all day eating and preaching on the ground" just to indicate how much we loved being together. Then, while I was still young, probably about twelve years of age, I spent a full day with my dad who was a skilled person in operating a massive machine simply called a "shovel." That shovel could lift enough dirt or rocks to fill a truck with one scoop.

But that is not what I most remember about that day when I must have watched just about everything that happened regarding Dad's work and relationships. Early that morning he seemed to be careful to introduce me to a black man. This gentleman was gracious and kind to me. But at lunch time I saw something that was not so beautiful. A group of local boys appeared to enjoy chasing that black man as if he were different from the rest of us. With a troubled mind, I asked my dad why those boys did not chase a white man.

So, about ten years later, at this Baptist College in Texas, a black student from Florida, came to my room. My Chinese roommate was not present so we talked fast and good. This new friend was an Episcopalian and as I had done, came to Wayland because it was, if not the first, one of the first such private institutions, in the south or southwest, to admit a black person as a student in what had been an all-white place of learning. This student asked me, "I have been told that you are willing to accompany me to an Episcopalian church Sunday morning. Will you do that?" I hesitated only briefly and said that I would be pleased if that was what was needed. However, I did not recall ever talking about any such thing with other students.

Then, on the following Sunday morning rather than going for worship at the College Heights Baptist Church where I was a member, I went with my new friend to what he hoped would be his new church. Just before we entered the sanctuary of that church, I asked him just what I was to do. He replied, "Just follow me." I did that and as my friend stopped to bow just before we took our seats, I hesitated. It was not that I thought his actions were right or wrong, it simply was that all of this was new to me. I grew up in a very small informal Baptist church. Now, this was undoubtedly a formal dignified church.

Following that time of worship, not so much for me because I was very nervous, but surely for that congregation and possibly for my friend, we walked out of the sanctuary slowly and quietly. Not one person spoke to us even after we hesitated a little outside the building, so we walked toward the college campus.

The following week, my friend again asked me if I would accompany him to the same church. I hesitated in my reply and then said, "I think it will be much better if you go alone." But I had more to say. I said, "I think that congregation thought of me as a 'radical' who had taken you to their church and all I was doing was to make them appear racial."

My friend hesitated but finally said, "You may be right so what do you suggest?" My reply was simple as I suggested that he go to worship alone and probably that congregation will think he is more like them and is simply seeking sincere worship of God. On Sunday, he went alone and was warmly welcomed before and after worship that day. This friend had found new hope and his friend, Jim, had learned a lesson.

When we returned from our first term in East Pakistan, I suggested to Betty that she, our two little daughters, and I attend a black Baptist church on Sunday. We did that for two consecutive Sundays and on that second Sunday, a black woman, undoubtedly a person who belonged to God, said to us, "I think I know why you come to worship with us but that is not necessary for we all know who you folks are and where you have been for we have talked much about you."

The kindness of that woman, and without a doubt she represented that black congregation, surely tracked us for years. We were helped greatly by her. While we may have helped that congregation or we may not have helped, we had been helped. Today, Betty and I can hope and pray that we, our children, our friends, and especially our fellow Southern Baptists, love people of all ethnic backgrounds as we know our God does love them and us equally. For whatever it may be worth, the pastor of that black congregation was a brother of the famous Dr. Martin Luther King. However, we did not know this when we attended worship with that church.

During part of my four semesters at Campbellsville Junior College, I was pastor of Central Grove Baptist Church in Clinton County. That church, through the years, has always been very good to me. Though I was their pastor for several months, I still like to think of myself during those months as one of their boys for they surely nurtured me as a young minister.

After graduating from Wayland Baptist College in May of 1954, my next all-important step was seminary training. There was never a question about where I would receive that training. That would be The Southern Baptist Theological Seminary in Louisville. This was Betty's birthplace. Her father was deceased but her mother still lived in there. Also, my mother and dad had moved to Louisville. So, after our marriage on August 20, 1954, we were to have the opportunity to be with parents before our overseas departure.

I graduated from the Seminary in January, 1958. While I was participating in seminary graduation ceremony, Betty was in the hospital giving birth to Cherie, the first of our five children.

Most of the time while I was a seminary student, I was pastor of the Mount Moriah Baptist Church, in Mount Eden, Kentucky, but this was only about forty miles from the home of our parents and we were privileged to have many wonderful times with them.

In April, 1958, we were appointed as international missionaries by the Foreign Mission Board of the Southern Baptist Convention. In late August we departed by train from Louisville and this marked the beginning of thirty-four years of journeys back and forth to East Pakistan/Bangladesh.

That first journey was not a simple one. Our train trip was from Louisville to Indianapolis. Cherie was moving toward her eighth month birthday when we began that journey. After a few hours in Indianapolis, we boarded another train which took us to Chicago. As we traveled we knew we were rapidly moving away from our beloved "old Kentucky home" and the thought of being away, especially from our parents, was not easy.

But the train from Chicago to Seattle, Washington, provided a wonderful trip. When we began that train ride from Louisville, it was only the second time Betty or I had made such a trip—earlier that year, we had gone by train from Louisville to Texas for a meeting of the Southern Baptist Convention. The beauty of the countryside from Chicago to Seattle was a plus for both of us. That beauty showed us something of the beauty of God's creation which we had never before witnessed and that helped some as we moved farther and farther away from our beloved parents.

Our westward movement on that train led us into northern California where the natural beauty, as we looked to the sides of the track, showed us more of our beloved country. Then, we turned north and traveled across Oregon and that beauty was different but not lessened by any means. As we moved into Washington, we knew it was only a few hours until we were to reach Seattle. Even though our deep feelings of being away from "home" seemed to increase, we did not miss the many significant differences in our final leg of that journey toward a land, "far away." God's created world continued to show its beauty and that helped greatly as we moved on to the place where we believed He wanted us to serve Him.

If the train ride across much of the United States had been different for us in many ways from previous experiences, the next part of our journey was to be even more different. Even the waiting in

Seattle itself was different to us. Our stay in Seattle was more than three weeks.

Soon after we reached the hotel where our Foreign Mission Board personnel had made reservations for us, we called the shipping company, Java Hoegh Pacific Lines, on whose cargo ship we were to travel across the Pacific Ocean, then to the Indian Ocean, and/ finally, into the Bay of Bengal, up the Karnafuli river to the port city of Chittagong, East Pakistan.

For two seemingly long weeks we stayed in the same hotel. Each day we called the shipping company and received the same reply from them. It was, "Call tomorrow, maybe we can give you our possible departure date." They were loading wheat and flour for parts of Asia and that meant food for a great number of people. Since I still had the heart of a farmer I knew that every ship loaded with grain meant more income for my farmer friends.

But as usual a better thing was in the making. On the second Sunday when we had attended a Baptist church in Seattle, a kind family invited us to leave the hotel and stay with them until our ship was ready for departure. Without hesitating, we accepted their invitation.

That Sunday afternoon we checked out of the hotel and the next day we called the International Mission Board, (the new name of our organization) to inform them of our new address and also, we called the shipping company. Now that we were in a home we had some beautiful help in caring for Cherie. In the hotel we had worked out a system for eating our meals in the dining room, with one of us staying with Cherie while the other one went to the dining room.

After more than three weeks, the shipping company called saying that we were going to depart the next day. So, the early morning of that next day our kind friends took us to the ship. Time was flying. We, at last, were going to be moving further in the direction of the place which was to be our new home. That pleased us very much.

Since this was a cargo ship, passengers were not the ship's crew's biggest concern. The cost of our ticket for those forty-two days of journey for all three of us was just a little over one thousand dollars. The captain told us during a casual time as we were crossing the

Pacific that they like to have a few passengers. Having passengers was another way to help in keeping the crew busy or at least giving them something to look at from our distance in the cabin area to where they were usually working.

There were four other passengers. We seven ate every meal formally with the captain, the chief engineer and the chief mate. As for the tableware, I often thought there was enough of it by each plate to fight the war of eating. The food was perfect and service also could not have been better.

We moved out of Seattle late one afternoon. I needed to take care of Cherie and I couldn't afford to be sick, so I had my seasick pills ready and decided to take the first one. Well, it turned out that I certainly did not need that pill. To my embarrassment, the ship docked again after a few hours and we loaded more wheat and flour in Tacoma, Washington. Betty laughed at me for taking the pill so early.

Then, we again embarked but stopped after a few hours in a Canadian port. It began raining and rained or at least misted small amounts of rain, for almost a week. Then, when the sky was clear we again loaded the grain and flour. Finally we were ready to depart. But we had learned why you didn't load grain or its products during a time in which it would become wet for this could cause an explosion in the hold of the ship. Looking back, we had no bad thoughts about the delay.

Our room was certainly acceptable even though we were on a cargo ship. Betty and I rotated who slept in the lower bunk of our bed area. Whoever slept in that lower bunk had the duty of caring for Cherie, who could be touched from that bunk. Her bed was a large basket with a small nice soft bedding arrangement. One night I was off duty, sleeping in the upper bunk, and Cherie cried out. Then, in a few minutes, or maybe seconds, she cried out again. I simply stepped out of my bunk, thinking I must be on duty, and landed on Betty who was arising to care for Cherie.

Needless to say, I received more care than Cherie did, for we spent a good amount of time caring for a cut on my foot as I struck the side of Betty's bunk. Anyway, we learned in the twenty-one days as we crossed the Pacific how to care for Cherie.

Those days were mostly beautiful. The most interesting thing to me was the thousands of flying fish, who leaped into the air and appeared to remain up several seconds. Name the ocean animal and we will declare that we saw it during that trip across the beautiful but not so peaceful Pacific. Some days the ship seemed to roll through the water. We watched as a sailor stood on the front deck of our ship, the Wonarata, and water covered him each time a roll was made. There were always many points of interest every day, so no one could say that we were bored.

But each day meant that we were farther away from home. After those twenty-one days, we docked in Manila, Philippines. We were immediately greeted when Hugo Parkman, a colleague who lived in Manila, boarded the ship and introduced himself. There was no question that we needed to walk on land again. But when I first stepped on the dock I realized, as I felt my body shake, that I was experiencing land shock. We had been told about this by people in our organization and in a few minutes, I "felt at home" on land.

After four days in Manila our ship was ready to move on to the next port which was also in the Philippines. As Hugo had met us in Manila, another person, of a different missionary organization, met us and took as ashore. Another pleasant visit for a few days but then we moved on to another Philippine port. We were met again. (We look back and remember the kindness of people, during most of our years as international missionaries; most of the time we had never seen them before and we have not seen some of them since.)

Perhaps the most beautiful time of our entire tiring journey was our travel through the islands of the Philippines. Sometimes, it appeared the ship almost struck some of the islands as it weaved back and forth. Just a glance at the ocean showed a beautiful scene. The water was as clear as any we had ever drunk. The many different types of fish were almost unbelievable. We were, again and again, struck by the beauty of our God's creation.

Travel with our God, as if He were the special Guest, was a new kind of experience. Most of the time, He surely made the arrangements so that we thought more about our destination than we did our departure from those we loved so much.

I truly believe that when we did look back to our two families in Kentucky, we had nothing but thanks for them. But we also remember well how they never even hinted in any way that they did not approve of our departure. Four years later when we returned to the United States for what is called "stateside assignment," we deeply felt that we had the strongest of support from our families. That was always a great encouragement.

After about four days in the Singapore port, and after beautiful encouragement from friends who met us daily while we were docked, we were ready to move on to our next stop and that was our final destination. From Singapore, we were soon in the Indian Ocean and then we moved into the Bay of Bengal. Our hearts seemed to beat more rapidly as our ship turned up the Karnafuli river of East Pakistan. We were aware that we had actually begun to turn west as our ship moved into the Karnafuli. We had been traveling primarily north from Singapore. For a few hours we were actually moving back toward Louisville—we had traveled more than half way around the world. Our journey had now moved into its forty-second day from Seattle.

When we had been appointed by our mission board back in April, Betty was twenty-six and I was twenty-eight. Hopefully, if we had not aged much, we surely matured some. But, for sure, we better knew and better understood our God.

Though the Karnafuli River was muddy and crowded with boats and ships of many kinds, it looked beautiful. It appeared even more beautiful as our ship, the Wonarata, eased into its spot at the dock. We had just arrived in the port city of Chittagong, East Pakistan. We had never met a Muslim person before.

Almost thirty-four years later, as we departed that part of God's world to end our formal international career, I rode in the backseat of the largest and most beautiful car I had seen in that land during those years. I rode in that back seat with a Muslim gentleman who had been a very close friend since December, 1970.

As I waved to my many colleagues, Betty and Jill were riding in one of our mission vehicles. Jill, our fifth child, had just graduated from Dalat High School, in Penang, Malaysia. In a few minutes we were at the airport.

The travel to the Dhaka airport was not an easy trip to make. Sitting by my side was the Secretary of Agriculture of Bangladesh. The date was late June, 1991. During the closing days of the Bangladesh War of Independence, I had been "assigned" the responsibility of trying to locate this man or his body if he were taken prisoner by the Pakistan military. The war ended abruptly and my friend was okay and I knew that because within a few minutes of the announcement of independence, he called to say he was okay.

As we looked down at the dock from high upon our ship, we saw a man we had never met, but we recognized him as Troy Bennett for we had seen his picture. He was the first of our missionary colleagues whom we met as he and the shipping agent boarded the Wonarata. The shipping agent was a Pakistani Muslim. He properly greeted us with a right hand salute to his forehead and spoke a "salaam" or greeting of peace. He was the first Muslim we had ever met. Since most of the crew of the Wonarata was Indonesian, for sure many of them were Muslim but we did not meet that part of the crew who seemed to be constantly working at painting the ship, moving the cargo, or whatever a labor force did. We were impressed by the kindness of that Muslim gentleman who accompanied Troy that day.

Troy had made arrangements for us to stay overnight with an American family who were also Baptists. Speaking of lasting friendships, about two years ago Betty Fowler visited us in Louisville. She had come to a meeting which was downtown, but she called and later spent some beautiful time in our Louisville home. It was in her home that we spent our first night in East Pakistan.

After checking with our freight shipment which had also arrived on the same ship, we made plans to move on to the provincial capital of East Pakistan the next day. That trip was on a DC 3 and as we walked into the cabin and moved toward our seats, it seemed like we were climbing up a hill. But years later we traveled several times on that type plane when we lived in Comilla.

Troy Bennett's family and the Trueman Moore family met us at the Dhaka airport. I remember only one of the vehicles in which we as a group drove from the Dhaka airport. That vehicle was a World War II jeep. This was perhaps one of the earliest changes in lifestyle we were to quickly notice. But that suddenly became a less important thing. The big thing was we had two new families of friends and quickly we would meet other friends. Some of them will be our friends right down to the end of life on this earth. About three months ago, we were with Troy and Marjorie and with Trueman and Jane Moore. It would not be incorrect to say they were our new family in East Pakistan when we arrived there.

That family was to grow rapidly as we met a host of Christians, Muslims, and Hindus over the next few years and the closeness of some of those new friends caused us to, down deeply within us, feel that they were to a degree, family with us. Above all else, we often thought of others as family members of our God's human creation.

Teaching Quran before school time.

Muslims praying on special occasion in Dhaka.

Muslims in Dhaka Stadium for special prayers.

Two muslim girls walking to school.

Muslim beggars.

Shitte Muslims mourning the death of Muhammad's last grandson.

CHAPTER ONE
One Year of Language Study in Dhaka

The house which the Bennetts and the Moores had rented for us in Dhaka could not have been better. But the house wasn't nearly as important to us as were our next door neighbors. Those neighbors were the owners of the house and our friendship, which began the next morning after our arrival at our new home, was very good from the beginning.

Dr. Latif, the owner of the house, was a gentleman in every respect. If he and his family ever tired of our calling on them, we were not aware of it. But at the same time, they never troubled us in any way. Mrs. Latif, a devoted Muslim as was her husband, was very proper with us as her neighbor and new "foreigners" in her country. The Latifs had, as best I can remember, three sons and three daughters. The middle of the sons was the most outgoing and if we ever had a question about the house in any way, he never hesitated in giving the answer. Whether or not the answer given was correct, Dr. Latif never changed what his son had said.

We were often invited to eat with the Latif family. We liked that because from the beginning both Betty and I enjoyed the hot spicy food which we were served. We did learn immediately that as long as you ate the food on your plate, more would be served. So, the custom of leaving food, though maybe not desired by either of us, was quickly accepted.

The quietness of Mrs. Latif, as we expected from a Muslim gentle lady, was always noted. But her kindness to us as a family was certainly equal to that of her husband. She dressed conservatively but her face was always uncovered. That helped us in our early days for we took that to mean that she did not need to cover her face in our presence. We were sure that she and Dr. Latif had discussed such matters when we were not present.

We slept in our new house the first night. The Bennetts and the Moores had again made everything as proper as could be for their new missionaries. One missionary family remained in East Pakistan for only a few months so when they prepared for departure, our colleagues had purchased their kerosene stove and refrigerator for us. We had a few pieces of furniture but it took a few weeks to get that from the port. However, all of our needs had been arranged by our colleagues.

Within a short time we were in language study and again, as far as we understood, everything had been arranged. Our teachers could not have been better at their jobs. One was Mr. Chakraborty who was a highly trained person and a convert from high caste Hinduism. Another was a woman and she did her job well though she did not have the experience of Mr. Chakraborty. The third teacher was a Muslim young man and though he was new at his job, it was right to have him as a language teacher, for the land in which we now lived was a Muslim land.

Though, even from the beginning of our missionary work in East Pakistan, we shared primarily the Good News of Jesus the Christ with Hindus, we were pleased to learn words from our Muslim teacher which we might not learn from the two Christians. This became evident because Betty was not free to walk the streets as I was, due to our being in an Islamic culture, I often heard words in simple conversation, which I did not understand, because those words were not what I call pure Bangla. This was because they were based on Arabic or sometimes, Urdu, the language which was primarily that of West Pakistan, the other part of the country, in which we now lived.

We soon began language study and we were told that the language spoken by most Christians in East Pakistan was pure Bangla based on Sanskrit or the mother language of Bangla and the holy language of the Hindus. Many of the Christians had been former Hindus or at least their older family members had been Hindus. So, having that Muslim young man as a teacher was helpful for we could freely ask him about words we heard but had no idea what their meaning was. Sometimes we had difficulty retaining the sounds of those words long enough to ask what they meant.

While international missionaries today often have opportunity to learn languages with more than one group, we can thank Almighty God for that opportunity early in our international career. When we moved to Feni in 1964, we had two of the Gospels of the New Testament (or Injil) in a special translation to help Muslims understand the Gospel better. In fact, if it is not too personal to say it, no more than five feet from where I type these words, I can see copies of those two New Testament books on one of my bookshelves.

But far better than that, today, the entire Bible is translated into Bangla for people with Islamic background. Though I rarely return to Bangladesh in my advanced age, I often read from that beautiful accurate translation and again thank our God for providing it for those who can better understand it. If I may add this word—three of my dearest friends, all Bangladesh Christians, one older than I, another much younger, and one about my age, were deeply involved in the production of that translation. This makes me feel very good.

Though our first child, Cherie, was only ten months old when we arrived in East Pakistan, her little sister joined us in August of 1959. With Betty expecting our Kathy, obviously she was not as free to study language as I was. So, one of the things I did was walk the streets of that city of then about 560,000 people and talk with anyone who would help me with the little Bangla that I was learning. One Muslim gentleman, who had a store on the main street of the old part of Dhaka city, helped me often and seemingly willingly.

One day that gentleman helped when I badly needed help. I was walking further into the old city and talking as best I could with anyone who was willing to try to understand what I thought I was speaking in their language, when this friend joined me. He joined me because from a distance, I was watching a man leaning against a telephone pole. All of a sudden, that man or that man's body fell to the earth and a cloud of dust ascended. I was astounded at what I was seeing. One man near where the man had fallen lifted his body up somewhat and leaned it again on the telephone pole. He walked a few steps away and again the dust arose as the body struck the earth.

That Muslim store owner touched my shoulder with his right hand and asked me to walk in the other direction with him. I am sure he had 'read' the look on my face and knew I needed help. But I wanted to talk with him right then. I did not want to try my new

Bangla language but speak to him in English. He then, carefully and slowly spoke to me in English saying that I need not worry because before long a bullock cart would come into the area and someone would speak to the man with the cart about that body lying by the side of the street, with his head now covered. That covering on the head was used to tell the "body pickup person" that this was a dead body. Burial, without any ceremony, would be in a common grave holding many bodies. And so the new international missionary learns much and learned it early in his career.

It seems only proper to say that I never feared Muslims in those early years because my primary example of a Muslim was the owner of the house, in which we now lived, and our next door neighbor, Dr. Latif and, of course, his entire family.

Though I had not heard much nor had I formally studied Islam, it seemed almost daily I heard and saw things which told me about that religion. Something which I witnessed early in my career was of a special sacrifice. Dr. Latif asked me if I wanted to watch as he and his sons made this special sacrifice or at least a special ceremony. Of course, I was most pleased to watch the procedure. One of the translations of the Arabic word for this event, into English, is Id-al-Adha.

The idea is that of remembering the sacrifice which Abraham (or Ibrahim) made of Isaac. To Muslims, it was Ishmael who was offered. But of course, God had intervened when He understood the willingness of Abraham to offer his son.

A special person from a near-by mosque came to actually make the sacrifice. I watched carefully and surely noted the solemn look on the faces of Dr. Latif and his three sons. Just before the main part, cutting the throat of the young calf, happened, Dr. Latif read his own name and then the names of his three sons. Then it happened. With one stroke of the massive knife, the throat of the calf was cut and all movements of that animal's body quivered and then suddenly, that quivering ceased. The ceremony was completed and the man from the local mosque departed.

Because I knew how much Dr. Latif loved his wife and daughters I wondered why he did not read their names also. So, after several days had passed, I asked him in English, why he had not read all the names of his family members. He was not disturbed by my question but simply answered that the animal was not sufficient for eight family members. That was the end of any further questions on my part. However, through the days following, I did understand that there must be many differences in the religious thoughts and actions of Muslims regarding men and women.

The broadest smile I think I ever saw on Dr. Latif's face was when I appeared at his large pharmacy in the old part of the city. He seemed most pleased that I had traveled so far just to see his pharmacy. Though I had, on several occasions when we were alone, asked him to let me tell him about Jesus (or Isa), he never seemed to let that be any hindrance in our relationship. But that day, our bond of friendship definitely was strengthened. I had seen how he was able to care very well for his large family. His business certainly seemed to be viable.

Across a little dirt road, and near the gate that led into our yard, was a large house where a group of young college students from West Pakistan had made their residence. They had moved into their house about three months after we had arrived in East Pakistan. Although we did not know much Bangla, we knew that these students knew none of the language. We became acquainted soon after their arrival and enjoyed getting to know them.

All of those young men were Muslim as most of the people of West Pakistan were. They did not have very many Hindus but there were far more Christians in West Pakistan than in East Pakistan. When we talked with them it always seemed they had as many questions about the people of East Pakistan as we had when we first arrived. We tried to be patient with them but at first, since they were also Pakistani, we had not even considered that they knew nothing about that part of their country.

We did notice that in action and in words, they did not look upon the local people, their fellow citizens, as highly as they seemed to think of themselves. Maybe we are all, as human beings, somewhat like that when we look at those with a different culture. But hopefully I am not writing too boastfully when I say that, in a few months of presence in East Pakistan, Betty and I felt deeply for the local people. So, naturally I was defensive of the East Pakistanis or the

Bangla people. These young men were social welfare students and had come to learn, among other things, some of the differences of the two parts of this huge nation.

The more we talked with the students, the more we understood how different people can be though they are of the same religion. Again, I may be unfair, but we went to know and to serve with Christians and in particular Baptists of East Pakistan. From the beginning we felt a nearness to not only Baptists, but to most of the Christians we met in our early days.

Today, I deeply believe our relationships with East Pakistani Christians were made possible by our God and those relationships were used by Him to help us serve with the Bangla people for thirty-four years and for our children to grow up loving the people with whom we lived.

An example of these students' expressing their feelings to us about the local people was the manner of the Bangali eating food with their right hand and not using any tableware. We later learned that many West Pakistanis eat with their right hand just as the people of Bangladesh do today. Maybe it was because I was a country boy that I liked that system of eating.

The right hand is carefully washed before eating. That hand is properly held so that as you eat it is "kept clean," for surely the food we take into our bodies is not dirty so how could food make your hand dirty? I always loved to eat bony fish with my right hand because I could feel every little bone and remove that bone from my mouth with my fingers.

I felt that at least some of those students simply felt they were much better than the local people and then attempted to find reasons to justify their feelings. Maybe I am too hard on them but I guess, looking at my own country and the ethnic differences and the poor manner in which we work with them caused me to notice the differences in other cultures and maybe to be too judgmental.

But God was teaching us and we slowly learned to watch our own behavior and not so much the behavior of others especially when it involved only trivial matters. We always enjoyed the movement from the nicest of tableware to the use of the right hand in eating.

After moving to a town that had an army base nearby, following our one year of language study in Dhaka, we had the privilege of getting to know several army officers from West Pakistan. In fact, if I remember correctly, the base commander during our three years of relationships with those of this base, was a West Pakistani. In fact, not many of the officers were East Pakistani.

Surely I am right to say that our God had known how much we needed to learn and to learn many things that would help us be better witnesses for Him so He let us, early in our international missionary career, live near these "foreign students." When we moved on to our next place of residence, those students were still learning social welfare and if they are like most of us, they are still learning regardless of where they now live. But for sure, they are not living in the East Pakistan because there is no such place. On December 16, 1971, East Pakistan ceased to be a part of Pakistan and became the nation of Bangladesh.

In late November we were ready to move on to a more permanent place for ministry but that ministry continued to include language study. In fact, as the system was then, I had a formal examination of the Bangla language at the end of each of my first three years in that part of God's world. Maybe I did not do so well each time, but I continue to study that beautiful language more than forty-seven years later. It continues to be a challenge.

CHAPTER TWO
Three Years in Comilla

Nothing better could have happened to us as a family of four than living in Comilla. Kathy had been born on August 11, 1959 and now Cherie had a little sister with whom she could share life. Going to Comilla was good for us because in a big city it is not so easy to learn much about culture; the people, as a whole, live much differently than those in smaller towns and rural areas. Though Comilla had a population of about sixty thousand, it was a rural town and we had the opportunity to meet many of the people and to get to know them in the three remaining years we had before returning to the United States for a state-side assignment of about eleven months.

There was a small Baptist church and an even smaller Catholic church in Comilla. We got to know the priest of the Catholic church soon after arrival in Comilla but that relationship never worked out very well. He made it clear to me early that he could not consider me a minister but that was okay with me. Several years later I became acquainted with the priest who followed him and that priest, Father Dan, became a beloved friend of my family.

Though I continued as an almost full-time language student, two Christian laymen and I began visiting Hindu villages and often we could share the Good News of Jesus the Messiah with them. This was indeed a joy, knowing that these people were so far from the Living Creator God, so every opportunity we were given we told the story of Jesus as best we could. I will always be deeply grateful to those two men, for from the beginning of our time in Comilla, they gave me opportunity to speak in Bangla and though what I said must have been weak and fragile, at least I had an opportunity to use the language as I learned it and to use it in a somewhat formal way.

But we will leave the subject of Hindus and talk about living with Muslims.

One of the earliest places the two Baptist men showed me was a Christian cemetery located on the right side of the road which led in the direction of Dhaka. That cemetery reminded me that Christians had lived in that area and had either moved to other places or simply died with no one left in that area. On the road from Comilla, in the Dhaka direction, there was one Christian family and that road distance was about thirty miles.

On the opposite side of the road from that cemetery there was a large market place. It was called Madhiya. Often, my Christian friends and I visited that market place and distributed small pamphlets and we also sold Bibles and portions of the Bible. Many Muslims seemed to deeply appreciate the Bible. They used to hold a Bible in both hands and then raise it to their lips and kiss it. There was no doubt that they deeply respected that blessed book. Although it may not have been in the language they would have preferred, they still read it often, without purchasing a copy. Though the price was low, yet it was too much for most of them to pay. But the portions were very popular. We had two of the Gospels and the price was very low so we were most pleased that these were available in a more applicable translation for Muslims to enjoy and understand more easily.

About eight years later, when the road from Comilla to Dhaka was completed, dozens of times I passed between the cemetery and that market place in route to and from Dhaka. Madhiya seemed to be a challenge to me. By challenge, I mean I remember two people, a father and son who lived near the market and had a small business there. They were community leaders and when they discovered we had special films of the life of Jesus the Christ, they asked us about those. We were excited that they were interested and in a few weeks, late one afternoon, we arrived at the market with all of the equipment for showing the pictures.

By equipment I mean we had a portable generator, a massive screen and all of the other accessories for showing the film. We arrived in late afternoon so we could prepare for the showing of the film. We wanted everything to be in perfect order and a moving picture such as the one we had was surely the first of such an event to be seen by any of those present.

There is no way of knowing just how many men and boys were present that night but possibly as many as fifteen hundred. The only light, other than the light from the projector as that film strip was positioned on the massive screen, was the light from the small lanterns positioned in the little shops. It was difficult in this first-time experience to believe that such a large group of men and boys could be so quiet.

The most beautiful part of the evening was when Jesus was presented as he was hanging on the cross with His torn body being shown so explicitly. Many of those who were watching so closely cried out, "No! No! He is a good man. Don't do that to Him! Stop! Stop!" I had never experienced anything like this. There was no doubt—Almighty God was present.

My colleagues had made all arrangements. Included was what followed the showing of the film, when I was to speak. I had asked that one of them do the speaking but they gave a clear "no" to my proposal. I remembered the first time I spoke to a group of Hindus, I made a most incorrect presentation by doing what my friends called, "going too far with the first presentation" to a group who had never before heard the Gospel. So, this was to be an altogether different situation. Most of the time, Hindus were more tolerant of other religions.

Added to the above was the fact I needed to use a somewhat different vocabulary for Muslims. I had worked for days with my language teacher but did not feel I was ready for this massive challenge. I had the Gospel of Luke, and it was translated into the best language for Islamic people, at that time. Then, I had to remember, as I prepared for this all important time, that I could not use notes since it would be dark. But I often remember the two gracious Christian men who took care of the light problem by placing a dimly lighted lantern at my feet as I prepared to speak. They wanted to help and kindness always helps, though the light at my feet really didn't give light to the materials I had.

When I began speaking in that deep darkness, I knew that I was receiving special help from the One who knows how to manage in every situation. I may have been a young man, in a culture that about twenty months earlier, I had never before experienced and I was not necessarily good at language, at least in such a situation. But I was almost overwhelmed. Never in my life had I nor have I experienced the presence of God so powerfully as when I proclaimed His Word that night, and I have been now doing this for fifty-seven years. I knew what God wanted was happening for when I talked of the cross and how Jesus died as He did die, the audience again cried out, "No! No! Don't do that to Him. He is a good man!" When I concluded, the perfect silence continued. Those men and boys began moving quietly out of the market place toward their homes. They seemed to go in almost every direction. Only a few carried lanterns. Most began to "feel their way home," which was not a new experience for them. When they reached home, still there was only a small light.

Some of the men who were nearer to me and my two colleagues touched us on our arms and shoulders and those touches felt wonderful. Even as we disassembled the large screen and placed all of the equipment in the Land Rover, there was hardly a word spoken. I guess we wanted quietness so that we could continue to hear God's silent voice touch our ears.

During the next two years, we returned to the area many times. The father and son, if they were present, always gave us a kind greeting of "Salaam." I had no doubt that they wanted peace for us and for sure, we wanted no less for them.

Several years later, I passed along the road between the cemetery and the market place and I noticed a great difference, for the cemetery had become a rice field. I did not see even one tombstone. Though buried in that former cemetery were the bodies of older family members of the two men with whom I had shared that wonderful experience "That night in the Market Place," the nearby cemetery was now a rice field. When I saw that change, I did not feel bad toward whoever turned the Christian cemetery into a rice field.

That day was much like today is—I can pray the whole world will know Jesus the Christ as He wants us to know Him.

This morning, October 11, 2005, as I type into the computer, there is a bookshelf to my right. If I stretched my right arm to the right, it would almost reach a copy of that beautiful Gospel of Luke telling one of the four beautiful stories of Jesus. It is the same translation I used the night in Madhiya, though I could not read it that night because there was no light. I can not quote it from memory as I did that night, and I love it and when I run out of anything else to do, I might attempt to re-memorize part of it. But I probably won't because I have a copy of the entire Bible in an almost perfect translation which is surely the greatest ever attempt in Bangla to make a translation which Muslim people can read with understanding for it has been prepared for them. Though I most likely will not have the opportunity to use that translation with a large group of people, I still often read it as if I were preparing to present it to Muslims in a group.

A sincere international missionary will most likely hope for and pray for an opportunity like "that night in the Market Place," but in the years of my ministry for our Lord in the Land of the Bangla people, I did not often face such an opportunity or such a challenge. But thousands of other kinds of opportunities did come to me.

Early in our days in Comilla a military jeep came near our house. In that jeep were two army majors in uniforms of the Pakistani Army. I never got to know one of those majors very well but the other one became a friend for our missionary career in that land. Those two majors came to our house to ask if there was anything they could do for us. We were in the midst of an awful windstorm. They expected the storm to become much worse so they, knowing we were new foreigners in their country, felt we might need some help or at least some encouragement. I must say that their presence for a few minutes was of great help to us. Of course, both of those men were Muslims. Even their names told us that. In our last week of our thirty-four year career there, Betty and I were with one of those former majors and his wife for a pleasant visit. Until today this family is constantly presented to my God when I recall the earlier years of our missionary career.

Since the major was the Brigade Major of that military base, he was directly responsible to the Brigade Commander, the Brigadier General, or a one-star general. The General was a West Pakistani and did not know the local language. However, it was most interesting that during our three years in Comilla, we were invited to the military base at least a dozen times to participate in a wonderful meal with the military and some of their local friends.

It was perhaps even our first delightful meal on the base when I detected a very interesting development that had nothing to do with the great separation of East and West Pakistan. However, it may have been a small part of their oneness. Remember that nearly all of the officers on the base were West Pakistanis. Also, they were to a degree perhaps, considered a little more formal than the East Pakistani who participated in those wonderful meals. But in that early evening, when the food was before us on a long line of tables, time came to eat.

Though we were standing, and these dinners were served outside of the regularly used dining room for officers, we knew how to manage getting the delicious food into our mouths. For the first few minutes everyone was somewhat overloaded with the multiple tableware eating equipment. But every time, soon after we began eating, some would lay all of their tableware aside and begin eating with the fingers of the right hand. It seems like it was only seconds away, when all of us turned to that convenient style of eating with our fingers. As the years passed, it always seemed that our children enjoyed that manner of eating as much as Betty and I did.

In those early years we did not give much attention to the political differences of West Pakistanis and East Pakistanis. But looking back, soon after we moved to Comilla, early one morning our yard was filled with local college students running and screaming. They were being chased by para-military personnel. When I noted some of the chasers, they looked quite unusual for military personnel. Their trousers seemed to be short and that caused me to look more carefully. They were West Pakistani military dressed in uniforms which had been made for those much smaller in stature, East Pakistanis. But things like that happened and then it passed from our minds since we really did not understand some of the things, which much later, we did come to understand concerning the struggle between these two peoples of Pakistan.

Most of the time, some local person, speaking to us in their language, seemed to want us to understand different events like the one mentioned. But we knew it was not proper for us to become involved in local politics even though, in time, so much happened between these peoples, that even as an "outsider," we did begin to understand a little, at least.

I suppose it is true in many cultures that there are great differences in careers, in employment, and in ethnic groups. However, I admit that today when I notice those in my own situation, it troubles me greatly. I want us to be one but I know that we aren't one. But I believe deeply that we must work to understand our differences. Differences do not need to be settled by fighting at any level, but by at least understanding and knowing that even in religion, of all the places, differences must not be confronted by fighting with words or arms.

Comilla was only a few miles from the border of India. Hindus often moved from East Pakistan to India. Through the years I met many Muslims in East Pakistan who had left India to come to a Muslim area of the world, East Pakistan.

So, I admit I was always encouraged when I met someone from West Pakistan who seemed to be pleased to be in East Pakistan. One of those persons was the Director of the Village Development Academy in Comilla. This gentleman seemed to know his work and to do it well. We got acquainted with him in an unusual way.

An American family was working at that Academy. One day the couple came by our house to tell us that five young women with USA Peace Corps had been assigned to live with us while they were in special training at the Academy. The couple was seemingly a little embarrassed since we had not been informed of the decision of the Director. But that was okay since it was not the United States Government doing it but local people, so we were not politically involved with our own country but with an institution which was training local people and internationals to help village people develop in such a way that life would be better for them.

I always say, "Keep your eyes open and watch, for God is going to show you something special." So, having those five women with us for about two months was helpful. Four of them were pleasant young recent college graduates. The fifth one, however, was unusually different. Her age was about seventy. She was a Buddhist convert from California. We learned about her in a somewhat unpleasant way. At our first meal time with three of the five, including the older woman, we were seated at the table and after I gave thanks for God's blessing of the food, I also thanked Him for letting us help by keeping those women in our home.

Looking back, I agree one hundred percent with that Director in assigning those women to stay with us during their time of training. The manner in which he did it is not important. He had probably known some Christian missionaries in West Pakistan and knew that we would be glad to help. But that first night, after the prayer to our God, Betty began passing the food. Remember, we did not know that older woman was Buddhist. We passed the meat to her but she refused. We passed other dishes and she refused. We did not understand what was happening. But one of the younger women spoke up and said, "We know that you were not aware of it but she is Buddhist."

About a month later when those three left us, we knew we had not helped one of them very much. But Betty never fed her any meat or used any cooking oil from animals of any kind, and though she ate very well, we felt a little relieved she was leaving us.

But growing out of the experience with the Academy we met one of the teachers, who had his doctor of philosophy degree from the University of Minnesota. He and his wife were Bangla people or Bengalis all the way. While the husband was doing special training for the beginning of the Academy, his wife had given birth to their first child.

This couple loved the United States. Probably the biggest involvement for the wife was that when her child was born in the USA, nurses let her baby stay in the bed with her and not in a crib. She had told the nurses correctly that when she returned to East Pakistan, the baby would always sleep with her. Now, is that great? Things like that make many of us, at least most of the time, be glad that we are Americans.

This Muslim couple seemed to think our home was their home and we liked that. Probably the most amusing thing in our relationships was that the wife might drop by at any time. Then, the least hint of an invitation to eat with our family was accepted immediately. This may be a slight overstatement but we just say every time that wonderful couple ate with us, the husband would put the cloth table napkin in his back pocket and take it home with him. You see, paper napkins were not available, so if you used napkins, they were cloth and sometimes, a most beautiful cloth. We always knew that after the wife had several napkins which she had taken from her husband's pockets, she would return them and she enjoyed a good laugh every time. We just thought of him as the "absent- minded professor."

As a family, we enjoyed the relationship with the professor's family as much, I think, as possible. So, one of the next things we knew was, they, with their two children, and we with our two children, began a two hundred mile journey to the only resort area in East Pakistan at that time.

That meant the journey would be at least eight hours of actual driving. Our friends did not have a vehicle, but we had a British Land Rover assigned to us by our organization. It was very much like an American jeep but perhaps a little larger.

How were we going to travel those two hundred miles? Remember that there were eight of us. But both families wanted to make the journey. About six o'clock one morning we were ready to begin the long trip on a road which was supposedly two lanes but if you wanted to pass another vehicle, that vehicle had to move off the road for you. Or if you met another vehicle, it was understood by drivers that each vehicle had to be driven with one side off the main part of the road.

But how did the eight of us get into the vehicle and be in a position to travel such a long distance? The spare tire of the Land Rover was in its permanent place on the hood of the vehicle just above the engine. Next to the driver there was room for one person. Then there were two seats in the rear portion with each one having room for two travelers. But somehow, for this journey, there were three in each seat plus a good part of our luggage for about ten days. The remainder of the luggage was on top of the car.

We had food to eat in route to save us some time. The fuel tank held enough for the entire trip so that was no problem. We made it to our destination before darkness. The cabins did have electric lights. We had, along with our luggage, enough cooking equipment for the preparation of all our meals. Most of the time, the cooking fuel was wood, so we had sufficient smoke to keep everyone's eyes watering and burning. Betty and the wife in the other family did all of our cooking.

For me, this trip was worth it all. The time was in early 1960. We had been in East Pakistan for a total of more than two years. I deeply thought God would give me the right opportunity for a verbal witness to my beloved professor friend. The time came as the two of us walked along the beautiful beach of Cox's Bazar, the location of the beach area along the Indian Ocean. I began talking about Jesus and was as careful, I thought, as anyone could possibly be. I did not want to make a mistake. I wanted this man to know Jesus. I had not spoken more than two or three sentences when he said to me, "Jim, if you want our friendship to continue then do not try to make a Christian out of me." I felt just about as bad as any sincere person could feel.

We completed our time there. Our four children, though young in age, had a wonderful time. Betty and I had probably never been that close to a Muslim family, so of course, we thanked Almighty God for this opportunity. We were friends and the years before us were to prove that.

In the summer of 1962, we made preparation for moving all of our furniture back to the capital for storage while we were in the United States for eleven months. During those days back in Louisville, we lived in an upstairs apartment just across the road from the campus of the Southern Baptist Theological Seminary. Every time there was opportunity I attended chapel at the seminary. I gave much time, especially during those beautiful times of worship, to thinking about mistakes I had made as a first term international missionary. I also thought much about how I could have done better in my witness both verbally and by actions in my daily life.

One day, as I walked from the chapel building, a professor walked up behind me and placed his hand on my shoulder. He then said, "Do you ever think you might be wasting your time out there?" He had spoken briefly but said all that was needed.

I turned to him and clearly said, "I am not wasting my time out there anymore than you are wasting your time here." Having said that, I left him. I hurt deeply.

Before I was appointed as a missionary, I had been pastor of two churches, and I had preached in dozens of special meetings in churches large and small. As a student pastor, I had experienced the "coming to know Jesus as Savior and Lord" by many people. Preaching in those special revival meetings, I had seen many more people come to know Jesus. But during the previous four years I had not participated in winning even one person to my Jesus.

Before that day ended in which the confrontation with the highly respected seminary professor took place, we were on the phone apologizing to each other for our rudeness. This was hastened by Betty, when I told her what had happened and by my professor friend because of the encouragement he received from his wife. I never felt bad toward my God for what sometimes seemed like failures, but I had and have a deep feeling that every sincere follower of Jesus the Christ should always make our witness for Him such that others, maybe many others, will come to know the God whom you know as Lord of their lives.

CHAPTER THREE
Learning to Live with Feni Muslims

While we were home in the United States from August 1962 to July 1963 one of the most beautiful things which could have happened to us as a family was that, our two daughters, even though they were very young, kept talking about going back home. That really meant that they were asking when were we going back to East Pakistan. Through the years we have noted that many international missionary children ask similar questions when they are back in their home countries. Though there are a multiple of ups and downs in family life of international missionaries, it seems that most of the time we have great support from our children when living overseas.

While we were in the USA for those eleven months we knew that when we returned to East Pakistan we would not be going back to Comilla for when we moved out, another family had moved into the house where we had lived for three years. Since our mission board had decided to build a hospital in East Pakistan and the location for the hospital was to be in a smaller town called Feni, it was decided we would be the first family of our group to live in Feni. That was okay with us.

But we also learned that before we were to move to Feni, after our time in the States, we were to fill in at an industrial school for about one year, then, we were to move on to Feni. When you become part of a team you must be willing to fill in at any position. So we, without knowing anything about how to do the job of helping the teachers and students of the industrial school, gave it our best and after about fifteen months, we moved to Feni.

That move was just about one of the most interesting things we have ever done. We loaded most of our belongings on to a country boat and watched as the boat, powered by sails and oars, moved out from the nearby dock. It was three weeks later when we saw the boat again.

Riding on the boat was a Muslim man who had worked for us and though all of the boat crew were strangers to him, he ate with them, slept with them and of course, traveled those three weeks with that crew. Though our belongings were most of our earthly possessions, we had no doubt that all of the boat crew and above all, the man so well known to us, would manage the arrival of our earthly possessions in good condition.

As we had traveled by road in the Land Rover assigned to us, we had a trailer attached to our vehicle. As we moved along, so did some of our "valuables" such as the refrigerator, stove, and record player. In addition, most of our clothing was among what we were taking with us. We knew the boat with our belongings had to travel on some massive rivers. They were to make many turns and this part of the world is frequently visited by terrible wind storms. So, naturally we had our most valuable possessions on that trailer.

Could you believe it? I don't even remember how we were first informed the boat had docked about seventy miles from Feni. I drove the three hour trip immediately. At that same dock, many trucks had come from the port city of Chittagong loaded with cargo to be sent on by boats to the East Pakistan provincial capital of Dhaka.

Shortly after my arrival at the dock, I noted those empty trucks were ready to move back toward the port city. I knew they had no choice but to travel through Feni. It was easy to make a deal with the drivers and in about two hours we had loaded our boat cargo on those trucks and then off we journeyed. When it was all over, looking back, it seemed a simple process and we knew it was a simple process because, even if our friend had become sick as he rode that boat for the long journey, those boatmen would have arrived with everything we had loaded back in Faridpur. Now, forty-three years later, I would expect Muslim men, in such professions, to be and do the same, meaning, they would be perfectly honest and complete the task they were hired to do.

I mentioned in a previous chapter that Feni was a small town of about twenty-five thousand people. But, even as I walked the streets, on many occasions, the heavy traffic was not motorized vehicles, but pedestrians going in every direction. At that time, 1964, in the nearby rural areas, the population density was approximately one thousand people per square mile. So, especially on market days, Feni was a busy town.

Since it was well known that we were in Feni to be a part of that hospital which was to be built, many people became friends immediately. Of course, we were there to make plans for the early stage of the hospital construction and it was true, we were there to make friends.

More than forty years before our arrival, Australian missionaries departed Feni and since that time, as best we could understand, only two "foreigners," young men with the Peace Corps, had lived there. But after a few months, because of some international conflicts, they were moved to another country by the Peace Corps. While they were in Feni, they were our friends.

The Australian man who had been in Feni, I learned, was still living, though certainly elderly. Eventually, I was able to correspond with him. As I read his letters over a period of several months, I felt he had a deep wish and the wish was that he could be in Feni with us. That attitude, through his letters to us, gave us greater strength.

One of our colleagues, living only forty miles away in Comilla, supervised the building of two residences and we were now living in one of the residences. I constantly watched for land which might be purchased for the hospital buildings.

However, nothing definite could be done until we had permission from the government for the hospital. One local lawyer became a dear friend. I learned early in our relationships that he could be trusted all the way. I knew he worked diligently to get local support for the hospital, but he never got paid for that work.

At that time, the government hospital in Feni had one doctor and about ten beds. Since the doctor and others who followed were government doctors, they were regularly transferred to other hospitals. All of them, whom I got to know well, seemed to welcome the idea of a missionary hospital.

There was no doubt we were gaining local support for the hospital. But at the top of that list of assured support was a public meeting in Feni. The governor of East Pakistan came to Feni for the meeting. At the time of open discussion with the governor, our lawyer friend asked him about permission for the mission hospital. The reply was not very pleasing to local leaders and I was disappointed he did not give public support for the hospital.

While we were living in Faridpur, just before we moved to Feni, I went to the heliport to meet a colleague who was flying to Faridpur by helicopter. I saw a not well dressed, seemingly polite man lingering as if he were waiting for someone to come to the heliport for him.

Seeing the man waiting, as we were ready to depart to our house, I decided to ask the gentleman if we could help him. In no time, he was riding in the vehicle with us. To our amazement, we learned he was a son of the governor. About one month later, we had an appointment with the governor.

In our group of five to visit with the governor were the missionary doctors who were ready to begin serving at the future hospital. That son of the governor had been faithful in arranging the appointment. The time was probably late 1963 and was before the governor's visit to Feni. However, several years later, we received a message in writing from the government that we could not be given permission for the hospital because we were planning to use too much valuable land.

But long before that happened, one of the doctors, a single woman, moved to Feni and with another of the doctors living in Comilla, we began a mobile clinic. Though I knew nothing about medicine, I knew when I watched those two doctors function, with knowledge of the local language how much our hospital was needed in that area.

Also, on many of those village visits with the mobile clinic I heard things I had never heard before. On one occasion, a man, much older than I, had brought his wife to be examined by our woman doctor. While that was happening, I heard many conversations but one stood out above others. This conversation was about the possibility of a war between India and Pakistan. The difficulty involved West Pakistan and border areas with India. However, these East Pakistani men were one hundred percent in favor of their fellow-countrymen. The one word, which I hardly understood, was "jihad." Even the older men were talking about going to West Pakistan and fighting with their fellow Muslims in the jihad or war against Hindu India.

But back to the older man's wife and her examination. Our doctor told me she did not find anything wrong with the woman to hinder her giving birth. She asked me to explain what she had said to the husband. I said he was standing by me right then. The doctor said, as she looked at that elderly man, "Oh, he is the problem." I asked him his age and learned that he had passed seventy years. His wife was probably less than twenty-five years in age. Oh well, we live and learn but sometimes we do not know what to do in light of what we have learned. Though we did not recommend it, he probably needed to adopt a child.

It was always pleasing to me when I felt I was considered to be informed about Islam, or the religion of the Muslim people. One occasion this occurred was when a properly dressed Muslim leader came to our house one day.

We sat on our front porch since Betty and our two daughters were inside, and I knew it was not proper to invite him to be seated in our living room. So, we talked and talked on the porch. But he seemed to be more nervous than I had ever noticed him to be, so I was patient. Of course, I went inside our house and Betty prepared a piece of home-cooked cake and a cup of coffee for this friend. He ate well and I knew he enjoyed it.

After a long time this friend said, "I have a religious question to ask you." I was pleased thinking he was going to ask about Jesus, but I was wrong in my assumption. He seemed to become more nervous but after a time said, "You know that I have three wives." No, I did not know that. Then he said, "And you know I do not have a son." No, I did not know that. He continued by saying, "Some of my close friends are saying that I need to take a fourth wife who can give me a son."

Well, I knew I wasn't about to get into that. But I had to, for he said, "I have come to you because you are a religious man and I want to ask you your opinion about my taking a fourth wife." How was I going to answer this extremely kind gentleman about taking a fourth wife?

Suddenly, I knew what I was going to reply. So, I said, "Well, I have only one wife and I do well to get along with her, so how could I recommend that you take a fourth one?"

He looked at me and seemingly he was searching for an answer. Then he began laughing loudly and said, "I am going to take your advice. I am not going to take a fourth wife."

He drank the last of his coffee and with a wonderful smile thanked me for a very good time and walked toward the gate. I opened it for him and when he reached the nearby road, he looked back with a smile and then continued his foot journey toward his residence. I watched as he walked. He seemed to hardly lift his feet as he rapidly moved on.

Soon after we had moved to Feni I walked downtown. As I was walking back to our house, a young man, a college student, joined me as I walked. He wanted to talk in English and I was pleased to do that. At least I was more relaxed speaking English and I assumed he wanted to better learn my language. The young man seemed very proper in every way and his use of the English language was good. The distance we walked was probably about one-half mile. The time passed rapidly. As we neared my house he said, "What I really wanted to ask you was do you have any pictures of naked American women you can give me?" I could have screamed, cried or blasted him with English words but I didn't. My guess was that he had either seen a filthy American movie or a friend had told him about one he had seen. I told him, "No I do not have pictures of naked American women and I am not that kind of person."

I could have given that young man stronger words but I only began thinking about why he would ask me about such. I also knew that there were dozens of young Muslim men in that town who were students of mine, Bible students, and they would never ask me such a question or even think of such themselves. The correct answer, as I look back now would have been directed, not at this young man, but at the American movie industry.

But also I remembered what many people across God's massive world think—that if you have light skin and speak English, you are a vulgar person. Most people across the world, at least in early 1965, had never met a sincere "American Christian." But they had seen some movies.

Early in our time in Feni I learned how to tolerate, without too much difficulty, the language or title some of the young boys gave me. Over a period of time, many people began to understand that I did know their language, maybe not very well but at least I understood most of what they said. These young boys apparently did not know that I understood the names they called me. The first time I heard it troubled me some but not enough to reply to what had been said.

The earliest name I remembering hearing was that of "white monkey." There are not many white monkeys anywhere, but I never saw a white monkey in East Pakistan/Bangladesh. So, I couldn't allow what they called me to trouble me too much.

But there was little or no doubt they were becoming proud of their feat for the number using various names for me seemed to grow rapidly. Hence, I began thinking of a reply. So, one day, after I had walked passed a group of boys, I heard the name, "Red Dog" so I turned around and said in their language "Which is worse, a "Brown Dog" or a "Red Dog?" That was the first time I had turned and faced them after a title had been spoken. They were shocked and their faces clearly revealed it to me.

One of the young boys said, "Oh, sir, we did not know you understood our language. We are sorry." That was the last time I was given a special name. Perhaps they feared I would tell their parents about what had happened. But more likely, they knew they should not do what they were doing and decided to let that pass. When I was their age I possibly would have attempted something as bad or maybe, even worse.

But one of the names I loved dearly was "Bible." We eventually had five Bible Reading Libraries in that district. Catholic young men regularly read in the library nearest where they lived, but they were few in numbers since there was only one Catholic church in that district. In time, in addition to international magazines, local newspapers and such, many people began going to these centers to read even the Bibles in English and in their own language of Bangla. We were pleased that we were permitted to have these reading centers. This also led us to have special Bible studies for those who wanted to participate.

In early 1972, after war had broken out between the people of East Pakistan and the Government of Pakistan, I was traveling sometime past midnight in a rural area when a young man walked out on the dirt road in front of the vehicle I was driving. I stopped immediately recognizing him as a local young man. As he walked to my vehicle door, I rebuked him for stepping in front of the vehicle. I said to him, "If this had been a military vehicle you would have been killed."

He replied, "Sir, you don't understand." With that he called out to a companion, "It's Bible, come on out." One after another, young men moved out into the road. They pointed out to me that one was carrying a hand turned siren.

The first young man who had walked out in front of me said, "Sir, if you had been military, all of us would have attacked you and your vehicle." Many nights in late March and early April of 1971, when I traveled trying to help helpless people, I heard voices say at road stops, "It okay, it's only Bible." Yes, it was okay, because Bible was not there to harm but only to help.

Though our purpose for the Bible Reading Centers was not there to keep us out of trouble, trouble always seemed to be present. But on many occasions they surely did create trouble. One day I was called to quickly come to the Center in Feni town. One of the readers had decided that there was practically nothing to read but the Bibles and other related books, so he decided he would close down the Center. When I arrived I discovered that he had thrown some of the Bibles on the floor but when I walked in he seemed to calm down for a minute or so. However, he demanded that we close down the reading room immediately. I proceeded to inform the police at once.

He didn't seem to like the word "police" very much, so he decided he would depart but gave us an ultimatum to close the Center. I later discovered he was a relative of the local newspaper editor and time would tell us how serious he was in his battle against us.

Perhaps it is true that people in many religions have special ways of attempting to bring harm to those who do not agree with what others believe and practice. History surely proves this does happen. One day, one of the young Christian men who worked with us was in a nearby market place selling portions of the Bible and other Christian books. East Pakistan was his home and certainly to me he was a faithful young man. There always seemed to be one in every crowd of people who wanted to, maybe not physically harm us, but to at least prevent us from presenting the truth about Jesus as the Messiah.

Well, this particular young man, Andrew, was well pleased for he sold a good number of books and he knew those purchasing the books would learn much about Jesus and maybe even come to know Him. But it did not happen that way. This one man, with some of his partners, began striking Andrew. While this was happening, Andrew noted a bus beginning to move toward Feni.

As the bus was gaining speed it came near to where he had just risen from where he had been knocked down. He reached for a handle near the open door of the bus and pulled himself inside the bus. No one on the bus hindered him in any way so he made good his escape. When I learned about what had happened, one consolation was that often when one Muslim hindered or attacked one of us, others were there to help us.

But one of the most dangerous events at the Center in Feni was when a political group of young men decided that when the room was closed for one hour for lunch they were going to have their meeting on the front porch and on the land reaching out to the main street. When I learned they were having their political meeting on our property, I knew it had to be stopped.

There were opposition parties whom I knew would blame us for giving them the right to have a meeting on our property. So, without hesitation, I asked the leader to stop his meeting immediately. The students stopped their meeting but the leader gave me warning that the time would come when they, using his words, "would get me."

Soon that time would come. A few days after Feni had been struck by two planes of the Pakistani Air Force, I was in a shop on the main street asking counsel from the owner. I knew he was respected by many of the Muslims of the town and would give me his best advice. While we were talking, that student leader walked into the shop. He heard part of what we were discussing and turned to me and said, "Sir, you do not need to fear our group. We know which side you are on in this fight." I am sure I had never said anything, at least publicly, about the struggle so his words were assumptions but I liked what he said. Nine months later, after the many, many deaths, Bangladesh became a new and free nation. Those students had fought for the freedom of their land.

One other beautiful thing which we were able to do right up until war broke out was Bible correspondence courses offered by mail. We eventually had about two thousand students, most of them Muslims, studying in a Bible course which belonged to another missionary group, but they gladly let us participate with them. During the time of war, most students were either across the border in India or fighting Pakistani soldiers in East Pakistan.

As a family, then with two daughters and two sons, we did not fear the local people even though there were groups of East Pakistanis who sided with the Pakistani Government. When I traveled from the capital city of Dhaka back to Feni during those nine months, I often saw many of our students. They always wanted to know how they could help us. We tried to always let them know that since we were foreigners, we had no right to expect any direct help from the enemy of Pakistan. I do not believe any of those young men ever blamed us for statements like that which I often made, though down deep, we were for their cause. We wanted them to be a free country but we knew we had no right, as missionaries, to say anything.

CHAPTER FOUR
Difficult Days in Feni

In 1967, near the time for us to return to the United States for state-side assignment, our missionary configuration had changed. The doctor who had lived in Feni had left and about that time, the doctor family who lived in Comilla had also departed.

It did appear the hospital permission would never be given. However, refusal had not been sent in writing and that was the form we believed the Government of Pakistan would follow. But a few years before our second departure back to our "old Kentucky home," many good things happened. Uppermost among those for our family was another missionary family moved to Feni and the wife in the family was a medical doctor. Local people were aware we were continuing our attempt to get permission for the hospital.

Some were saying we never intended to build the hospital but others knew we were making every attempt. One of those was our lawyer friend whom I mentioned in the previous chapter. He and a large group of his friends very much wanted a hospital and they made this clear to the masses of people in the Feni area.

We departed Feni in July of 1967 for the United States. This assignment was to be about eleven months again and a wonderful eleven months to be with our two families. Our children were to have another opportunity to become reacquainted with those they deeply loved but rarely saw.

Those kinds of experiences did happen. Four years had passed since we had been with our family and time, as it is always expected to do, had caused our love to deepen. Now that love deepened even more during the months we were in Louisville, where Betty's mother and my parents lived. Being with our families only made us realize, in a fresh way, how much we loved them and how much at times, we had missed them.

While we were in the States, we learned the Pakistani Government had made a decision about the proposed hospital and that their decision was permission was denied. Since we had Pakistani visas, we could return to that country and especially to Feni, East Pakistan.

It was soon time for our Feni missionary colleagues to return to the States, so we missed them very much.

During the next four years, life in Feni and in all of East Pakistan was to radically change for the local people and for us. Though in 1968 there was relative peace, yet often there were riots in various places against the Government of Pakistan. But this had happened before and we never thought of anything bad really happening. By bad I mean the destruction of human life by political groups, one against the other. Often, it seems that the most innocent of people are the ones who receive the greatest amount of damage in one or another way.

But one thing was clear. Our missionary group had been refused permission for the hospital we had hoped would be built. However, we had no choice but to live with the decision of the national government. The sad thing is radical groups were to accuse us of never really planning for the hospital. They broadcast in different ways that we had deceived the local people by saying we wanted to build the hospital, though the great majority of people seemed to acknowledge we had made every plan for the hospital, we had done our best in our efforts to receive government permission, and it was the national government who denied us the permission.

Just before we went back to our home country in 1967, we received another four year multiple entry visa for serving in Pakistan. My visa application clearly stated that I was a missionary. In this book, I must say several times, the Government of Pakistan had been gracious to many of us as international missionaries and I attributed this to the fact that many of their officers had known missionaries in West Pakistan and some of those officers had even attended missionary schools. During 1971, when massive numbers of East Pakistani people were killed, I met many military officers from West Pakistan who spoke highly of the international missionaries they had met in one way or another in their part of Pakistan. So, really the trouble seemed to be that local Muslim leaders from East Pakistan and particularly, the East Pakistan Governor, had taken a position against us.

Though I do not want to write too much at this time about 1971, news sources told of one night in which the former governor's body was dug up from his grave a few months after he had died. His death came one night when a group of freedom fighters knocked on his door and afterwards declared that they had brutally killed him. Further, those men declared they had thrown his body into a river for the soil of East Pakistan was too sacred to hold that body. Perhaps it happened in this way. But let's wait for the next two chapters to write about such experiences.

Feni was again our home. But we now knew for sure that many Muslims would believe the gossip we had never planned for the hospital. Others, some of them I would call strict Muslims, always stood with us and blamed the governor for the refusal.

Always remember, as you read, that this missionary family wanted above all else, for people to know Jesus the Messiah, as their personal Lord. So, with not just young men, but often older men, coming to one of those five reading centers in the district, to read the Bible and related books, we were pleased.

We were always grateful to be in a land that though primarily Muslim, gave us freedom to do our thing. You will remember that in Chapter Two I wrote about the love many Muslims had for Jesus. Also remember that I wrote about the fact that I did not consider myself a good student of Islam, but that I did know many devout Muslim people and many of them spoke often to me by calling Jesus, "your Isa." Of course, I loved those kinds of statements. There was never even a temptation to deny that He was our Jesus. But more than that, we were His through a personal experience of salvation from our sins and a new kind of life because of Him. So, He was our "Isa" or Jesus.

An update on our family when we returned to East Pakistan in about July, 1968, shows that our two boys were ages four and two and the two girls were ten and eight. Betty was their teacher and the most I knew about their "home school" was the five sure were a disciplined five.

Though home schooling ended for them at grade eight, they all became college graduates and two of the first four received post graduate degrees. Jill, our fifth child who joined us in 1973, always attended regular school.

There were two Christian families living in Feni, and the children of one family often came and played with our children. Many of our Muslim neighbor children also came to our house almost daily to play and to enjoy the good home-made sweets Betty kept prepared for them.

One day Betty called me to the kitchen and when I walked in she motioned for me to be quiet and for me to come near the window. One of our children was talking with one of the little Muslim girls and what we heard was beautiful. Our daughter was trying to learn her little friend's language. So, the little neighbor girl would use a Bangla word and our daughter would reply, "Say it again." Then our daughter would attempt to repeat what her friend had said. Then, they moved from single words to sentences. One thing for sure, our daughter's mom and dad loved what they heard and saw. Needless to say, that daughter's Bangla, through the years, without a doubt, sounded much better than that spoken by her mom and dad.

Since I was one of the older evangelical missionaries living in East Pakistan even in 1968, I often had the opportunity to work with other Christian groups. That did keep me away from my family but I guess, down deep within me was an assurance that if Betty needed help there were a host of people who would have taken "their last step in life" for my family. Looking back now, I am sure I had the right to feel that way.

Early one morning the above paragraph became reality. A devoted Muslim friend came to our house and asked Betty where I was. This friend had just read the new bi-monthly local newspaper where the editor had written about how local people had a right to question who Mr. McKinley really was. The charges or doubts about me were severe. There was no doubt what the editor wanted to accomplish. He wanted the local people to think of me as a spy or secret service agent of the United States government.

My Muslim friend wisely suggested that Betty try to get the information to me immediately which she did. The friends, with whom I was staying during the days I was speaking in meetings for them, called me to the phone. Betty was on the line. She simply and briefly told me about our friend's visit to our house and a statement or two about the news article. I assured her I would immediately depart for home and hopefully, I would arrive in the late afternoon.

The distance to our home in Feni was about eighty miles. I was traveling by train. As the trains traveled through densely populated areas, they stopped often for passengers even when there was not a station. Even that day, stopping for village people as they did was commendable. So, I had sufficient time to think about what I would do when I reached Feni. Included in my thinking were the names of several people whom I knew I could count on for help. Though the day seemed longer than usual and I rode three different trains to make the journey home, I arrived in Feni late in the afternoon.

Riding from the train station, I encouraged the rickshaw man to go as quickly as possible to my home. I didn't need to tell him where I lived because he and just about everybody else in that area knew where the foreign family lived.

When I arrived at our gate, Betty was there to meet me. It was as if she knew about when I was to arrive. That was encouraging to me. Then Betty said, "What are you going to do?" She did not have any suggestions. Her question, even in such a dangerous situation, caused a smile to tickle my face. She had just said, without putting it into words, "Do what you think is best and do it quickly." I said, "Darkness will soon fall and we may need to make a special decision before that happens."

Those slow train rides had given me sufficient time to think and before the third train of the day pulled into the Feni station, I knew what I was going to do after talking with Betty. I had ridden the rickshaw from the station with the top up covering me or at least causing most people to not notice me as I rode through the town. But my decision, after talking with Betty was to say, "You may need to pack a few things for each of the children in the event we need to travel as darkness will soon be approaching."

I briefly described to Betty what I intended to do immediately. I was going to walk down our street into town and to walk each of the main streets going on one side and returning on the other. That would mean most of the people in the streets would notice me and

I knew that news travels quickly and they would have an opinion about the news article.

I further told Betty that I would greet as many people as possible with a "salaam" of peace with the hopes that many of them would return that greeting. In a few minutes I began walking toward the main part of Feni. As I walked, I remained on our side of the road. Also, I felt little pressure for I knew most of the people on both sides of our street would greet me kindly. I only recall one person who refused to return my greeting of peace.

That person was the imam of the mosque located on our side of the road. But many times I had attempted to talk with him but he always ignored me as if he did not even understand what I was attempting to say. So, his refusal did not trouble me too much. Obviously, I tired as I walked. It had been a long day with deep tensions. The question had roamed through my mind as I traveled on those trains "What will be the response of most of the local people?"

The longer I walked the better I felt. I do not think it is an overstatement to say roaming through my mind was the thought, "The Lord our God loves us far more than we are ever able to love Him." I also thought, "He knows how to manage the thoughts of the people of a town of about twenty-five thousand people." This was a market day and though night was quickly approaching, there were still many village people in town winding down their business for the day.

I was pleased to reach the opposite side of the road leading back toward our house. But my mind was still roaming even as I gave the peace greeting. I did not believe local people would physically harm Betty or our children.

However, I had no doubt that there were some who would delight in severely harming me physically and I could only imagine what reaction this would bring to Betty and our children. But all of a sudden a beautiful thing happened. It was as if the entire incident had dropped down from Heaven. Of course, that would be my Manager at His best.

Well, what could so suddenly happen? The answer is one of my friends called out to me right in front of his shop. He said, "Come in and let me serve you a cup of tea." Though the cup was small the tea was hot and my friend had already added both milk and sugar. I must admit that tea felt wonderful as it eased down my dry throat. It had disappeared quickly and I had been greatly helped with that small cup of tea. I had to hasten on toward our house which was only about fifteen minutes from my friend's shop. So, I said to him, "I must go and get home quickly." A strong "No," quickly rang out and he added, "I must talk with you."

Never had I seen my friend so seemingly nervous. Then, all of a sudden speaking with a strong voice he said, "We are going to kill that editor."

I was astonished and replied, "What editor?"

My friend said, "The one who lied about you."

I truly believe I was relaxed so I calmly said, "No, you are not going to kill him."

Then he replied, "But he is a communist infidel and you are a man of the Book." Again my "No" was calmly stated and it was followed by, "Well, when we discussed this we said you would probably refuse us."

Now, try to remember that this friend's shop was directly or almost directly across the road or street from the mosque where the imam had refused to give me a greeting of peace. But my friend had more to say. "Well, we will burn the building that houses that editor's press."

My quiet reply was, "No, you cannot do that either."

Then a seemingly desperate statement came forth, "But what can we do? You are our friend and we want to help."

I easily replied, "You have helped and I will go home and tell Betty and our children that we do not have to leave Feni. We have many friends who will stand with us as needed." The walk home was swift and easy.

Again, Betty was waiting for me at the gate. She didn't ask for details which seemed to be a way of life for us as a family. I simply told her that everything was okay. But as I walked home and passed a particular house I remembered a recent incident involving the friend with whom I had just talked and been so encouraged.

This friend came to our house at about ten o'clock at night and asked me if I could possibly take his nephew to the Chittagong hospital. Of course, I could do that. It was apparent that the young man was very sick and the local hospital probably could not adequately care for him.

So, about an hour later we were moving toward the port city and as I drove I remembered well that Chittagong was our first real look at Pakistan back in November, 1958, or about eleven years before. The trip was never easy. Most of that road had little more than enough room for one vehicle and when vehicles met, someone had to give a lot of space to the other. If the on-coming vehicle was a loaded truck, it was only right to keep them on the main part of the road with their heavy load. So, it probably took us about three hours to travel the sixty-five miles, or at least about that many miles.

We reached the hospital at about two o'clock in the early morning. I remained in the vehicle while my friends made all of the arrangements. About an hour later, my particular friend came to me and said the young man had been admitted to the hospital and that he would remain with the family members. I got down from the vehicle to have a stretch before beginning my journey back to Feni. When I opened the door the interior light came on and when that happened, my friend screamed, "You are bleeding."

As we had traveled that long journey without stopping, I had been a little uncomfortable at times but if I twisted my body a little, it seemed to help. While sitting in the vehicle at the hospital, I had not known that I had been bleeding through my trousers and onto the seat. Driving long distances on terribly rough roads often caused hemorrhoidal bleeding.

So this was not the first time this bleeding had happened nor was it the last time. As I told my friend that it was okay and I had very little pain and I would be okay to drive back to Feni, he seemed to accept what I had said. I reached home at about six o'clock or just as the sun began to rise.

While walking home from my friend's shop that day, encouraged by the many things that had happened as I walked, I had no doubt that my God knew how to manage in the most difficult of circumstances. The beautiful thing is those kinds of experiences continue to happen because my God never tires.

In 2002, during the later part of October, I was traveling down the road on which we had lived for about eight years and the same road I had walked by in 1968 and I was watching for a particular shop which I understood was owned by my friend's son. All of a sudden I felt I had spotted the right shop so I requested the rickshaw operator to stop. I got down from the rickshaw and walked into the shop. Though everything on the road was very different I believed I was at the right place.

As I walked into the shop I knew I was in the correct place for a gentleman, dressed in a dark suit arose from a chair and came toward me quickly. As he walked in my direction, he screamed, "My father's friend!" He put his arm around me and embraced me tightly. He spoke many quick words about his father and the relationship I had experienced with him. I had no doubt that this son loved the Christian missionary man as much as his father had loved me.

When I had last seen this man he was a young college student. But standing in the shop that day, I was beyond speaking. Everything was highly emotional to me as I tried to recall some of the things which had happened on that special day in 1968. I hope this is not supposing too much but I guess I believe today that my friend was waiting for a special word from me, and then he would have been ready to risk his life to carry out what he believed would have been a religious decree. Of course what he wanted to do was certainly not within what I believed as a Christian and I do not have the right to say that it would have been acceptable to religious leaders of Islam. So, I think it would have been a violation of Islam to think that his missionary friend could give such a decree. But I do say that I loved this man for the fact that he wanted to help me and my family when I was in what could have been a very serious situation.

Quickly I made my way back into the street in my rickshaw. I had told my friend's son a goodbye and as the rickshaw moved away, tears gushed down my face. The most important thing I thought about as I moved on to a few other places I wanted to visit in the short period of time I had left to be in Feni was whether I had failed my friend. Was there some other way that I might have presented

Jesus to him? I don't know but I know I loved that man and I knew he sincerely loved me as well as my family.

Times were changing in East Pakistan during the late 1960s. There was great political unrest. People seemed to hardly understand what they needed to believe or say or do. There appeared to be tension almost everywhere. Betty and I discussed that maybe we should take the children to the capital city for a visit with missionary friends. She and our children had gone six months without seeing any of our foreign friends.

So, early one morning the six of us started out for Dhaka in a Volkswagen Microbus. We had traveled this road many times and felt at ease as we moved along. I knew there would probably be mobs on the road, but I did not expect them to hinder or harm us. But about half the distance to Comilla we came to a road block. The in-charge men seemed to be apologetic when they told us we had to turn our vehicle and return to our home in Feni. It was a big disappointment to all of us. Actually, it was years later when we again saw some of those friends we would have seen in Dhaka had we made the trip that day.

Once, I was telling about a time when threats were made against us. Much later, Betty said to me "Don't you remember when we stopped in Comilla to purchase special bread at a bakery and a group of men threatened us?" No, I did not remember. Another time the older of our two sons heard me talking about some of the more difficult times and he said, "Dad, bad things happened often. How do you expect me to remember a particular one?" He was probably six and his little brother four when the following happened to the three of us.

I knew of different missionary mothers who diligently taught their children for many years and I knew Betty was one of those. Though I may have not been nearly as grateful as I should have been, at least, on occasions, I tried to be thoughtful and helpful. So, one Thursday night, I suggested to Betty that since I had a full day's journey ahead of me the next day, would it not be good if the boys went with me. She immediately accepted the suggestion even though the boys would miss a day of school. But since they were much younger than their sisters, their missing one day of school would do no harm.

So the big day began for us when we backed out of the driveway and on to the road. We had our lunch. We had our drinking water so we started out that Friday morning by eight o'clock so we could visit four of the reading centers and deliver many correspondence courses to students in that area of the district. The boys seemed to be pleased but of course did not consider that we would return home late in the afternoon. They drank lots of water but we had a sufficient supply.

The younger of the two boys had red hair which was a new color for most of the people we were to see that day. That red hair was certainly noticed throughout the day. For most and maybe even all of the people who saw us that long day, little light skinned boys had never been seen before in that area.

Before the day ended, our journey had taken us about fifty miles west and almost to the massive Megna River. If we stopped for just a few minutes without getting out of the vehicle, lots of men and boys looked through the windows to see the two unusual looking boys in the vehicle. I could only imagine the way most of those who saw my sons that day were to describe them to other family members when they returned to their homes.

But we did our job which included visiting with each of the young Christian men in each of the centers. We offered every possible encouragement to them. They had all come from Christian villages and were not accustomed to being with only Muslims or occasionally with a few Hindus. But they were now to relate to those of other religions and to share their faith in Jesus.

The last center we visited was the one farthest from our house. We probably departed there at about two o'clock in the early afternoon. As most of the roads were, the ones we traveled that day were narrow and so we rarely passed another vehicle. The vehicles we did pass were usually buses which were stopped off the road to pick up passengers.

We had gone about thirty miles when I noticed that off in the distance the road was filled with men walking in our direction. The road was level and perhaps I first saw this group when they were a mile or two away. But as we moved on toward them, I understood without a doubt that this was a mob of angry men and boys.

However, I didn't think too much about the scene except to remember carefully how I would react to the crowd. I planned to do what I usually did in such circumstances. I would bring the vehicle to a very slow forward motion. Then as we got near the crowd, I planned to touch the horn lightly thinking that as many times this had happened in the past, the leaders would come to the front and move their people to the side of the road so that there would be no harm to anyone. I did my thing but the leaders did not come to the front.

This large group of maybe one thousand people had leaders but it appeared they did nothing to stop their mob. In just a few minutes the vehicle was surrounded. The road where we had stopped was about twenty feet above the fields on each side. I guess I thought they would pass on by and then we could move on toward home. But they didn't pass on by.

No one attempted to speak to us. Maybe they thought we could not understand their language and surely in a rural or village group like this one, probably no one knew any English. But we soon learned they spoke Bangla and spoke it clearly. The first statement I heard was, "Rock the vehicle!" My first thought as they began rocking the van was that they were teasing us. But then I thought they were going to roll the vehicle over the embankment. I never thought of trying to get out of the vehicle. Even if all three of us got out we would probably be separated and I did not even want to think of what might then happen.

They seemed to be enjoying rocking the Microbus. In those moments, dozens of thoughts rapidly passed through my mind. No doubt, they hated the government of Pakistan and they hated it even more because the government was military.

But, why us? I doubt that anyone among them knew who we were. Not at that time, but later, I concluded that because we were foreigners, we possibly owned the vehicle or at least had it in our possession right then so we in a sense represented the elite and they were poor people and I have no doubt that all of them were Muslims.

I never thought of this at the time of all that confusion but later I found myself wishing that a few of our devoted Muslim students had appeared on the scene, we would have had them as friends but that did not happen.

They continued rocking the vehicle. I could see my boys in the mirror. They did not make one sound which I heard. But then I heard an awful hateful sound. It was "Remove the gasoline cap," and I knew immediately when that had happened. I knew because I could smell the gasoline as the vehicle was being rocked and it undoubtedly sloshed out on the side of the van.

Then, no more terrifying words could be heard by a father caught with his two sons in such a horrible situation. Those words were "Who has a match?" Remember that every word spoken was Bangla and my boys understood those simple words. But finding a match was not a simple undertaking. You see, in a group like that probably no one owned a cigarette lighter and possibly no one had even one match and certainly not a little box of matches. If they smoked, most of the time, there was a place by the side of the road which sold cigarettes and they had a lighted jute string and that was used by any and all to light their cigarettes.

Since we were on the high part of the road, there wasn't much standing room. There were men and boys crowded on each side and in the front and back of the vehicle. Suddenly, an elderly looking man dressed in a white prayer cap, a white shirt and trousers began forcing his way to my side of the vehicle.

As he pushed and screamed, I marveled at his power. He was too old to do things like that. But he made it to my side door. The crowd pressed against him and I noted how his chest shook. You see, I had the motor running and had the gear shift pulled down into the lowest or most powerful gear. I had done all of this when they had first stopped our van.

Here that elderly small man stood by my door with a look of compassion on his face. Then he spoke the kindest words I have ever heard uttered. With a sad expression, he said in English, "Sir, you are in much trouble." But he had more to say, "If there is any way to get you out of here, I am going to do that."

I replied, "Please do that."

In that horrible situation, I marveled at what he began to do. He pushed, he shoved, he screamed. He did the things only an athlete was capable of doing. The young men in the crowd seemed to think he was funny so they began pushing and shoving and screaming. Some rolled over the embankment. Then, not some but many of the younger ones were pushed over that embankment and some seemed to just jump. Actually, in a very short time, I noted fewer men in front of the vehicle but the elderly gentleman continued his venture.

Then, all of a sudden, as if he knew what he was doing, he motioned for me to move the vehicle forward but I could not do that for there were still a few men on the road in front of the vehicle. But seemingly again, with one plunge he knocked those in front of our vehicle and the road was open enough for us to flow out quickly. I did take care to make sure I did not stall the engine for that would be the end of all efforts. But the engine did not stall and we were out of there.

Still, I had not heard one word from my boys. I kept watching the rear view mirror but noted that no one in the crowd chased our van. After a few minutes and several miles down the road I pulled off to the side and turned off the ignition. Though the engine had stopped, the vehicle seemed to continue shaking. I guess it shook because my entire body was shaking. I said nothing to my boys for I did not know what I needed to say.

We quietly sat there in the old vehicle by the side of the road. During all of that time and during the incident we did not see another vehicle.

Then, the older of the boys said, "Dad, they were going to kill us, weren't they?"

I replied, "Yes, they were going to kill us." I thought, "Dear God, give me something better for my boys," and He did for I was able to speak clearly, "But they didn't kill us, did they?"

They replied, "No, Dad, they did not kill us." After a few minutes, we drove on home.

Since we were late, Betty was at the gate and she opened it for us to enter the yard. I gave no attention to the boys as I stepped out of the van. Betty immediately said, "Did you have trouble?"

I replied, "Yes we did."

Then she added, "Are you okay?"

I answered quietly, "Yes, but I am not sure about the boys." Betty never asked me more about what had happened that day. Again, that was just the way we did it as one missionary family living with Muslims.

However, the next day I heard that a mob of men had attacked a police station, practically destroyed it, and left six policemen dead.. I never shared that with Betty and our children for years.

On several trips, when I traveled on that same road, I asked about the elderly man. One reply I received one day was from a man who said he had heard about that story and had often wondered who the elderly man was.

He continued by saying that he had asked many people about the elderly man but the answer was always the same. They, too, did not understand who he was but knew that it was a very ugly situation and that elderly man had saved the missionary and his sons. This particular man said that day, "So, you are that missionary man. Why, I have seen you many times. I had no idea they had attacked you. They should not have done that to you and your little boys." I was pleased that he added the boys.

The above incident probably happened in early 1970. I first wrote down, as best I could recall, most of what I remembered in late 1991 and then attempted to tell the story as best I could at the Sunday morning worship of the largest Baptist Church in Kentucky. I didn't do very well telling the story. Now, years later, though much of the story has been printed earlier, it is certainly highly emotional to me. I can only add that for international missionaries who have children with them, those children are as golden as gold can be. I can only hope that these above words of the day with my two boys have expressed with enough feeling and description to have you feel what happened that day.

Regarding the elderly man, if you are a believer, then your ideas about him are as good as mine.

CHAPTER FIVE
A Wedding, a West Pakistani,
and Our Muslim Visitors

Until the dates of November 12-13, 1970, one day could be very quiet and pleasant and the following day might be filled with activity of every kind. Sometimes though that activity wasn't against us as a family, yet there was often physical danger. We understood this and were very careful about the different places in Feni and the surrounding areas, which we knew we should not visit for any reason.

But the above mentioned dates changed the course of life for East Pakistan's people. I still do not know an accurate estimate of the number of deaths when a forceful cyclonic tidal wave struck the primarily southern coast of East Pakistan.

I may have mentioned earlier that an estimate I read early this year listed 300,000 people killed. But recently, our local newspaper here in Louisville gave the number of deaths as 500,000. That is the number I had been using through the years and I do recall that many news reporters gave this as the first estimate. But whatever the correct number of deaths, surely the total number killed was the most killed in any natural disaster across the world, since a flood in China in 1932.

Sometime before that disaster happened, Betty and I were invited to a wedding in Feni. Both of the families involved were known as distinguished people, and though I did not know the family of the groom, I knew the bride's family very well. This family owned land, and a considerable amount of land, but they were also business people. So, the wedding was a big event.

From the beginning, it was apparent the wedding was a traditional Muslim wedding. When we first arrived, Betty was taken to a section of the larger building where the bride and the women who were family and friends were located. But the area of most activity was with the groom. Of course, it was immediately noticed by most of those present, that Betty and I were among the invited guests. In such a situation, it was most always noted, if you were alert, that some or even most of the people welcomed the foreigners who were also Christian missionaries. But the refusal sometimes, to even giving a greeting of any kind, was practiced by others. Those people probably wondered why the head of that family had invited such people as Christian missionaries.

I think it is correct to say that most of the time Betty was welcomed more at such occasions than I was. But that had become a way of life and it is only at times like now when I am writing that I ever give much attention to those negative feelings of people we met who, without a doubt, considered themselves much more devout in their Islamic faith.

A few years after retirement from the now International Mission Board in 1992, I made five trips to Israel and Gaza to be involved in a special study regarding international missions in those two areas. In a special section of Jerusalem, on several occasions, a friend pointed out to me the special dress of some of the religious leaders of the Jewish people.

I always noted the special cap worn on the back of the head which was usually black but could be a small round white cap. Often those men had deep black beards and there were other distinguishing parts of their clothing. But, though I had lived with Muslims for about thirty-four years, this was very interesting to me and since then I have been more alert, for whatever it may be worth, to the garments worn by religious leaders of different groups of people.

But when I thought about the way the Jewish leaders dressed, I remembered well that, when it came to variety, they were much like the Muslim leaders I had known well through the years. But all you need to do is keep your eyes open and you will notice that among more informal Christian leaders, there is much variety in the clothing even the most distinguished ones wear.

I have been watching a DVD that has six parts and I have noted four different beautiful sport shirts worn through the first four sections by the famous pastor speaking. I look forward to the two remaining teachings and also to the two remaining sport shirts.

So, as I recall the different styles of clothing the Muslim religious leaders wore, even at that wedding, I knew that clothing, "never made the man inside the clothing." But I saw it all when we attended that wedding in Feni. Some of the seemingly more pious ones may have attempted to add to their piety with the special clothing but all of us knew this made no difference in their true being.

Among the many interesting things that day, the food seemed to take precedence for all of us. That was a perfect time to fill your stomach with the best of food and I attempted to do my best with the eating.

At the present time, Betty and I have five children and eleven grandchildren. I have decreed as one of the grandfathers that there must be at least two more grandchildren, because I have a great interest in and a great love for children. That day of the wedding I think my most interesting action was that of watching the little children. Many of them knew they were among relatives, but they could not, apparently, sort out who was who, but on the other hand, that did not matter. This was a big occasion, and they were privileged to meet new friends whether those friends were relatives or not.

Since the room where the bride was located was very crowded, most of the children stayed out in the open and the location of the groom was in a large tent with all of the sides, except the area just behind the groom, which was open. Those children, when the formal part of the wedding was completed, could have probably fully described everything which had happened to that point. Dressed in their best, they truly seemed to be excited.

I was nearby when the religious leader came to the groom and seemed to mumble a few words. When he stood to depart, one of my friends said, "They are now married."

After some time had passed and I was standing near where the groom was sitting, the father of the bride came to me and said, "In just a few minutes I will take the groom to meet my daughter, the bride." He did everything carefully and I had no doubt, he wanted me to understand everything which was happening. Then the father added, "I want you to accompany me when I take the groom to my daughter." I could not believe what he had said though he said it in English.

A few minutes later, the father spoke to the groom who stood and began walking toward me. The father briefly introduced me and we were on our way.

For sure, I had my camera with me and protected it as if it were the most valuable of possessions. The father led the groom, his new son-in-law, into the room filled with women. It took me some time to locate the bride. She was seated on a carpet.

The father had the groom sit by the bride. Of course, they were now husband and wife. Betty was also seated on the carpet nearby. Except for some space just in front of the couple, the room was jammed with women. The father of the bride stood at a distance and I stood with my camera ready.

Betty and I learned later that both the groom and the bride were college graduates and most pleasant people. The bride, according to custom, sat with her entire face covered with her beautiful red sari. One of the women standing directly behind the bride had a hand-fan and almost continuously fanned the bride. I am sure that in that non-air conditioned room with all of us crowded in that the kindness of that woman with the fan was deeply appreciated.

In that extremely warm room, the groom undoubtedly decided to have some fun in that women-filled room. He reached over as if attempting to lift the veil from his new wife's face and as he did that the woman standing behind the bride struck his hand with that small fan. There was a roar of laughter by the women.

Though this couple had been friends for several years, they tried to act according to custom and of course, they knew well that many of the people attending this wedding followed the strictest customs. For many of those present that custom meant that marriage is planned by the two families and that often the couple see each other for the first time when they have just been married. This old Christian missionary man thinks their customs may be as bad as ours. Also, I know that in many sections of Muslim people, friends have found ways to make sure the ones to be married have the opportunity to at least meet, somehow.

Days like the wedding day always helped us to manage in the midst of difficulties. We knew that we had many friends among the many Muslims of the greater Feni area. A few days after that wedding, the couple came to our house for a short visit. The bride was beautifully dressed and the groom wore an English suit. They had seen enough to understand, even on their all-important wedding day, to know that we had deeply enjoyed their wedding so they came to thank us for accepting the invitation.

Buying gasoline in Feni became a problem for me. There were two service stations and two of my best friends were the owners. Business competition was fierce so I attempted to purchase the gasoline every other time from each of my special friends, the father of that bride being the owner of one of them.

In late 1970, a new political officer came to Feni on his Pakistan government assignment. He was a very pleasant man and in the early months, he, though he did not speak the local Bangla language, seemed to be accepted by most local people. His home was West Pakistan and this was his first visit to our part of his country. Soon after his arrival, his wife from West Pakistan joined him in Feni. I am not sure when I first met this gentleman, but it was natural for him to willingly accept me as a friend. Since I did not know his primary language and he didn't know Bangla, our only way to converse was in English. I understood early in our relationships that our speaking in English, especially before others who did not understand what we were saying, was improper at a time of turmoil between the parts of Pakistan. Hence, I did hear occasionally the question about why the Feni people needed to be ruled by someone who did not know their language.

A few weeks following the horrible tidal wave, elections were held for a new Pakistani Government. Two men from the Feni area were elected and it was later announced that one of those men had received more votes than anyone else for the National Assembly.

One of those men, the one who received the large number of votes, was a very close friend of mine. Soon after the election, the government officer invited me to a special meeting. Among those present, and we numbered about one dozen, were the two newly elected members of the National Assembly. At that time, the military was in charge of all of Pakistan. It was not an easy time with the newly elected government waiting to take control of the country.

Among those present at that special meeting was the editor of the local newspaper, who had nothing to say to me. Nor did I attempt to say anything to him. Two matters were presented to the group by the officer. Those two were the possibility of badly needed lighting for the town and a park especially for children, but which could also be used for meetings of different kinds.

When he had invited me, the officer told me that the matters to be discussed would not be political in any way. I had accepted that and the only thing I said at the meeting was that I certainly did support the two matters. The meeting went well with plans for other meetings scheduled. No one seemed to resent my presence except the editor. Though I knew little about the faith of most of those in the meeting, all were Muslim except me. As for me, I was pleased to be a part of a group that could help the people where we lived.

We never met again. Our planned second meeting didn't seem important in light of all the political unrest. Though I went downtown regularly, I never felt completely at ease. Feelings went deep and I sensed that most people did not seem to know where to vent their feelings.

In the midst of all the confusion, we decided it was right for us to invite the West Pakistani officer for dinner. We had learned that his wife had gone back to their home in West Pakistan. He came that night with a guest of his whom he had mentioned to us when we invited him for dinner.

But as they entered our home, we felt bad about that second guest. He was a Pakistani army captain and of course, was from West Pakistan. Their jeep, that night, carried a large black flag which was supposed to indicate they were against the atrocities being committed across East Pakistan by the army.

To our dismay as a family, the captain carried a pistol in his holster and placed a deadly sten gun on a table in our living room upon their arrival. Our living-dining room was combined and even when we sat to hopefully enjoy the good food Betty had prepared, that sten gun was nearby.

The evening visit was brief. The few comments the captain made were too crude for all of our six family members at that time. The Government officer, who had told us of his many Christian friends in West Pakistan when we first got acquainted with him, was certainly not comfortable because we were sure he knew we were uncomfortable with the captain. Betty and I understood that the captain was really the in-charge person. We came to understand that night that the captain also considered himself a good Muslim.

An elderly man became a very devoted and faithful friend of mine. He seemed to hardly notice the political ups and downs of life for the people in his area and even less for the vast areas with millions of East Pakistanis often fearing what might happen next in their land. I became acquainted with this gentleman in an unusual way for a foreigner living in his area of what was to soon be Bangladesh.

The way I got met him was an older son of his had apparently gone into town early one morning and had spent a good amount of time drinking some form of alcohol. There was no doubt that he had taken into his body a good amount of that junk stuff. I knew he was by the side of the road just in front of the house because I heard him calling out for help. When I saw him, I knew he did need help. He wasn't on the road but down in the ditch between our house and the road. Several people who had been walking from town saw the man and were devoting their time to watching him. This was also a new experience for me though, as a boy, I had seen many drunk people.

But I must admit that he was in an unusual situation. The ditch was not so much for carrying water during the heavy rains but it was also a conveyance for carrying all kind of debris, including the over-flow from the outhouses. Sometimes when there were small amounts of rain falling over a period of time, those ditches became quite stinky. That day was one of those days even though, earlier, I had tried to keep the ditch open so it would really serve as a drain, but often the debris just didn't flow freely.

I really did not recognize the filth covered man as a son of my loyal friend. But I got him out of the ditch and I will not tell you how I did it. Then, after some strenuous effort, I got him in a cycle rickshaw, I climbed in with him and off we went without a hindrance since the rickshaw man knew exactly where he needed to be taken and that was to his father's house.

His father was home and that made things easier for me. I simply told him his son became too weak to walk home so I had helped him. That elderly Muslim man thanked me graciously and I got a clean rickshaw and made my way home. By that time I had probably dried enough in the hot sun so that Betty and the children did not smell me too much when I entered our house.

A few weeks later, at about nine o'clock at night, that elderly man came to our house accompanied by at least a dozen Muslim women. I have always supposed that he thought of me so highly for doing what I did to help his son, that he thought it would be proper to bring those women to our house. When they came that first time, I was in our bedroom but heard all of the voices so naturally I went to our living room.

One village Muslim woman saw me and since she was standing near one of the window drapes, she began wrapping herself in that drape by twisting until she was hidden. The elderly gentleman unwound her from the drape and then with kind words, he assured that woman that I would not harm her. We were pleased as a family that these people from a nearby village came to our home. We know they were pleased by the long conversation we had with them and even more by the fact that the elderly man came many nights with large groups of women.

One night I had gone to bed and I always slept in long pajamas especially during the cooler part of the year. That night, when I was at least one-half asleep, several village women moved from our living to my bedroom and the door was open as usual. Those women gave me a greeting of peace and continued to move about the eighteen hundred square foot house.

But on another night, a group came and each time a group came they seemed to be more relaxed than earlier groups. No doubt, they learned from one another and no longer had any fear of me whatsoever. But this one night, one woman, who was the leader except for the older man, seemed to know her way around the house. I was in the living room and heard one of the women scream. I ran to the place of the scream and with two or three other women in the bathroom, she was hanging on to the bright shiny steel handle on the commode. Apparently, this woman had pushed down on the handle and the toilet began flushing. Then, with no idea what was happening she probably thought she had broken something so she held on to that shiny handle. I pulled her hand from the handle. The water had now stopped flowing and the in-charge woman reminded them clearly, as they were walking in our house, she had told them to not touch anything.

A few times in the days which followed, I thought about those pleasant visits and the longer they lasted, the more pleasant they were. But in thinking about culture and the life I knew as a young boy, I remembered much about my mother. Mother, I remembered, had always called any refrigerator, Frigidare, because our first re-frigerator in about 1939, was a Frigidare or made by the Frigidare Company.

I remembered that my mother always called all soft drinks Coca Cola. She grew up in an era when it was probably the only soft drink. So, if mother wanted an orange soft drink in a restaurant, she would ask for an orange Coca Cola. Others, at that time did the same.

We learned much from that elderly Muslim gentleman and all of those village people who visited with us. The most important thing was that we had nearby friends. This was deeply proven when one night after the first Pakistani planes attacked our town that same elderly man came to our house to inform us that our house was marked for protection. He said there had been an area meeting and since we were foreigners and the meeting was what he called "politi-cal," they decided not to inform me of the meeting. We slept better at night because of kind Muslim people like that elderly gentleman. We knew there was little these friends could do against an army but a type of assurance always comes when friends stand by you "in sickness and in health."

Let's move on to chapter six and begin by learning about that horrible cyclonic tidal wave which killed so many people and caused massive destruction to that area of the world.

CHAPTER SIX
What to Do? At Least 300,000 People Had Died

My family of six (Jill had not yet joined us) flew from Bangkok, Thailand, to Dhaka, East Pakistan. We arrived in the early afternoon so that gave us time to move on toward home. But of all the vacations we had experienced, this stood far above the others. We had relaxed on a beach in southern Thailand, but now we were anxious to be back in Feni. We must again say that our God knows how to manage because that vacation surely helped us in the next fourteen or so months.

I first attempted to tell this story in 1978, but most people back in the States had not heard much about that time of awful destruction by a tidal wave. Though what I had written about the event was printed, the book was sold privately. That means it was not available in book stores.

But that tragic time certainly had much to do with a war through which the nation of Bangladesh was born. This chapter and the next few chapters will tell of some highlights or better said, lowlights for there is no way to know exactly how many people died in that cyclonic tidal wave and the war which followed.

But as we flew over the southern part of the then East Pakistan and had we observed carefully, it is likely that we could have seen the water flowing back into its place in the ocean. We were thinking more about the long and often tiring trip on to Feni and we didn't watch out the plane windows as we sometimes did.

But the trip home, or near home, told us that there had been a damaging storm. Feni, directly south of the capital city, was about twenty miles from the ocean. Later we learned that the water had been driven across the fields and it came within six miles of our house. A few trees were blown down in our area, but storms often happened in October and November. The day we arrived home was November 13, 1970. That forceful ocean water had been blown or pushed across the land beginning the previous night just after darkness was arriving.

News traveled slowly since many of the people had been killed and even police stations were wiped away. So, on Saturday, November 14, I did hear from ear to ear sources, that the storm had killed many people. I got in touch with one of my international colleagues and asked him if he would travel with me on Sunday to see what we could learn. We traveled to Maijdi Court, which was the primary city or town in what was then the Noakhali District. From there we traveled a route that I had never heard existed. Going directly south was a dirt road built up in most places about fifteen to twenty feet high.

After traveling a few miles on that road or levy, we began to notice massive amounts of rice straw which had been pulled from the earth and carried by that rapidly flowing water to points along the levy. My colleague, R.T. Buckley, and I determined that on our return up the levy, we would count the number of dead cows lying with the straw, against the levy. As we moved slowly along the road/levy, probably both of us felt that though the storm had been destructive, it was not as bad as we had thought about from the stories we had heard.

But we soon learned that we were very wrong in our doubting for when we stopped and began searching or watching others search for rice which had fallen from the straw, we began to note the human bodies. It was not long until we ceased counting animals, knowing that for every animal killed, there probably had been several humans killed. Most of the men who had survived that tragedy kept busy searching for grains of rice. Some of them had family members, but now no houses or food. All we could say was, "May our God bless them." After about ten miles on the levy, we had no choice but to turn around, for the levy had been broken and our vehicle was not capable of going on that washed out road and completely destroyed levy.

As we drove back, we understood that regardless of what the rest of the world might be saying, death had struck forcefully and as I type into the computer right now on October 18, 2005, I gladly go on record that when the counting or estimating was complete, this had been, and still is, the worst natural disaster since the one in China in 1932. You could never have convinced me that 500,000 people or even 300,000 people had died on those two days, but on the day my colleague and I had viewed the rice, the rice straw, the dead animals, and human bodies, I could believe anything.

But it was not many days later that we would have probably accepted much higher numbers as we had traveled across many areas where few if any vehicles such as ours had ever traveled. All I can say is at that time there were no official records of the people who lived in that greater area. But we met people who told us of the previous number of family members and then the number of those who survived, and we certainly believed those survivors.

A few days later the two of us traveled west from Feni for about forty miles. Then, we located a road going south. We moved down that road/levy for thirty miles and came within a short distance of the ocean.

We began walking east on the ocean levy. But most of the time, we found there was no levy remaining and as we looked to the north and south of the levy, we saw glistening bodies of humans as the hot sun pulled the remaining oil out of those bodies. That oil from those bodies told us that many people had died. We learned later that the survivors, with the little strength they had remaining, had covered many of those bodies with earth. That earth represented the funerals and the graves for the present time. We were also told that after a few days, due again to the burning sun, most bodies could not be identified.

Those trying to help us understand what had happened showed us a former village where maybe one hundred houses had stood. Now there was nothing left but the slick earth which had been the floors of those little houses. One young man, without a shirt and with a deeply scarred chest, told us of how he climbed a tree. Apparently as he climbed, the thorns had torn his chest, but he continued his climb and lived. He said, "As I was climbing, I did not feel any pain." Undoubtedly, to him life was precious, for he was very much alive.

One very handsome young man had walked with us that day. He was tall for a Bengali, probably about six feet two inches. I marveled at his gracious spirit. When we had seen enough for us to make a strong recommendation to our organization for funds to help the survivors, we expected this young man to make a strong request to us. I knew it would be difficult to say "no" to a person like him, but there was no need for a "no."

Before entering our vehicle, we told the small group who had been with us along the Bay of Bengal or Indian Ocean, that we were going to see some other areas and we might not even be back in their area. The reaction was almost overwhelming. The young man spoke for the group. "That's okay, but we thank you for coming and walking with us and letting us tell you what had happened."

Later, we did put down some wells for drinking water in that area and were most pleased that we could do that. It was interesting then and maybe even more interesting today, that all of the people we met on our survey trips of the area were Muslim. But more will be said about Hindus when we reach the time of the war which was to begin a little more than four months later.

But what were we going to do to help these people who were suffering so much? R.T and I had no doubt about the approach to take, at least in the beginning. So, I went to the District Commissioner's office to inquire about what they thought we might do. We did want to do something which this office would know that other people might not do. The answer in that office was explicit. They would be most pleased if we as missionaries would accept the task of sinking tube wells for clean water.

We well remembered that the ponds which were their primary water source had been contaminated by every kind of dead animals and by the bodies of human beings. We had never been involved in anything like sinking wells but we never indicated that to anyone else.

We could learn and learn quickly. My colleague was able to recruit workers from Comilla so that meant we had an advantage with them since they were away from their home territory. We knew we must do this all important job properly and with the outside men, we probably would be able to do that job better.

By the time we asked our organization for money, news, though maybe not accurate news, had covered much of the world. The people in our Baptist churches wanted to help and through our organization, the money came quickly.

We were ready to begin work of sinking tube wells. The tube was a galvanized metal pipe one and one-half inch diameter and about twenty feet long. A small hole about two feet square and about one foot deep was dug at the site where hopefully the well was to be. Then, a simple arrangement was made with two long poles extending up into the air, about twenty feet high, and driven down into the earth about two feet. Those two poles then had cross bars of bamboo to be used as a ladder for one of the men. He climbed to the highest step and positioned himself so that he could work for an hour or maybe even two hours without climbing down from the structure.

Then, that long galvanized pipe was fastened so it could move up and down. It was moved up and down because one man pushed down on an attached handle and then, watched the pipe rise. Next, he would let that pipe drop and its weight would sink it into the ground a few inches. The depth it would sink was dependent on the texture of the soil. But each time when the man on the ground was ready to drop the pipe, the man on the top of the frame had his hand on the pipe, but as it hit the earth, he lifted his hand and once everything was functioning, water squirted out of the pipe. The water which came up through the pipe was the water which was in the little hole that had been dug.

Rarely ever did you find water twenty feet down and as you added sinking pipes, they became heavier to raise up and down but their weight also caused them to sink more rapidly. Could you imagine a simple mechanism like that enabling those pipes to reach down into the earth for maybe two hundred feet? It happened. Of course, someone had to keep water in the little hole but it was beautiful to see the mud which you knew was moving that lowest pipe way down into the earth. The man who had his hand on the top pipe was very important. Most of the time when the pipes were down about sixty feet or maybe even less, the top man felt the texture of the soil as it came up through those pipes. He was feeling for coarse sand. It was in coarse sand that the water was stored.

The deeper the well the more six feet long filters were attached which gave the little pump an easier task when it had been fastened to the pipe. But before the water was thought to be in that coarse sand and the extra feet had been sunk that long or short pipe or pipes were gently lifted up out of the ground.

Another type of pipe was the one used for the filter and one or more was attached then the first pipe and another pipe or whatever number you used to reach down to the level where that course sand was located, were screwed together. The last pipe usually extended a few inches above the ground. Next, the hand pump was fastened to the top pipe.

Now, the most serious time had arrived. First, the handle of the pump was grasped by one or two men and they began to move the handle up and down knowing that way down in the earth or in that coarse sand, water, hopefully, would begin coming up those pipe as the pump sucked that water through the coarse sand. Most of the time water began flowing in a few minutes. Pertaining to health of human beings, nothing was more important than the flow of that water as it was literally sucked out of the earth.

But flowing water in a coastal area was not final. After a few minutes of pumping, the water appeared clean but someone had to taste it. Why the taste? It had to be salt free especially in areas near the ocean filled with salty water. We discovered that often local people let us sink wells in areas where they had never been able to find sweet water but had always found salty water but because we were religious people, they thought where we sunk the pipe, we would find sweet water. Most of the time, we did find that valuable sweet water but sometime we did not, and that was terribly sad.

The men who did this laborious task were paid by the depth of the completed well so we encouraged them to work long hours so we could more rapidly find good water for the devastated people who lived through that awful disaster. When we had done the sinking of the well according to the promise we had made to the local government officer, we felt good about what had been done. Water, clean water, is essential to human life. We always felt that the money we were using was being used properly.

The most difficult thing for me during that time was hearing the stories of the people. Before the tidal wave, the village where I helped to sink the first well had twenty four people. When we sunk their well, an elderly man with a teenage grandson and two little granddaughters were left. The other twenty had died in that disaster. The four had done their best to make a little house from branches of the trees which had survived. I had prayed that we might locate an abundant supply of water for those four, but it didn't happen like that. Clean water did flow but it was a meager amount which flowed through that hand pump. However, the elderly gentleman seemed extremely grateful.

If a situation can be worse than the one just mentioned, I think I found it early one morning. I was working with two teams of men and trying to watch carefully to learn about any games they might try to play. So even though most of the time the wells were at least two miles apart, sometimes, they were separated by a greater distance.

On Sunday morning, I was moving rapidly between two well sites when I heard a woman screaming. The screaming was not unusual for many people seemed to feel there was nothing left to do but scream. Of course, I never in my mind blamed them because they were desperate.

That morning I felt I should stop and look and listen. After all, it was Sunday morning and surely the missionary could learn something about God by listening to the crying of a poor woman. I squatted on the path and searched for the woman with my eyes.

I located her and saw that she was seated on something like a clay pot but a large one. How it had survived the massive flowing of water across her village, I will never understand but unusual things seem to happen in such circumstances. Her face was thrown back as if she were looking into the sky. She never ceased her screaming.

Sitting there on that little path early that Sunday morning, I reviewed a few of the reasons why I should be grateful to God. I knew I was losing weight but I did not sense that anything was wrong physically. I also knew that in a short time, Betty and our children would ride cycle rickshaws to the worship place which was one of the reading centers in that area. Four or five of the young Christian men would be present as would be the two Christian families. It would be a holy time as they were to sing, to pray and one of the young men would bring a good message from God's word. But I had no complaints about where I was at that time. I just knew my God was present and that was what counted most.

I had heard stories so I could only imagine what had happened in this woman's village. One story was that the people heard a loud roaring noise. Then, they noted quiet water at their feet, and quickly it began to rise. One mother had searched for her baby but in their tiny little house she could not find the baby. She lived but her baby was never found. Another mother had her baby held firmly in her arms, but a mighty wave of water sucked the baby away and the little one was never seen again.

Suddenly, as if God had touched me on the shoulder, I stood up and began moving. I knew I had experienced a great time even in a most difficult situation because, again God had spoken to me. As I thanked Him I walked, then I walked more speedily and soon I was running to make sure I let those working men know that I was aware of everything they were doing. We must find good water.

We did find good sweet water in many places across that devastated area. Also, it was probably the most interesting experience I had ever known. My colleague, R.T., was one of the most faithful people I had ever known. He knew what hard work was, and by the time the terrible war began, he had given four full months with me and had left his work, forty miles north of where we lived. During that time, his family hardly saw him. But without him, I probably would have broken down in distress. I could say what I needed to say to him and I knew that was as far as my words would go.

In the beginning, because this was his first term of missionary work, I wondered how he could manage in all of that devastation. His true feeling came through late one afternoon when I was home in Feni and he came by our house from the disaster area. He had attempted to sink a well in an area where the nearest good water was about eight miles away. He had the pump, pipes, drilling equipment and filters strapped on the top of his van. We unloaded everything in our yard and by that time he seemed emotionally able to tell me what had happened.

His crew had sunk the pipes six times in that remote area and each time the end result was salty water. All of that material was of great value. The cost, especially of the steel pipes, was high. In a few minutes, he got into the van and I watched the tears flow down his face. We certainly had become or already were, members of the suffering people's closely knit human families.

I suppose mentally and emotionally, we had suffered a little with them. To have left those people without a new source of water was not easily done. I accepted there was nothing further we could do to help this particular group of people.

However, the next day, a group of four or five men came from that area. They had a proposal to make. If I would give them the materials, they would try again to find good water. Ordinarily, and especially since I did not know any of those Muslim men, I would not have even entertained the thought of giving that expensive equipment to total strangers.

But, and maybe I should give God the credit, I decided I would give those men the pipes. I had no idea how they could manage the pipes and other materials over the main road for about twenty-five miles. Then, they had to travel on a dirt road for about five miles before moving out across an area where there were only little paths for about eight miles. I did not ask them how they could manage the movement of materials. But everything was lying in our yard just as R.T, and I had placed it the day before.

I had nothing further to say to the men and went inside but heard them moving everything out to the side of the road. A few minutes later I knew they had placed everything on top of the bus, and they joined the materials by climbing to the top themselves and away went the bus. I never asked how they had managed everything but when they came back to our house a few days later, they carried smiles on their faces. They announced they had found good water.

There was only one thing for me to do and that was to travel with them to the new well and taste that water which was coming out of the earth from about twenty feet below. Two and a half hours later, I tasted the water and it was as good as any I had ever tasted.

There was only one thing wrong and that was that they had sunk the well in a low area which would become a mud hole when it rained. I had only one choice and that was to move the well about fifteen feet to a higher level and then I would search for an expert who could tell me if I should leave the well in that location of the eighth sinking.

A few days later I went to Dhaka and one of the important things I had to do was talk with a man who knew everything about such situations. I explained about the well location in the mud hole and that we had moved it to a higher level nearby. I think he thought that I should have known that the second location was okay. He explained that water in that area was located in only coarse sand, and I knew that. But he continued by saying when water is in that coarse sand and is pumped up, it is drawn through the sand and that sand does its task of filtering the water. Yes, I had heard that also, but never actually experienced working in such a place before. He added that even the twenty foot depth was okay.

I had done my job. One day when I seemed to have lots of time to think, I was sitting near where a crew was sinking another well and I began thinking—wouldn't it be good to stand before the staff, faculty, and even some trustees of John's Hopkins University and tell them they were linked to that well sunk only twenty feet deep and only a few miles from the salty ocean water. You see, the person whom I consulted that day was Dr. Henry Mosely who was the first Director of the School of Public Health and Demography at John's Hopkins. I usually say that in such situations, it is the seemingly small things that count most.

When R.T. and I were taken to the first area where we would be sinking those wells, a government officer traveled with us in his vehicle. He had two armed policemen with him. As he moved about pointing out the area where we were to be involved, those policemen were always near him. To me, it looked stupid with death all around us and the survivors had everything on their minds except politics.

But when that officer prepared to depart he told me, "I will leave these police with you for in these times you never know what may happen."

I had only one statement to make and that was, "No, we do not need your police. If we can't work helping these people without police protection, then we can't help them." He departed with the police and though we had some occasional tough times, we managed without police accompanying us.

Many friends in other organizations came to see what we were doing and to help us. But one experience involving another of my colleagues was the effort of Tom Thurman and the Bangla pastor, Pastor Halder. Early one morning, at about the break of day, I said goodbye to this good team of workers led by Tom. They had two wells to sink out near the ocean. That would be more than a full day's work. I had no idea how far they had to walk to reach their first site and they had enough good common sense to know not to ask me about the distance.

With my two teams I moved on quickly because we had a long distance to walk carrying the materials for three wells. We never slowed our pace and as we walked through two shallow streams of water I knew that within twelve or thirteen hours, those areas would be filled with ocean water as the tide came in.

If the crews ate lunch that day I was not aware of it. I had a small lunch which Betty had prepared for me early that morning and it was in the vehicle when I reached home just before midnight that day. Sometimes, others things are far more important than eating food. The first two wells were completed and pumping sweet water by the early afternoon. Then, the two crews combined to sink the third one and it was sunk quickly and again, sweet water flowed.

As darkness began to fall, we were walking toward the location of our vehicle. The first channel of water seemed too deep for us to cross, so one of the workman said to me, "Remove as much of your clothing as possible for if your clothing is wet when we reach the other side, you will be very cold as we continue walking." I removed as much as my missionary modesty permitted and with a worker on each side of me, we waded through the neck deep water. After we crossed, I redressed.

We walked rapidly and soon reached the next channel. It appeared to be deeper than the previous one. We went through the same procedure, however, and one man, as he had done earlier, carried my removed clothing on his head. I did have one advantage on the two men guiding me in the darkness of the night through that chin deep water. I was taller than they were. I also knew that if I fell, I could not swim, so there would be real trouble.

But how those two men managed me, I do not know. They may have been a few inches shorter than I was, but they knew how to do what had to be done. My clothing was again dry and I gladly redressed. We drove on to a market place and I waited for Tom and Pastor Halder. But I had told Tom early that morning that I might return home without them that night since there was no way to know whether or not they had completed their two wells.

I did wait probably for about two hours. However, I was busy listening to the radio news with the men in a little shop. News of the election which had taken place that day in most of East Pakistan was being broadcast. It was apparent that an East Pakistani, Sheikh Mujibur Rahman, had been elected even without the votes of those in the disaster area who would vote a few weeks later. The market place people were wild in their rejoicing. One of their own had been elected by such a majority that even if most of the people in West Pakistan voted for someone else, Mujibur would win because though East Pakistan was smaller in area, in population it had several million more people. This was the first truly open election for all of Pakistan since they had become a nation back in August, 1947.

It was now near midnight and driving home was a short journey in light of what I had experienced that day. But it was a good day. Early the next morning, I was moving toward the area to hopefully find Tom and Pastor Halder. I located a high area of earth so that my vision would maybe reach out a few extra hundred feet. I wanted to know that my colleagues were safe and had been able to complete their work of sinking the two wells.

I looked and looked thinking I was seeing them but then understood it was just an image of some sort. But I didn't give up on looking because that was my task at the time.

Then I noted a group of men walking in my direction. One man seemed to be several inches taller than the others in the group. A few minutes later, I knew the tall one was Tom and I soon learned the job had been completed the previous day but the tidal water kept them in the ocean area. They had slept in a stack of rice straw with

Tom between two of the workers who shared their little blanket with him.

Through the years, I often wished that all missionaries were as kind and faithful as R.T. and Tom and others of my colleagues. But I must add that I knew many others, who had they been where I was located following that disaster with my family, would have been as faithful as R.T. and Tom.

On the second of our trips into this area, R.T. and I had noticed large banners proclaiming mostly in English, "Our foreign friends are here, where are our West Pakistani brothers?" The national government had not acknowledged that the disaster had struck for at least several days and hence, offered no support. Eventually troops moved into the area, but I am sorry to write that they did nothing to help. Their presence was only an agitation to the local people.

Another thing must be mentioned. Though I supposed that the Pakistan military had helicopters which could have distributed food in those early days, they didn't do that. Later, I was glad there were no military helicopters around for they would have been used to kill innocent people.

However, a pleasant sight in the devastated area was the helicopters from the then West Germany, from France, and from the United States, which flew over our heads carrying food to most of the remote places and especially to the small islands out in the Bay of Bengal. But later, dumb regarding local and international politics as I was, I regretted that those three countries did not leave their helicopters in East Pakistan so that they could help in other disasters. After March 25, 1971, I was glad those three countries had not left their helicopters for they would have been used to kill innocent people.

One afternoon, I returned home from work thinking I was sick. I had little to say to Betty and the children for I felt miserable. Betty and I often wondered how she did it, but she did keep the children quiet or if they were not quiet, I surely did not hear them.

I slept and slept and when I awakened for a few minutes I seemed to ache from head to toe. But then, after a short time, I journeyed back to sleep. In the dead of the night I awakened feeling great. I had not been sick. I was exhausted. Though I had lost weight, I knew the reason was seeing others without food and water. I didn't seem to want to eat. Of course, I lost weight.

After I had awakened feeling good, Betty told me that a most gracious man had come by wanting to see me but when he learned I was resting, he, Mr. Alam Chasi, refused to let Betty call me. He came by later with a friend, Abdur Rab Chaudhury. At that time, Rab was serving as the relief coordinator for the districts of Noakhali and Chittagong.

Mr. Alam told us that Rab had lost twenty-two members of his greater family in the tidal wave. Mr. Alam had served with the Pakistani Embassy in four of the world's largest countries. He called his previous role as being a beggar for food for Pakistan. He definitely was now a diplomat turned farmer, for he was working with a friend of ours who was with British Baptist.

The mission of the two gentlemen was to ask us to join them in the building of a village in the disaster area, primarily for those who had lived near the ocean or one of the main rivers. The idea was to get those families more into the interior of that ocean area.

All I could do, as tired as I had been but then feeling very good, was tell them that I would share their concern with R.T. and we would let them know our answer. We were coming to the end of our promise to the government about our sinking the wells and I was in a good position to help because I had about sixty-thousand dollars in a local bank in a separate account. This money had been given to me by concerned people who felt I could better use their money than they could use it.

Soon R.T. and I were involved in the village construction with our two new gentlemen friends. Those two friends did all of the tedious work such as acquiring the land for the village. Immediately, we dug a massive pond in the middle of the area where the houses were to be located. That pond would be used for just about everything such as bathing, washing clothing and for growing fish as high protein food. It was great that we did not have any responsibility for the administration involved in building the village.

So, as if God had dropped them down from Heaven, blankets by the hundreds were given to us for distribution. That did not take much of our time and no money was involved which simplified everything we did in the distribution. I will mention two areas where we made distribution of the blankets. The time we took blankets to one village, the list of two hundred names had been prepared by their leader. One person, with a strong voice, called out the names. One hundred and ninety-nine names were called of people present. I handed the last blanket to the leader and told him in front of the great number of people present, that he was to give that to the person who could not attend the distribution.

It was my understanding that during the struggle for independence, that village leader became a captain with the freedom fighters and survived the horrible war. Though I was in this same area once or twice during the war, I was always glad I did not see this friend. We were too close to be found together at such a time.

When we arrived to distribute about two hundred blankets in another area, a massive crowd was present. We did not know the leader. He had several policemen present to supposedly assist in the distribution. He had a list but apparently his list was "his" list for when names were called out a great roar came out from the crowd. This meant they did not approve of the names being called. How we longed for the discipline of the previous village leader!

But we had a job to do with or without a good leader. At times, I aided in pushing the rushing crowd back as they came to the table where the blankets were located. While I was pushing, R.T. climbed up on top of one of the tables and began what I call "running off at the mouth" by saying, "Look at my older missionary colleague. He sure knows how to push, doesn't he?" That may or may not have helped, but as I pushed I laughed. Eventually we distributed the blankets. But don't ask me to declare that those blankets were given to the right people. I always remembered that you don't always win them all.

Near the last market area, on that road south from the main road, across Noakhali District, we began the construction of houses in a nearby area which we had not known about earlier. Those for whom we were hoping to build two hundred houses were all Hindus. But the person supervising for me was a highly respected Muslim young man who owned considerable property. I had no reservations about trusting him. This was the last work we began in the total area of that almost overwhelming destruction on November 12-13, 1970. About one year later that work was completed.

Though I have not told you about telling the stories of our sharing what our God had done in offering life-changing experience of eternal salvation through Jesus the Messiah, I have told you of a few things international missionaries can do when they live with Muslims.

CHAPTER SEVEN
War Begins — Maybe Three Million People Will Die

At about four-thirty, long before the break of day, I moved out by myself in the old microbus. My hope was that I could cover the forty or so miles to Comilla and that my trusted colleague and friend would be, if not on the side of the road, at least would come running to the vehicle so that we could proceed immediately toward the capital of East Pakistan, Dhaka. R.T. was ready as he always seemed to be and off we went even though I was already tired of driving. As we drove out of Comilla on the western side, by six fifteen or so, we were on the army base. But that was no problem. A brief check and off we were again. We reached Dhaka without difficulty.

We met with some of our colleagues and, like us, they didn't seem to know much of what was happening. But it was only right that we could, at least, meet with them. It was years before I saw some of those colleagues again. During the days, the weeks, the months and even the years to come, I often missed those with whom our lives had been so closely linked.

After meeting with these colleagues, R.T. and I drove down Mirpur Road which was the beginning of the route to Calcutta, India (or now Kolkatta, India). The road was not as busy as usual and it was almost lunch time, but about eight blocks away from where some of our missionaries lived, and on that road leading west, we noted too many military vehicles parked near the home of Sheikh Mujibur Rahman. This was the gentleman who had just been elected the new president of Pakistan. Those military vehicles gave us a warning. We quickly made our way to the Intercontinental Hotel for lunch. The hotel was filled with international reporters.

While eating our lunch, we kept our ears busy hoping to learn something new about the political situation in East Pakistan. We learned only that those reporters probably knew less than we did so we ate quickly and moved out of the city with only one destination in mind.

R.T. wanted to reach home in Comilla which was located only about six miles from the border of India. But to reach his house, we had to again pass through the army base and knowing that something was in the making after seeing the military vehicles near Sheilh Mujib's house on Mirpur Road in Dhaka, we realized there might be many questions about who we were and where we were going. But those questions were never posed to us as we entered the military area.

Perhaps, the army was too busy to give time to us. In a few locations on the base, we only slowed the vehicle and were motioned to continue before we stopped. Once we were stopped but only for a few seconds. It was as if they wanted us to get out of their way and we were most glad to move on toward our families and our homes.

R.T. climbed out of the microbus near his house. Looking back now, I probably thought that it was great to be so closely related to someone like him at such times. I did have a brother who was four years younger than I who lived in southern California. There my "little" brother was serving the God and Savior whom I served. But I probably knew R.T. better than I did my only earthly brother. About fourteen months later I saw R.T. again.

I reached our home in Feni just before eleven o'clock. However, I was fortunate indeed, for before reaching Feni, just as I crossed a one-lane bridge, another vehicle decided we could meet on the bridge. But with about one-half of my microbus across the bridge, he struck me forcefully. I was sure my van would go off the road, but it didn't. I stopped but the other vehicle didn't stop. So, after taking a rapid look at my vehicle, I began moving as rapidly as seemed possible to me. I thought that perhaps the automobile I met had someone in it who knew more than I did about what was happening in some places even at that very moment. Maybe they were moving toward home as was I, so I do not cast any fault in that driver's direction even today.

As soon as Betty saw me she asked, "Is there trouble in Dhaka?"

I replied, "No, why do you ask?"

Then she told me of different people who had either come by our house or who had called by the telephone, which actually worked a few times, to inquire about where I was. She said these friends feared trouble and wanted me to be present in Feni if the trouble reached there.

About the time I reached home, the army had struck with apparently all of their power in Dhaka. At about the same time, they also made their attack in the port city of Chittagong, about sixty-five miles south of Feni, our home. We learned about these attacks the next morning on a radio station we had never before heard.

There was no doubt that we had a large number of friends in Feni. I doubt if most ever thought of us as being anything other than their friends. Though for religious purposes, they might down deeply have some hate for us. We knew enough to be alert but at the same time, we were not necessarily afraid. At least, during those first days we were not afraid. The editor, who apparently hated me, was too busy thinking about what the army might do to him, so he would not trouble me.

But remember that our chief government officer was a West Pakistani, and his guard was the Pakistani who was fully armed when he came with this officer to our house for dinner. His behavior was full of hatred as were his words. So, Feni was probably in for some real trouble.

I remembered that Mr. Alam Chasi, whom I mentioned earlier concerning the building of a new village for some of those who had been so severely struck by that terrible cyclonic tidal wave, had given me a special task a few weeks earlier. That task had been that of delivering some special bricks, which were made primarily of sand but with enough cement to make them stronger, to a man on the northeastern side of Feni. When I delivered those brick, I remembered I saw some soldiers of Pakistan but thought nothing about it then. I had been on a mission of mercy and was not necessarily interested in the military.

We have to remember that the first meeting of the newly elected National Assembly of Pakistan had been scheduled for March 3, 1971, but that meeting had been cancelled and that Assembly, as they were elected, never met. From that time on, it was generally considered by East Pakistanis that the armed forces of Pakistan would never permit one of theirs to be head of state and rule the country. Now, they seemed to be ready to enforce their will upon the people of East Pakistan, or upon the Bangla people.

The new lighting system had been partially installed as a result of the efforts of this leader and in other ways he had been kind to the local people so that may have saved his life or at least given him time to get out of East Pakistan. On a later date, I went to his office only to learn from the military that he had fled and perhaps had returned to West Pakistan. I was glad for that.

On March 26, 1971, people walked past our house by the hundreds. This road led them to the west, which meant they were moving farther away from the border of India. Most or at least many people with whom I talked in those days felt that India would support the people of East Pakistan against West Pakistan. Of course, that proved to be correct during the following nine months of war.

On March 27, 1971, people walked by our house by the thousands. Many of them were from Chittagpong area which meant that they had traveled about sixty-five miles by foot. Most of them were without shoes. Their feet were swollen. In no time at all, I moved the Volkswagen Microbus, which was assigned to me, out into the road headed to the west. I called out for twelve people to join me by riding in the vehicle. Dozens gathered around the vehicle. I then spoke slowly and carefully in their language that first women and children could ride and if there were older men they could also be included. However, there were very few older men.

After a few trips back and forth over a road mileage of about twenty-five miles, I was amazed at the discipline of these poor people. When they over-loaded the vehicle, I asked every time that the number be decreased down to twelve people. If they ever tried to cheat me in that number, I never noted it. It was as if they clearly understood that the vehicle would be destroyed on those many journeys if it were overloaded. I think, as they walked, they discussed that the vehicle would be returning and maybe they would be in the next group to ride. Going east, there were very few people so there was no problem of overloading.

As time moved on and a few days had passed I began trying to understand what was happening militarily. I walked downtown and talked with Abdul Malek, a shopkeeper. While sitting and listening in his shop, I overheard him tell a friend where dynamite was located for destroying a bridge east of Feni. I did ask him if it was necessary to do that destruction. His answer was clear. He wanted to do everything possible to keep the army out of Feni and destroying the bridge might help. I said nothing else.

But while I was sitting in Mr. Malek's shop, a student leader, who had earlier threatened me, came into the shop. He looked at me with a smile and then said in English, "Sir, you do not need to fear us for we know you are our friend." There was nothing I needed more than a few statements like that spoken in a public place. I knew the student leader meant what he had said.

We had no television but we did have a radio which was both electrically and battery powered, so we located some foreign broadcasts as well as the local station apparently controlled by the rebels or freedom fighters. Those sources from the radio gave us a lot of information that we needed. Of course, the six of us were nervous but as a large family we seemed to be doing very well. We ate well. We slept well, and Betty, as always, continued the teaching of our children.

Other beautiful things began to happen in the midst of all the chaos. It was almost unbelievable but one morning the "Editor," who had written the lies about me in his newspaper, came to our house asking me to advise him. He was troubled by what he should do. I had no doubt that the army would immediately arrest him as a communist. They would do that because the radical Muslims, who supported the army, would tell all they knew about such people. So, I simply said to him, "As soon as possible, take your family and cross the border into India," and I added, "I have nothing else to say." I did not want him to write lies about me or some other missionary in the future.

I thought of him more as a Muslim who never read his holy book but did only the things that might help him prosper financially. So, The "Editor" was no exception to many people who were as cheap as humans could become but at the same time, became afraid so easily. He did not ask how Betty and our children were doing in this terribly dangerous situation. Nor did he ask what we were going to do. Had he asked, I probably would have simply said, "We have not yet decided what we will do." Since we had not made that decision, I would not be lying.

One night I took what was almost an unbelievable trip. I traveled west about forty-five miles and then south for about twenty more miles. I had to inform a New Zealand missionary family that we as a family did not know what to do about leaving Feni and that sometimes, we became anxious about the nearby border of India and their possible involvement. So, in the middle of the night we talked about many possibilities for both of our families.

I felt much responsibility to this good family because when they first moved to the area where the new village was to be constructed, I had taken the mother and two sons in our van. The father had his jeep loaded with their belongings. That night they explained to me that they could cross some rivers and it would not be too far to a location where one of their missionary families lived. That satisfied me.

But also, near where they were, Mr. Alam Chasi was staying in a little shop which had an attic where he slept. He, without a doubt, was glad to see me and decided he would ride part of the way back toward Feni with me. I was pleased to again be related to this gentleman who was so gracious and helpful to poor people.

But soon, the vehicle was loaded. As we traveled, there were two very interesting things which happened. One was the conversation among those riding with me. Soon I knew one of the men was a communist leader and it was not clear whom he would support in this war.

The dumb thing was he said in the conversation with at least one other person in the van, "I will go with which ever group China supports." Any person, who could read or hear, knew that China was for West Pakistan and India was for East Pakistan. So, here he was with his unholy position. It did not matter how many of his own people were killed in the days ahead, he was for China. I was glad when he signaled me where he wanted to get down. I was even happier when he actually left.

The second interesting thing, and I liked this one very much, was every few miles, there were road stops commanded by local people who of course, were my friends. They knew the vehicle because it was one of only a few which was traveling those roads during those days. When I would stop as signaled, they would flash a light and scream out to their forces, "It is okay, it is only Bible." How I loved that name! Please remember those reading centers and some of them were called Bible Reading Libraries. I was pleased, in a land torn by war, to not just help as many people as possible but to be called, "Bible" by many of the common people.

Mr. Alam Chasi got down where the road led south to the major town of the district. He did not even hint that I take him down that road about six miles to his destination that night. He just wasn't that kind of person. I knew he wanted me to get home before the light of the new day began to rise. But I saw him again soon.

A few days later Alam Chasi sent word to me in Feni that if at all possible, he wanted me to come and meet with local leaders and plan to help the devastated people in additional ways. I went and we drove out to some of the areas I had not seen.

The men all seemed to be sincere. They only wanted me to assure them that I would help if the political situation permitted that. I knew I could help because there was still money in the local bank for helping others. But of course, that opportunity did not come, for the days before us soon became much worse.

Earlier, I mentioned taking brick samples to a man in the northeastern part of Feni and that day I saw Pakistani soldiers whom I did not know were present in our town. I soon learned that local people had decided to fight them.

One young man came to our house and asked me if I would like to go with him and watch the battle. Of course, I would not do that under any circumstance. Then, that same young man told me that he couldn't fight. He said, "Mr. McKinley, I wanted to fight because we knew that the West Pakistani soldiers had killed all of the East Pakistani soldiers in that little camp and I should fight." He continued, "When I saw the dead lying all around me, I became too afraid to do anything. So, I knew if you went with me that would help." I still didn't go with him.

All of a sudden that afternoon, we as a family learned what war was like. It came to our town. Our four children were playing in the back yard probably about two hundred feet from the house. Betty and I heard screaming and we ran to the kitchen from which the sound had come. Trembling, Kathy said, "Look."

We looked up and saw two planes flying low across the rice fields. We looked and I saw Cherie trying her best to get her hands on both of her little brothers. All I could do was signal to Cherie to pull her brothers down to the earth. Though those little boys thought the planes were interesting, Cherie knew what they were about to do.

Those two Sabre 86 jet fighters of the Pakistani Airforce spewed bullets and hundreds died from those bullets. I ran to Cherie and we got the boys into the house before the planes made a second attack. We all moved into the long hallway of the house and waited in fear. After several flights over the town, spewing those killing bullets, they departed. There had been no danger to the pilots but they had killed many people and wounded hundreds of others.

Soon everything became quiet. In just a few minutes hundreds of people could be seen running across the fields and west on our road, carrying the dead and the dying. As soon as it quieted a little, I told Betty that I must go down town and see if I could do something to help. That may have been one of the best things I did while living with Muslims for thirty-four years.

As I walked east or downtown, hundreds and hundreds of people shared the road, but they were going in the opposite direction. They wanted to move west and to get out of town and farther away from the border of India.

Screaming people cried out to me "Sir, be careful. They will kill you, too." I just wanted to help somebody. My family came near a horrible tragedy but we had escaped with no physical harm. The children, as usual, were expressive and maybe that helped, but they were just as interested in others as were their dad and mom.

The first person I saw as I entered town was a man lying with one of his legs bent not under him, but back on his chest. The leg had not just been broken, but torn apart with just a little flesh holding it to the upper part of that leg. Some volunteers and I picked him up and carried him to the hospital. The only doctor on that hospital staff simply shook his head after a brief check of the man. He was dead.

It seemed that all who were left in that little town which a few minutes before had probably numbered maybe even fifty thousand because it was market day, seemed to want to show me everything they had seen. I think, above everything else, they wanted that foreigner among them to see what had happened to them. They wanted sympathy and I hope many of them knew that I knew how to pray and that I would do that for them and I did.

One man led me to a body. The head of that man had been ripped apart by a line of bullets from those planes. We asked some men to carry that body to the little hospital so that maybe, before night, it would be claimed by someone. I am sure that body was claimed for the next morning when I entered the hospital I quickly learned that though the front door was open, the hospital was closed.

But on that day, April 6, 1971, I attempted to see every person who was in the hospital and I think that happened. One was a local communist. He pulled me to his chest but there was no cry cursing me but only a question, "Sir, what will happen to us?" I did not know was all that I could reply.

One man, whom I knew well, called out to me and I immediately made my way to his bed. He pulled back his sheet and I could see that most of one of his feet had been shot off. Perhaps the rest of the foot was lying somewhere in the street. I stood near him and he pulled me to his chest and gripped me tightly. He was a rickshaw puller or pedaler but now he, had operated his last rickshaw.

I moved away from the hospital and one man ran to me and said, "Sir, look!" I looked and saw his hand filled with bullets which he had picked up from the streets. Maybe some of those bullets had torn through human bodies or maybe just "wasted" as they missed their marks.

But among the beautiful words I heard that late afternoon was, "Sir, we are glad you are with us." Let me say that is enough to make life worth living. You are needed and you can do something to help someone right then. That something may be to just be with someone, or maybe even with many people.

I knew I needed to get back to the house and be with Betty and the children. As was often what happened when I was away from home, Betty and the children were standing at the gate. I didn't even need to open the gate. One of them opened it for me...and what a beautiful welcome that was, given by those who love you so much. I suppose they loved me more because they knew I could help others and often did that and hopefully I continue that service of helping.

Yes, we slept that night concerned but slept well. When we first went into our three bedrooms, the darkness of the night was very powerful so we could see large splashes of light as we looked out the back windows. That light came from Pakistani ships firing from the Bay of Bengal at civilian locations as well as at East Pakistanis beginning to respond to all that had been done against them. It was only about twenty miles to some of those ships, but that was 1971 so those guns could not reach even near us.

Morning came and we appeared to be a family united, a family who cared for others and a family that did not seem to be afraid. But that day, April 7, 1971, was a busy one for me. A report had come that there was fierce fighting about fifteen miles away on the road to Chittagong. Local people by the hundreds had gathered to stop the army from getting to their families.

Many of the people who I knew were killed, but after several days of fighting, the military of Pakistan turned back south toward the port city of Chittaong. It seemed to me that no one expected me to watch the fighting or have any part in it whatsoever. They now seemed to know that the missionary man with them did not kill or physically harm anyone and I am sure they understood that I was not a spy for the United States of America, my beloved home country.

So many people, after that first attack on the main cities by the Pakistani army, had asked me, "Sir, you won't leave us, will you?" And I usually replied that I would not leave them. But that day of April 7, many people were changing their minds about departing from Feni. Among these dozens of people was a bank manager who earlier had assured me he would not leave. He came asking me to take his family to an area west of Feni. I did that. As far as I was concerned, he was free from his promise of not departing.

During that day I transported Alam Chasi from an area near the main city of our district to Feni. I didn't see him again until

January of 1972. He had been made Secretary of the Ministry of Rural Development. He was the one with such a deep respect toward the poor that I in turn had deep respect for him.

Early that day I did go back to the hospital and I had found it closed. But it was so sad for me to hear that my friend, Dhanu Mia had died that previous night. He was the rickshaw puller who had his foot shot off. However, the previous day he probably was not even aware of that, because of the many places on his body where bullets had stuck—that there were several bullets in his stomach. Where did my friend live? What about his family? I learned that his body had been buried and where his family lived. I went there with some blankets and money for his wife and six little children. This was the man, who was very poor and had a large family, yet, who said often to his missionary friend, "But Sir, I should not charge you when you ride in my rickshaw. You are my friend." He never did charge me but I gave him money anyway.

Three days after the first air strike, they again struck with force. We knew the day was not too far away when the soldiers of Pakistan would strike Feni. Betty and I talked with our children about that. I told the children that if we heard the army coming that I would walk out into the road so they could see I was a foreigner. Again, this showed how little I knew about war and fighting. After the army actually came into Feni, friends told me they shot everyone in sight. We had been gone about ten days before that happened.

After that second air attack, the streets of Feni were almost vacant. One of the men who had been elected to the National Assembly which never met stayed for several days to do his best to prepare for an attack. He became very angry at me for one Sunday morning we went to the Reading Room for worship.

In route to the church, there was a road block. I climbed down from the van and removed the materials in the road block. Then, I drove through. But I stopped and put everything back in place. We were ready to move on a short distance in the vehicle when this National Assembly member arrived on the scene, very angry because I had removed the road block. Finally, he seemed to cool off and we drove on to the worship place.

I had known another member of the National Assembly very well. In fact, one day during the election, he came to the house to ask for my support. I said without hesitation, "This is my support to you. Do not come back to our house until after the election and if you see me downtown or anywhere in this area, do not even speak to me."

He seemed to sit quietly for a few minutes and then replied, "I understand and am departing right now." After the election, of course, he was welcomed to our house. He is the one who received the most votes of anyone in that election. But things were different now. He wanted my advice about what to do.

So, I said plainly, "Get into India immediately if you want to live. The army will kill you if you remain here in Feni." I understand that he and his family crossed the border in a few hours.

No parent could have missed the apprehension of our two daughters. The boys seemed to be okay. Cherie's was now thirteen years old. Kathy was eleven, and the boys were seven and five. It was understandable that the boys kept on playing in the yard. We attempted to keep them in the backyard, but they didn't necessarily feel the need for that. At night I read long Bible stories to all of them and as usual, they listened beautifully. Yet, Betty and I knew we had to make a change, but what change? That, we did not know.

We often thought of the Buckleys in Comilla. On two occasions, I hired a man to walk that distance of about forty miles and to try to visit with the Buckleys. Both times, he entered Comilla but could never reach the Buckleys. On one occasion, he thought he saw their house but didn't see them. But he was faithful and he learned from someone that the Buckleys had been able to reach Dhaka. We accepted that as fact.

Other than that location of Comilla, we also had missionary colleagues in Faridpur, but between us and Faridpur was one massive river and several smaller ones. We finally connected with them and just as we were okay, they were also. That knowledge helped and would not hinder us from departing to where we did not know. We never troubled about our colleagues in Dhaka for there were several of them together.

On two separate days we made two extended visits. One was a journey of about thirty miles. We did not know whom we might find upon reaching their area but we decided to make the trial run. We did and it was an almost perfect visit. It was the Canadian Catholic Mission. We had heard a little about it because the priest had encouraged the Catholic young men to enroll in our Bible correspondence courses.

When we first arrived, there were two sisters present. Sister Stella seemed to be the in-charge person, and she immediately asked Betty if they could prepare lunch for us. Of course, that pleased Betty and all of us. Later the priest came to the house where we were but could not remain long but we already knew of his wanting a relationship with us because of the correspondence courses for the Catholic boys.

Just before lunch, Sister Stella quietly asked me if I would have the blessing for the food. She explained that she wanted it to be exactly what we did at home because that would make our children feel better. In a district where about ninety-nine percent of the people were Muslim, we found a place for lunch where the in-charge person wanted, first of all, to please our children with a prayer to Almighty God that would make our children feel better. May our God bless her today, wherever she may be, and may she remember that two Baptist missionaries will always remember her extra kindness.

When we prepared to depart, we had to remember that planes might attack again in our area. As we moved along the road, we had it almost all to ourselves. The three older children rotated in attempting to keep their head out the window to watch for planes. I do not know what we would have done had planes been spotted.

Another day we visited on a shorter trip of about eight miles. We went to visit with a man who had retired from the government of Pakistan only a few weeks before. He had been Secretary of Communications and had been located all the way on the other side of India where West Pakistan and the national government was located. But he was now back in his village home.

He and his family seemed to be most happy that we six suddenly appeared. We talked and talked. One statement he made was,

"Mr. McKinley, we are all equal. We are all poor. We all seem to be almost helpless." Just before we departed I asked Mr. Rashid if there was something I could do for him. His reply was, "Could you possibly bring some coffee for my wife?" I was never able to deliver that coffee, I am sorry to say. Times were rapidly changing and we had to quickly make some of those changes.

Then, the man in what I understood to be the last family in Feni other my family asked me if I could take them to a village area. I gladly did that. I repeat parts of this because now Betty and our children would be the last woman and children to depart that town. We had kept our promise which was "We will not leave." Now we felt free totally of that promise.

On April 14, I talked with a cousin of Dhanu Mia, the rickshaw operator, who had been so brutally killed. We were ready to leave and needed his help. This man had many questions. He asked," How far do you want us to go?"

"I hope we can reach Comilla," was the answer.

"But what if we find the army in route? What do we do?"

I answered, "If you know at any time that we are near the army, you can turn back to Feni and we will cross into India as refugees."

He seemed to be willing so he asked, "When do we depart?"

My reply was, "At the break of day."

"I will be here with six rickshaws," he replied and left for his home.

From the few men left in Feni, I inquired concerning what they knew about the road between Feni and Comilla. Their understanding was that it had been blocked in many places by local people. But they also added that many people had walked that road. I knew enough now about the road. If we chose that route, then it would take extra time because of the road blocks. However, the India border was never more than six miles from the road.

But that night we arranged for one of the young men who worked with us to travel as a helper. Daniel consented to make the attempt. We knew it was far more dangerous for him than for us as a family because if the army saw him near the border of India they might think of him as an enemy. I did not want him to travel with us because of danger to him, but I needed help in lifting and doing other things in route. Thanks to him.

We gathered fresh food from our good garden. We prepared a gallon of drinking water. Betty arranged for a total of four suitcases which included all the school books. We took the tires and batteries off the two vehicles. The second vehicle was a small truck which we had used some in the cyclonic tidal wave area. We placed the tires in our store room which was in the middle of the house and carefully locked that door.

Perhaps most important of all talk was the talk with our God. We knew how to pray and by that I do not mean the necessarily proper words for public prayer, but to talk with our God. I really needed clear contact from Him since I had to decide which of three routes to attempt to travel. When I had talked with the rickshaw operator, I felt that we would most likely travel the old road with which we were well acquainted.

That night, just before we went to bed, I told Betty, "We will travel the old road." Suddenly it came clear to me that the route we knew would be far better for the children. Even if we had difficulty they would feel better knowing where we were and that proved to be true.

The alarm awakened us about one hour before daylight.

CHAPTER EIGHT
Traveling over 100 Miles in Thirty-Six Hours

The morning of April 15, 1971, was a sad time for the six members of our family. When the rickshaw operators arrived as darkness began to disappear, we were ready to travel. We surely hoped that we would be able to travel north and then slightly west to Dhaka, the capital city of East Pakistan.

We knew the main road very well since we had traveled it often. However, we knew that there could be many things to take us in different directions and one of those directions might be east or into the hill area of India.

The six men in whose rickshaws we were going to make the first part of that journey were cheerful and ready to go immediately. I had one deep fear. That fear was those men thought I could arrange anything and everything and I knew that I could not do much.

As carefully as I possibly could, I instructed the rickshaw operators how to line up their rickshaws and keep them in that same position as long as we were riding with them. They understood and I think that helped them greatly.

Remember, these men were relatives and friends of Dhanu Mia, who had been my dear friend and was killed by those attacking planes on April 6. They also knew that I had given blankets and money to Dhanu Mia's widow and of course, they liked my doing that.

When we began loading the rickshaws I again felt the operators appreciated that I had organized the lineup. Seven year old Keith and I were in the first rickshaw. My being in that first rickshaw simply reminded them I was in charge. This would help if we were stopped by anyone other than friends, since I would do the talking. That protected them, at least in their minds, and saved their energy for pedaling the rickshaws.

Cherie and Kathy rode in the next two rickshaws and each one of them had a large piece of luggage. I had no doubt that Betty should be in the next rickshaw though that did place her a great distance, in such circumstances, from me. But she had our youngest of the children with her and that was five year old Wade, so since the two other pieces of luggage were in an extra rickshaw just in front of Betty, she was in the fifth rickshaw. That arrangement was so that if one rickshaw broke down, we had an immediate replacement. In that last or sixth rickshaw was Daniel, our friend. If someone hindered us from the rear, then Daniel was to be the first target and he understood that since he knew I was riding in the more dangerous position in front.

Our friends, the rickshaw operators, were even more nervous when I had asked them to line up with the direction west. They knew we were going north and to go north from our house, you went east and then north from the main street of Feni. Then, when we were ready to depart, I explained that we wanted to avoid downtown Feni and that there was a road or path which we could travel that would keep us from downtown. After going about one mile we turned northeast and that soon led us to the main road.

It is putting it mildly to say that morning was a "once in a lifetime" event for us. Everything was an "if," but we knew the One who could work through our mistakes and we believed He was more than capable of "directing our path" that day and for everyday. We had prayed for help when we had shared a snack early that morning. I said to Betty and the children just as the rickshaws moved out, "Don't look back at the house because we may never see it again." I meant that more than the value of that house to us was that we must look to the front or future. My family and I did not have any idea what the day before us held.

Previously, I had told the children that it might be necessary for us to sleep in a road culvert or maybe in a near-by village that first night. They had no problem with that. They knew we had to do something to get out of Feni and surely, Dad would know what to do. But they also knew that all of us had a beautiful connection with our God who knew well how to manage.

We traveled the first ten miles in about two hours. That seemed almost impossible. I had watched the rickshaw operator of the first one in line. His feet, his arms, his hands all seemed to be busy constantly. I had never noted a rickshaw moving as fast as these six moved. I knew that these men would tire early but said nothing about their almost miraculous speed. I was all for our moving as rapidly as their strength would permit.

It probably took us as much time to travel the next five miles as it had the first ten, but that was understandable, not only because of a loss of strength of the operators but because of the many road hindrances. The biggest hindrance was that over the forty miles to Comilla, there were nineteen destroyed bridges or culverts. Thankfully there was always a way around.

An even greater hindrance was trees lying across the road. Local people, in order to hopefully stop the killing army which they felt would surely come down that road, wanted to stop them or at least slow their advance. Several times, we got down from the rickshaws and watched as village people from both sides of the road helped the rickshaw men lift those conveyances over the fallen trees. Those kind village people seemed to be challenged by Betty riding in that fifth rickshaw so she could watch her four children and her husband. There is no way to know what all they thought about a western woman, yet it was obvious they had great respect for the one they saw that day.

Could you believe it—on several occasions, before Betty and Wade got down from their rickshaw, those village men lifted that rickshaw over the fallen trees. They did it carefully so Betty had no fear of falling. As we crossed a hurdle and began moving on, those kind people, though in fear for themselves, gave a salaam of peace as they saluted.

Now, at least, they had a different kind of story to tell about western women. Anyone with even the slightest amount of knowledge of this area knows that people such as those in the villages along our route that day had heard numerous stories describing half-naked western women. Most of them had never seen a missionary mother traveling as Betty was that day, with her husband and four children.

We knew that people in the dozens of villages near the road as we traveled were aware before we reached their area that a line of rickshaws was approaching. We learned they had designated men on the lookout all of the time. They even had guards posted all night long. What good would that do? They could always run deeper into the countryside, hopefully out of reach of the army.

We stopped to eat our lunch before we reached a large market area we knew was only a few miles away. There were no complaints about our lunch and the rickshaw men ate in the small nearby market. We ate celery and raw carrots as if it were Thanksgiving Day. Betty had several small boxes of cookies for dessert, and standing by the side of the road, we feasted.

Ordinarily, most of the men and boys in the nearby market would have come close to us but this was a different time, so no one looked on as we ate. The drinking water tasted like ice tea or lemonade. I believe that it even had a heavenly taste here on Earth or more specifically, there by the side of the road in a land of Muslim people. The rickshaw men returned after everyone finished eating, so we were ready to move on—to where, we were not exactly sure.

Those men had learned much in the small market where they ate. Though I did not ask them even one question, I knew that before long they would be requesting permission to turn back toward Feni and more importantly, back toward their families. This soon happened when we approached the big market which was near the middle of the distance between Feni and Comilla. So, we were one-half the distance to our projected first stop in Comilla.

The rickshaws pulled on to a little path on the western side of the road. We all got down and dozens of people from the nearby village joined us. They did not crowd around us as other people had often done and I heard some of them whisper to others, "I recognize them." We had traveled that road for seven years and recognition surely did not harm but helped. We talked as if we were long lost friends and for sure, we had a lot in common. We feared the Pakistan army and especially feared the army in such a remote place by the side of the road.

From where we were standing, even weak eyes could see the Pakistan flags waving in the market place. My first responsibility was to the six men who had done such a perfect task of taking us for about twenty miles through a dangerous area. I immediately told them they were welcomed by my family to return to their families near Feni. Of course, even without my welcome, they would have done so. But the seven of us stopped some distance away from the crowd and I had the money arranged for each of them. I gave it to them and asked them if it was okay. With smiles they nodded affirmatively. I hoped the payment was enough for at least a month of food wherever it was available.

Those men immediately climbed on their rickshaws, salaamed us gracefully and moved onto the road quickly. I had never seen a more disorganized group. They were all over the road and were busy passing one another. They were tired physically but more importantly they were "on their way home" with the blessings of the six of us.

We knew the border of India was only a few miles east of the road. Looking in that direction did not help me. I realized that if we crossed the border we could be in much more difficulty, as if that were possible. So, we began talking with the village leaders about the nearby big market place. They were sure the army had not yet arrived but how far away the army was on the north side of the market, they had no idea.

They didn't appear to want us to cross into the hills of India. Proof was within a few minutes six men with their rickshaws came out of the village. They were ready to take us north. The charge for their services was not even mentioned. Did they know we would pay them well? Or did this not matter to them at such a time? We didn't know but in a few minutes we moved out in the same order as before but not before we spoke words, hopefully filled with kindness, to those village people.

Remember there would be no East Pakistani Hindu people living that near the India border. If they had previously lived there, they would already have crossed into India for safety. So, as were the previous rickshaw operators from Feni, all of these people were Muslims, who certainly didn't hate or despise the Christian missionary family who was so desperate.

As we passed through the big market place, men and boys's eyes were filled with questions but they had no opportunity to ask who we were and where on earth we were going. Why would we be going in the direction of the army undoubtedly was on their minds. Not far beyond the market we began to hear fearful noises. Massive guns were being fired to the west. That location was near a place called Laksham and the north and south road through this area was one of the possible routes I had considered the previous day.

I have never apologized for saying that the rickshaws quivered as the road under them shook. Huge shells struck the earth and we did not know how many miles away those guns were located. We never slowed down.

Occasionally, the man guiding and pedaling the rickshaw in which Keith and I were riding looked back at me but never said anything. But they were helped greatly because we reached an area where water was flowing profusely. Evidently the rain had fallen that previous night, mostly in nearby India. We reached a stopping point. The bridge across the road had been destroyed. The rickshaw men were ready to turn back toward their village. I immediately paid them and quickly they began their journey.

All of a sudden, young armed men began to appear from the border area of India. One of the first ones coming in our direction called out, "Mr. McKinley, what are you doing here with your family?" I told him our story and his reply was, "You don't need to cross here. Go with me into our camp and we will find rickshaws for you." The young man had been in many Bible classes I had taught at our Feni reading room. He and other young Muslims had loved it when we talked about Jesus, or Isa, from the Gospels, or Injil.

I told him clearly, "You know we should not enter your camp." He accepted that but in a few minutes left and quickly returned with six rickshaws on the other side of the flowing water. Then, from a hidden spot nearby, a man riding a crude looking boat came to our side of that flowing stream.

That conveyance had been constructed primarily out of huge banana stalks. A rope was tied on each side and as two of us at a time boarded the boat, the man on the opposite side of the stream pulled us across. Quickly, we disembarked and the man on the opposite side pulled his rope and in a few minutes, we had crossed the stream of rapidly flowing water with all of our luggage.

That young man, or the spokesman for the group of freedom fighters, said to me, "Now you will be coming back so when you reach this area, come through our camp and we will do whatever is needed to help you." I had no doubt that he would help me, regardless of the situation. We, as a family, had been greatly helped by this young man and his companions.

We were probably about six miles from Comilla. There had been no need for sleeping in the road culverts or villages that day. We had no idea what to expect in Comilla, but you might say we couldn't be stopped.

The rickshaw operator and I talked some as we neared Comilla. He had been into the town but stayed only a short time for he didn't feel safe with all of the heavily armed soldiers seemingly everywhere. I asked him if he knew where the Catholic mission was located and he did. So, I asked him to go directly to the mission and then after a few minutes, we would go on to the Buckley's house. Though we felt they had left (as the young man had brought that news to us in Feni), we hoped to stay in their home.

As we entered the city there were very few people in sight. When we moved on to the main street, we immediately met an army truck with machine guns pointing in almost every direction. Hoping that it was not too apparent to the soldiers, I kept watching behind me for our other five rickshaws. What I saw could not have been more perfect. They were all in place and close together. We soon reached the Catholic mission, but no one was there.

We moved on toward the Buckley's house having no real idea what or whom we might find. In route, however, we met Father Dan walking toward his mission. You would have thought he had been given the right to formally receive us into the city of Comilla. He couldn't have been more pleasant. He was good for me and no doubt, good for Betty and our children. We talked only a short time but he did tell us that the Buckleys had gone to Dhaka and that also, at least one of the sisters who had fallen and broken some bones had gone and maybe one or two others. We took leave of Father Dan and moved quickly to the area where there would maybe be one or two Baptist families.

As we moved through the gate to the Buckley's house, beautiful screams rang out from the Roy's house next door. "It is the McKinleys, are you okay?" Yes, we were okay. Then we heard, "But how did you get here?" Our reply was short and to both them and us, it was almost unbelievable. But I first had to pay our third group of transporters so they could be on their way home. One of the Roys opened the Buckley's house and we moved our suitcases and other items into their living room.

The trip had only taken about ten hours and had you asked me in normal times about such a journey, I would have simply answered such would be impossible. Our First Class Manager had shown us just a little of what He was capable of doing. We had traveled those forty miles or so in about ten hours. We had crossed a stream of rapidly gushing water on a banana stalk boat. We had traveled in three sets of cycle rickshaws. We had stopped to eat in route. We had seen the rickshaws lifted over broken out bridges and culverts. But more than that they had been lifted over dozens of trees which were lying across the road. That's how we got there.

The hot tea at the Roy's was wonderful. We talked and talked about the recent days. Several Christian families had gone into India. The Poddar family had been taken away in an army truck but they were returned. Later we learned that one of the Poddar sons had become a freedom fighter. Had the army known that, we can only guess what the army would have done to the rest of the family.

We learned that several young Muslims were shot just outside the Buckley's gate and that R.T. had been caught outside during a round of intense firing. He lay in a ditch until he was able to slip into the house.

The town of Comilla had a population of about one hundred thousand and they were all without electricity and running water. We rested while Mrs. Roy prepared a good dinner of curry and rice.

Just before we began to settle down for the night, I hired a friend to go to the bus station and inquire about the possibility of our traveling the next thirty miles or so by bus. It happened that the next morning buses were to begin moving in the direction of our hopefully final destination.

As night approached we went again to the Buckley's house and prepared for sleep. There was no doubt that the tension of the day had depleted our energy so we were ready for a good night's rest. Wade slept with me and in a short time, he was sleeping soundly.

That was good news. Soon, April 15, 1971, would become history for our family. There were to be other difficult days not too far away, but probably none filled with more tension for our whole family than this one had been.

Early the next morning a Christian young man informed us that the bus going toward Dhaka was to depart soon so we made our way to the bus station on the western side of Comilla. Betty found a little rice and some salt in the Buckley's house and she gave that to the Roys.

The good breakfast which Mrs. Roy had prepared helped us to feel better as we thought of the day before us. The Roys treated us so kindly that it reminded us of the way all of the Christians treated us in 1959 when Betty, Cherie, Kathy, and I moved there as new missionaries with only one year of language behind us.

As we prepared to depart in the rickshaws for the bus stand, Mrs. Roy came to me and said softly, "When the war is over, we want you and all the missionaries to come back." The previous night I had said that after reaching Dhaka, possibly Betty and the children would leave for America. I also added that it was likely I would be returning in a few days.

But that morning of April 16, 1971, after Mrs. Roy had spoken, I dared not open my mouth for even one word. If I had done that, there is no doubt my emotions would have taken over right in front of our children. As we moved on toward the bus stand, I thought, "It is at times like this that the best comes forth from many good people." In Mrs. Roy, the real self was full of faith.

We boarded the bus and took seats near the front. Passengers soon began filling the remaining seats. Each seemed to make as much room as possible for others. There was not the usual pushing, shoving and arguing over seats or at least, over the preferred seats. We were living in a very serious time in that part of God's world.

We were waiting for the bus to begin moving when all of a sudden I recognized a man approaching the bus. He was one of the workers who had helped R.T. sink tube wells following that awful cyclonic tidal wave a few months earlier. We had spoken only a few words when he said, "I will be returning in just a moment," which he soon did with a bunch of small knotty bananas for us. He was a poor man and now unemployed. Those bananas may have cost him the equivalent of one-half day's pay. The bus moved out and it was quiet for most, if not all, of the passengers knew that in a few minutes we were to reach the army base.

The bus stopped for a complete search by the soldiers. The soldiers climbed to the top of the bus where most of the luggage was stored. One soldier called out forcibly, "Where is the key to this metal box?" It was not our metal box but I climbed out through the window to the top of the bus and as I did one soldier said, "We are not looking for yours. We will not open yours. Only these people are bad."

With that I quickly climbed back into the bus through the window and asked who the owner of the metal box was. One man pointed to a woman whose face was covered with her black cloth. That meant I should not speak to her but I did. I said to her," Give me your key and I will watch as they open it and I will not let them take anything."

I knew this was "big talk," but I determined to protect her belongings and I did not believe she had any kind of arms in that box. Though I knew the soldiers did not understand me promise to the religious woman, they did know I watched carefully until that metal box was relocked. Again, I climbed back into the bus through the window and handed the woman her key.

As the bus moved out I knew I had depleted much strength and my body even shook a little, yet I had no doubt that Betty approved of what I did. Maybe even more importantly our children were learning a little about the true Christian life.

We continued our journey and once one of our children asked, "Daddy, why are the houses burning?" Some of the passengers suggested that we pretend not to notice anything. But soon all of us were talking about that man-made tragedy. Eventually, it was sure that there were no friends of the army on that bus. I often remembered that we were to hear and then do what is right. Hopefully we were doing what was right in the eyes of the Living God as He watches us and over us. Hopefully, as we traveled, we did what was right.

After twenty miles of the journey, we had to leave our bus since a large bridge had been destroyed. It was easy to arrange for our luggage to be carried across a plank bridge about two feet wide and then on down to the rickshaw stand.

We had about twelve miles to the next river and we had no idea what we would find there. But we quickly got a line of rickshaws ready for departure on the next leg of our journey. We did meet a bus and we knew that bus would have to return but we had no idea when that was to happen. So we kept moving on toward the next river.

We reached the river and our rickshaw drivers acted like they knew exactly what they were doing as they saw a large ferry boat docked. So, they drove not just down to the boat, but upon the boat.

We soon had all arrangements made and we knew that boat was going to take a long route but it would reach within about fifteen miles of Dhaka. Mile after mile, as we rode the big ferry boat with only one vehicle on it and only a limited number of other passengers, we saw where villages had been burned and even some were burning as we passed.

Our boat docked and we had no idea how we were to make the rest of our journey. But before that happened, some soldiers, though I think this was not typical of Pakistani Muslim soldiers, teased Betty, Cherie and Kathy. These soldiers, supposedly friends of our home country, were unloading boxes of military supplies with markings of the United States. That was difficult to take but absolutely nothing we could do.

Then a beautiful thing happened. Two men walked down near the boat and said they were taxi drivers and willing to take us to Dhaka. That was to be their first trip to make with passengers since the night of March 25. We were pleased that they were willing to make the attempt to get us into the city and we were probably just as pleased as they were to have some business going again. With our luggage, we filled the two taxis.

The total trip was about eighteen miles since we had to cross the city to the western side and we had entered from the east. As we traveled, the two drivers without pointing kept saying, "Look to your left or look to your right."

What they showed us was bad. Vehicles, like the two in which we were riding, were charred metal. Buses and trucks had been burned or bombed. Buildings, large and small, had been burned. Rickshaws even had been smashed apparently by large military vehicles. As we moved along on the final leg of our journey, the road was left to us except for an occasional military vehicle.

The buses blasting their horns, the trucks moving at a dangerous speed, the cycle rickshaws, the push carts, the bullock carts, the cumbersome cattle pulled carts, the few private automobiles and the tens of thousands of pedestrians simply were nowhere to be seen.

As we passed through the main streets, occasionally a man or two would peep around a corner to see what the two vehicles actually were. It was as if we owned the streets and everything had been cleared for us. There were no obstructions in our way. And before March 25 this had been a city of about two million people.

As we began to reach the opposite side of the city, we talked about what we would say when we reached the guest house and talked with our missionary families. As we came nearer to our final destination, we remembered we had been in the only two vehicles seen since we left the ferry boat except for the military ones.

The guest house door was locked. A note told us where we might find the key. That note brought us to a low point, a very low point.

CHAPTER NINE
Dhaka — A Place of Security!

As you read, kindly remember that we needed to see some of our colleagues. The last one I had seen was R.T. the night of March 25, just a few hours before the army had made its attack on the people of East Pakistan. We now had news that the Buckleys had gone to Dhaka and our source for that had been Father Dan in Comilla and then the Roys. But that is all we knew except that a runner had told us the Thurmans were still in Faridpur. However, there were four families we knew nothing about when we reached Dhaka.

But as is often true among international missionaries, those in organizations other than your own often care much about you and you care for them. So, the note at the guest house made it clear that Phil Parshall, of the International Christian Fellowship, knew about our missionaries and where they were.

Betty and our children waited outside the locked guest house. I was immediately able to locate a cycle rickshaw to take me to Phil's house. At the sound of their doorbell, my name rang out clearly. Phil said, "Jim McKinley, where did you come from? How are Betty and the children?" Then Phil continued, "We tried every known way to get some news concerning you. You are the answer to the prayers of every Christian in Dhaka."

We were soon joined by Ed Welch, one of Phil's colleagues. I began asking about my missionary colleagues. "What about our missionaries?" I asked.

Phil replied, "Four of your families have gone to West Pakistan and possibly on to the States. The Rythers, we understand, have gone to Faridpur and are with the Thurmans"

Phil tried to briefly fill me in on others by saying, "My family, as well as Ed's, left for West Pakistan. He then asked, "What are you going to do?"

I replied, "It is impossible to say now. We will have to wait and see how Cherie and Kathy feel."

Phil and Ed had been most helpful. Phil handed me the guest house keys and said as we walked to the door, "I'll come over tomorrow and give you some money from your mission as well and some financial records and the safe keys." I was deeply grateful to Phil and Ed and quickly climbed into the rickshaw which had been waiting for me. As we rode along I began thinking about Betty and the children again. I knew about an hour would have passed by the time I reached them. That was a long time to be sitting on the steps with luggage on one of the main streets of the residential area of the city. In normal times Mirpur Road was always overcrowded with every type of vehicle and pedestrians. However on that day the streets and Mirpur Road were empty.

In fact, in difficult times like that, it seems that the streets may be ready to explode. For his own reasons, the rickshaw operator often rang his bell which was fastened to the handle bar of the rickshaw. It seemed that every time he rang the bell, people would look out over the brick walls to see who was on the road at such times. As we moved along I knew this city had taken a beating by the army of Pakistan.

Immediately Cherie asked, "Daddy, where are our missionaries?" I answered exactly as Phil had told me. Cherie asked further, "But Daddy, how can we live by ourselves with all that is happening?"

I answered her by saying, "Cherie, I don't know, but let's try to be patient and wait and see."

Kathy, and most of the time you did not need to wonder what she was thinking for she would tell you, said, "But Daddy, why did our missionaries leave?"

I began by saying, "Kathy, we have seen enough since we left the ferry about two hours ago to cause anyone to leave this city. Most likely, they thought we had crossed the border into India." That seemed to suffice for the time.

As we were unlocking the door, the guest house cook and one helper suddenly appeared. It was great to see them and their help would make life much easier for Betty and our children needed to be busy with their school work. The cook also could buy the groceries meaning, at least in the immediate future, I could be nearby for my family.

As best I can remember, the ground level of the two level building had four rooms. The living room was the mission office and on one side of that room there was a bedroom and bath. Then, on the other side were two bedrooms and a connecting bathroom. The Moores had been living upstairs.

So, where do you suppose we slept that first night as a family and for the full following month? We six slept in the same room. There was never a question about that. We did sleep well, even the first night, after that extended trip from our home in Feni.

As darkness approached I felt it best for our children to know that about one month before March 25, when we feared trouble and maybe, bad trouble, was on its way, I had written what to me was a special letter to each of our missionary family units. I primarily said two things. The first one was that each family, in light of the situation, should make its own decision about what they should do. I added that the rest of us should support others in their decisions.

Then, I commented that Aunt Fran Buckley had been fighting hepatitis. We also learned quickly that Uncle James Young was desperately sick with the same difficulty as Aunt Fran. The Moores were scheduled to go on stateside assignment in two months and for sure there would have been little they could have done in such a situation as we were facing in those two months. The Moores knew that their children's school was closed indefinitely because it was located in Dhaka. Then also, the Joneses were transferring to Taiwan and two of their children were in West Pakistan in school so they were in a real sense cut off from those children.

It seemed that our children accepted the situation without their friends very well. Until this day, I still admire them for acting so well in a very difficult time. But we never forgot that we were in a difficult situation.

As the weeks passed and as I met more military people of Pakistan (and again by that I mean West Pakistan), I wanted to correct their poor opinions, especially of the local Muslims. I constantly heard from them that East Pakistanis had mixed Hinduism into their Islam. Through the years, I have not minded going on record that Islam, from the beginning, had chosen to adopt the Arabian culture and even the name of one of the pagan gods of the Mecca area as their God. I know they make it clear they did not accept idolatry but I say that only to say the Islam of East Pakistan/Bangladesh never reminded me of Hinduism.

On at least a dozen trips to West Pakistan and knowing many who came to East Pakistan for work or for visits, I felt that the East Pakistani Muslims may have been more conservative than most of the West Pakistanis. Of course, I must add that many news sources lead us to believe that the Islam of the West Pakistanis has produced many terrorists. May the living God protect the people of present day Bangladesh from those of their own number who even consider terrorism.

But you learn many things by living with people which you most likely would never learn otherwise. We did not fear the people among whom or with whom we lived during that war of liberation for the people of East Pakistan.

Night time deepened our fears for we began hearing terrible stories. The army of Pakistan had to be considered an occupying army. They, with their commanding general, had refused that the duly elected person, an East Pakistani, become head of the Pakistan government. So, this only weakened the morale of some of the soldiers.

If they thought the local people were not faithful Muslims, they considered the young women free to be taken as they pleased. Many people, primarily Muslims, told us story after story about the treatment of local women by the soldiers. I know there were warnings issued by the government in power to "beware of rumors," but the difficulty was that I knew many of the so-called rumors were true.

In July of that infamous year, an international reporter and I had a conversation that could not be called "smooth." He told of more than five hundred young local women being kept on the army base in Dhaka. I questioned him and even said, "You cannot prove that." Then he proceeded to give the name of the doctor who refused to abort babies for some of the young women who had been forcefully taken to that place. Now, please remember that I will tell other stories about Pakistan soldiers who, to me, were to be highly respected in their attitude toward the Bangla people.

You can be assured that we slept in the one room and carefully locked all the doors every night. We never knew what might happen before the light of the next day began to shine. We knew the hatred grew as the days moved along with so many killings. In fact, one army officer told me that they knew how to produce a new race by getting the local young women pregnant.

But I will add that right up until December 16, 1971, on only one occasion did a soldier even hint any harm to Betty and our daughters and that was on April 16 when we were getting down from the ferry outside of Dhaka.

I have said and continue to say that during our first few weeks in Dhaka, Betty, Cherie, and Kathy did their best to remain inside the guest house. We did not want to draw attention to ourselves and that could happen so easily due to the location of the house in which we were living. However, it was also to our advantage to live there because it was such an open place in that city. Gradually we learned that probably foreigners were relatively safe.

In later years I heard that Henry Kissinger, the United States Secretary of State, had flown from a secret air base in West Pakistan to China during the time of war in what was to become Bangladesh. That trip, in later years, was heralded as the beginning of the peace movement between the United States and China. But the war was a price too great to pay for a visit that years later had ultimately meant little or maybe nothing, between my home country and China. The price for the journey was the blood of the common people of East Pakistan. I had and have great moral and mental difficulty with such behavior, especially if such action involves the "land that I love."

But back to the Islam of some East Pakistanis who cooperated with the Pakistan army. Later, as I traveled to different parts of East Pakistan, I learned that not a few East Pakistani Muslims cooperated with the army. I must add that most of those whom I met didn't have much courage. Their cooperation with the army only meant cheap politics and in the end they lost badly.

Soon after we reached Dhaka I informed the American Consulate that we were now in Dhaka. We always tried to keep them informed when we changed locations. Doing that, at least at that time, was proper. We might need information from them or our families might need information about us.

The Consulate officer asked if I would come to their office and give them a report concerning Feni and our travel to Dhaka. At first, I hesitated and then decided that was the proper thing to do and Phil Parshall volunteered to go with me to help. That was helpful. Though he would not interfere in what I was reporting, Phil's presence meant that I had at least one person there to support me. I knew only what I had read in the newspapers about Mr. Blood, the Consul General. He had helped much following the tidal wave and I sincerely appreciated that.

So when Phil and I arrived at the consulate, Mr. Blood took us into a room filled with dignified looking people. There was no doubt that our coming from an area that was still under local control and we had traveled a distance of over one hundred miles without any harm to us in any way, was of great interest to this group.

Among those present were an American army colonel and a British major, both dressed in civilian clothing. I did not understand their presence and naturally guarded my remarks. I, as an international missionary, no matter how much it may have appeared, was not a carrier of military information.

Another person present happened to be the Deputy Chief of Mission. He had come over from the US embassy in West Pakistan to learn about the situation in East Pakistan. I don't think I was introduced to him but learned from someone else who he was. He didn't seem to be interested in what was going on and sat some distance from the rest of us.

The early questions asked concerned how we had lived in a border area and no harm had come to us. Then, they asked about how we had traveled that great distance especially with four children. All of that, I did not hesitate to answer as best I could. .I suppose my answers gave the information that no one, not the army or the local people, did anything to harm us. Thinking about this and reading what I wrote earlier still leaves me angry at the so-called gentleman who sat at a distance as if he had more important things to think about. Hopefully, it doesn't sound too arrogant but if he thought he was too important to be a part of such a discussion, why did he sit nearby?

Then, I was asked, "Are the local people armed?" I answered what I knew.

Then someone asked, "Do you think the Bangla people can hold the Feni area?"

I immediately answered, "No." Then I added, "The local people are up against a well trained and well equipped army, and they have only meager arms. With their planes, the Pakistani forces can drive the local fighters into India or kill them." They all knew that I knew what those jets could do.

Again, looking back more than thirty years since that meeting, I think I would not have said what I am next going to write had that "gentleman" sitting at a distance not been present. You see, I had and still have the deep feeling that to me there are no big shot persons and there are no little shot persons. Then, again, I guess my arrogance broke through as we were talking about arms and I said, "When my wife and my children were lying in the hallway of our house, I knew the planes zooming over us were made in my country. They were killing our friends and our neighbors."

Then the "gentleman" so nicely dressed and still at a distance, loudly remarked, "You cannot prove those planes were supplied by America." I knew I could not lose to such a statement.

About six years earlier, when India and Pakistan were fighting each other, many news sources said that the Saber 86 jets of Pakistan were supplied by America. Maybe so, or maybe not so. However, I knew that those Saber 86 jet fighters which knew how to strafe and kill hundreds of common people who knew nothing about war were American planes or at least manufactured by us. So I also added, "As those planes moved away from Feni, on one of their killing missions, they attacked a near-by market place, where there is no reason to believe anyone there had a weapon of any kind." Earlier in this conversation, I had mentioned our children and that first plane attack in Feni.

I even added that after those planes attacked Feni, I inquired whether or not the local people had weapons to shoot them down.

Now, looking back and well remembering, I believe the first guns I saw near the India border was when we were attempting to cross that steam of water where the bridge had been destroyed. I had heard stories about the fighting on the eastern side of Feni and at a bridge east and south of Feni, but I had not seen any weapons.

Again, looking back, America did not own me in such situations, my God owned me and the next involvement was ownership by my family. Only a miracle of my God saved our children that day. One question I heard a few years later was, "Why were you in such a place, anyway?" A person who asks that kind of a question would never be able to understand the reply, "We are in this place because of God's love and we are not afraid to share that love in both word and deed anywhere in the world."

I must say that the Consul General and the American colonel and the British major could not have been more polite to me. Mr. Blood would not accept my refusal when he asked if I would like to send some type of cablegram to the United States. He even refused a short message I prepared in his office in a code address at the then Foreign Mission Board. I finally wrote a longer message to our "Boss" knowing that he would get all of the information to our families in the United States. Then the Consul General asked me if we needed transportation out of East Pakistan. I replied something like this. "No, at least for now we will remain here in Dhaka for it is 'a haven of rest,' compared to where we were before we made the journey to Dhaka."

As we departed, Phil's presence with me helped greatly so by the time I reached the house, I had settled down somewhat. Phil said, "Jim, I was proud of you. It may not have helped but you gave the Deputy Chief the right answer." I must add now that to me, no person, anywhere, loves his or her country more than I love my country. They may love as much but not more. That love moves you to want your country to be most careful in all situations. We should not be in the business of killing innocent people or enabling others to kill.

On Sunday, our family of six was with five others at the International Church in Dhaka for worship. The eleven of us were proof that most foreigners had departed that land. But one of those present was Mark Tucker from Texas, who was at that time with the Cholera Research Laboratory, with a purpose of understanding and preventing infectious diseases. Mark said that if we were interested, he would be pleased to show us different parts of the city the next day and Betty and I agreed.

Mark showed us a place which had been police barracks. But the massive shells on the night of March 25 left that place a shamble of primarily ashes and other debris. Some of the concrete buildings showed deep holes where shells had struck and we knew, as we looked, what had happened to the police in those buildings. The old section of his historic city revealed that those people located in that area had suffered much for many former wooden buildings were flat with only ashes to tell you what they had been.

Perhaps what hurt most as we gazed were the bustee areas, or the places where the poorest of people lived on land in the poorest of little houses and on land which wasn't theirs. Those bustee areas were ashes. Local newspapers, now totally controlled by Pakistan, published stories about how the military government was cleaning up the city.

As we drove back to our new "home," Mark pointed out a bustee two blocks from where we were living. He remarked, "I wonder why they left this one?" The next morning I passed by the same place, but it was now a clear spot of land for the little houses had all been burned and nothing left but ashes.

Again, please remember that East Pakistan's Hindus, or at least most of them, went into India as quickly as possible for them to travel that distance. So, even in a city like Dhaka, on the night of March 25, there had been primarily Muslims killing Muslims. But at times like that, people like us think of people killing people not necessarily Muslims killing Muslims.

Then we learned that the area we loved so much had been taken by the Pakistan army on April 24. We could only imagine what all had happened there. Everything we owned was in our house in Feni.

As time moved along, buses began to travel the streets of the city. Rickshaws were seen and their bells heard again and "yes" those bells sounded good. Cherie and Kathy began to walk about in the yard. Also, without a doubt, news traveled in many directions for people came by the guest house to talk as they learned we were missionaries. Most of those people were nearby new neighbors of ours. As they expressed themselves about what had and was happening, they seemed to feel totally free to say anything they wanted. We at least thought they understood that they were able to trust us. We knew they badly needed to express their anger.

Often, strangers said, "Why do you remain here with your family? It is dangerous."

I had no difficulty answering, "We believe God brought us to this land. We believe He wants us to remain." Often these statements were the extent of our verbal witness to some people.

The days were tough and seemingly longer than usual. But many friends helped greatly. Many people seemed to primarily want to just get a look at our children. I could have told all of those people that our four were absolutely great.

A real shock came in late April about two weeks after we reached Dhaka. A cablegram came from the American Embassy in West Pakistan to the Consulate in Dhaka. That cable said, "Ryther's daughter emotionally ill." Carla was in boarding school in Murree, West Pakistan. We still assumed that her parents were with the Thurmans in Faridpur, East Pakistan. Faridpur was probably a day's journey from Dhaka or about one hundred miles away from us.

The cable arrived late in the afternoon. Somehow, we had to get that message to the Rythers, but how at first we did not know. I had and still have a childhood saying, "If there is a will, usually there is a way." So, what was that way? The way was that someone had to take that message to the Rythers. Bangla friends had done enough for us. That meant I had to make that journey, somehow.

The gravest and almost unthinkable situation prevailed. I counseled with Betty and our four children. In that conversation, Cherie, our eldest, said, "Daddy, you have to go." Kathy and the two younger boys seemed to agree without hesitation. Often in such conversations, Betty did not need to say anything. The children knew what to say and they said it. I hope they are like that even today. I would not consider any of our five children today, "bossy," but their mother and I often receive unsolicited counsel which is still welcomed.

I am sure that our children thought of themselves in such a situation. They surely would want their parents and that meant Carla wanted her parents. But my family was to be left alone on one of the main streets or roads of Dhaka. But remember, we had two missionary friends only about three miles from where we were living and their families were not with them. That meant I had to get to Phil and Ed and then back to my family before darkness made its visit.

So, off I went in a rickshaw to talk with Phil and Ed. The reception I received was much more than anyone had any right to expect. I had only asked my friends, "Could one of you stay with Betty and our children while I am gone to Faridpur?"

Phil replied far beyond what I could have ever anticipated, "Ed, if you stay with Betty and the children, I will travel with Jim."

Obviously, I objected and said, "If there is trouble, it is better that only one person be involved." My statement was ignored. Early the next morning, Phil and Ed reached our house. Ed stayed with my family.

Phil and I reached our first traveling obstacle. There was no ferry functioning at the Padma, also called the Ganges River. On the western side of East Pakistan, the India River, the Ganges, actually turns south and hence, flows near Kolkata, India. But that is only a small stream compared to the amount of that river's water, which flows into the then East Pakistan or today's Bangladesh. Anyway, the Padma is a massive river.

Phil and I found a relatively safe place for the vehicle we were driving and we began flowing downstream in a small boat on that river, as if we knew exactly where we were going. The tide from the ocean was down so the boat flowed along beautifully. There was no doubt that the boatman was extremely nervous. After sometime, we turned up a small river channel toward the regular ferry dock. The boatman said without hesitation, "I will have to turn back here."

So, since the army was in control of the dock about three miles away, we got out and paid the boatman well. Perhaps we were his first passengers in many days but he feared the dock where the military personnel were located. We began walking the three mile journey in the direction of the dock.

Time passed rapidly. Every direction we looked during that walking journey was terribly sad. Dogs chewed on human bodies along the river bank. There was no doubt that many people had died. As we neared the dock, we saw that the little houses had been burned. You might say that this is the way the army cleaned the area.

Just a short distance from the dock a soldier stopped us. We had no way of communicating. We, Phil and I, could speak English and Bangla but that soldier knew neither. But we pointed toward the dock and we walked with him. We walked on when we reached the dock, but he stopped us and pointed toward the dock where there was an army officer who knew English.

We didn't want to be delayed but the officer insisted that soon a jeep would come to the dock and we could ride in that jeep to Faridpur. We waited for two hours, but still, there was no jeep. We had about fifteen miles to travel. Of course, there were no buses. I said to Phil, "Even if we walk the entire distance, we may not arrive there before dark," but we began walking.

Just before we reached the main road we saw a rickshaw. The passenger in the rickshaw got down and paid the operator. From our distance we noted that as the passenger walked away, a soldier walked toward the rickshaw and stuck out his hand and received something.

When we reached the rickshaw operator, we immediately knew he was deeply distressed. "What happened?" I asked.

"The soldier took all of my money," he said. We didn't need any further explanation. That was this man's first work in several days. He had been paid and anybody who had any common sense knew this operator badly needed that money so he could buy food for his family.

So, we asked him to take us to the next road where we might find another rickshaw but he was too tired to do anything since he had been so emotionally depleted. Well, it was not to be the first time or the last time I had tried something radically different. I climbed on the operator's seat and Phil and the rickshaw man climbed into the passenger's seat and off we went but we went wobbling and at a very slow pace.

Then, my new machine didn't seem to do everything I attempted and I noted we were headed quickly to the side of the road and started over the embankment. Phil and our new friend jumped out of the regular seat and I leaped off of the driver's seat, but we managed to hold on to the rickshaw and prevent any bad damage.

Perhaps Phil would not agree after all these years, but I thought I began to do a little better as a rickshaw driver. But I could not pedal it sufficiently to get up the hills or grades. We pushed it and then all three of us rode downhill. But, after about four miles, we found another rickshaw driver who wanted to go toward home in Faridpur, so we had a good deal. We paid the man who had lost his money very well and I can assure you he had much more after we paid him than he had before the soldier took his money.

After a few miles in the second rickshaw, we found another one waiting anxiously for work so we moved on with Phil in one rickshaw and I in another. They gave us speed since each rickshaw carried less weight.

On that long journey we counted houses which had been burned. Dozens of houses in village after village were no more. We noticed that occasionally houses that were probably the best in each village were spared by those who burned the others. I suppose that like the military had cleaned up Dhaka, they were also cleaning up rural areas. As we traveled, we estimated that seventy-five percent of the houses had been burned.

Nearing Faridpur, I began thinking about how we were to approach the Rythers with the difficult news we carried. Eventually I said to Phil, "Let's wait until we can get Carl alone and then tell him the news we received. Then, he can tell Jean."

Gloria Thuman had gone into the kitchen to prepare food and Jean Ryther had gone into another room so that left Carl with Phil and me. I was too emotional to speak of what had happened so I simply handed the cable message to Carl. Though they had traveled from Dhaka to Faridpur a few days before, circumstances had radically changed. Carl, like a mature "man of faith" said, "We will go to Dhaka tomorrow and then to West Pakistan as quickly as possible after that." I wanted to help but it seemed, for once at least, I had little or nothing to say.

Like mature Christian parents, the Rythers began making plans to depart early the next morning with Phil and me. I had no doubt they were doing the right thing. Their young high school daughter needed Mom and Dad. We knew they were ready to go to that daughter.

That night, we talked considerably about the past few weeks and that all of a sudden, at least parts of the three Southern Baptist missionary families were together for the night along with our beloved friend, Phil, who probably should be credited with keeping me out of difficulty with some military people.

By daylight the next morning Jean, Carl and their youngest child, Tim, began walking a different route than the one Phil and I had taken to reach them. We wanted to avoid the dock where we knew dogs were still chewing on the remains of human bodies. When we reached the big river, we rented the only available boat. This boat was made for cattle transportation and because it was so heavy, it did not make very much speed since two men couldn't provide much power with only oars. We were traveling upstream and that made the situation even more difficult.

We baked in the hot early morning sun and then, as we reached near to noontime, it became hotter. Eventually, we found a smaller boat for Jean and Tim so with the three men walking along near the boat on the river bank, we moved much more rapidly those last ten miles to our vehicle. When we reached it, we immediately saw that changes had taken place overnight. Navy personnel had moved into position near the van, but since we all had passports, they delayed us only a short time.

The van had not been harmed and though we were tired and sunburned, we were pleased to be moving on our last leg of the return journey. Just before we reached Dhaka, we were moving slowly along a very high new road embankment leading to a bridge. The headlights showed us what was happening. Soldiers were on the embankment with a lone Bangla policeman.

One of the soldiers, apparently having fun, pushed that policeman down the embankment right in front of our moving van. I jumped out of the vehicle. I assumed, as I often did in similar situations, that if the policeman saw I was a foreigner, then he probably would not fire his weapon and he did not fire it. Of course, none of us thought such behavior by me was dumb during that time of chaos in East Pakistan.

Two days later, the Rythers departed for West Pakistan. Upon arrival there the government gave them twenty-four hours to depart as they claimed the Ryther's visas were not in order. I have always said that the disorder was what this good family had experienced in the Dhaka-Faridpur areas.

We soon heard that Carla was not "emotionally ill," but disturbed about her mother, dad, and little brother. The same feeling prevailed among all missionary children who were separated from their parents.

Though we were one hundred percent for the reuniting of the Ryther family, we faced a different kind of times. Our missionary group was down to two families. The city of Dhaka was desolate. Daily, we watched as military trucks moved down the road fully loaded with Bangla men who were their prisoners. The stories of the treatment of Bangla women mushroomed. Cherie and Kathy seemed to grow more impatient.

Then, two beautiful things happened. We met a newly arrived Presbyterian couple at International Church. They were the Wilkens family and when our home-grown school started later, Mrs. Wilkens became Kathy's teacher.

About a week later, after the Ryther's departure, the Thurmans came to Dhaka. This was truly a boost to us as a family. Philip and David Thurman were both younger than our youngest, Wade. Our four received those two as if they were little brothers.

Several times while Phil and I were in Faridpur I wanted to ask the Thurmans to join us in Dhaka but I just could not bring myself to do that. They had responsibilities there with friends and living conditions were not too bad. Also, the border of India was at least sixty miles away. However, the next morning as we had prepared to depart for Dhaka, I said to Tom and Gloria, "If you want to come to Dhaka, you will be more than welcomed by my family."

I believed the Thurmans moved to Dhaka because of our need and not theirs. They were the kind of people who are always helping others. Our family surely received a boost from their arrival.

CHAPTER TEN
Traveling in War-Torn Land

Without a doubt our family loved the Thurmans and we loved to be with them. Perhaps our days in East Pakistan would have been shortened had they not come to Dhaka. Tom and I had similar feelings about what was happening in our second homeland. We had deep feelings about the local people and most of those feelings certainly favored the people with whom we lived.

Soon after the Thurmans arrived in Dhaka I began thinking that the time had come for me to visit Comilla and Feni. You remember I had said in Feni, "We will not leave you." Then in Comilla, I had told Mrs. Roy, "I will return." I knew that the God I love and serve was the kind of God who, if it were humanly impossible for me to do that returning, He would put aside what I had said. Therefore, this was my desire to return. It was not my consciousness of a mistake being corrected, but it was the honoring of my word given. In one sense, there was no reason for my not returning.

Early one morning, I was off to Feni in a vehicle and after about sixty miles of having the road primarily to myself, I reached Co-milla. Without a doubt, the Comilla Christians with whom I talked were glad to see me and I was just as glad to see them. After a good visit, I began thinking that I could drive all the way to Feni since the newspapers carried the words, "All is normal in East Pakistan." But everything was far from normal!

One village was still burning. People saw the van I was driving and ran in the opposite direction. Eventually, I was able to talk with one man. I asked him why the army had destroyed a large bridge on the road to Feni. He said, "The army did not do that. The freedom fighters did that to keep the army away from our people." With the road and bridges destroyed, I knew that the vehicle could not help me move on toward my destination. So I began driving back toward Comilla.

As I drove slowly, I remembered that a Muslim friend lived in one of the nearby villages. Soon I knew that my God had again managed everything beautifully. We talked only momentarily. Then

I asked my friend if I could leave the van in his village. His immediate reply was a strong, "Yes." Then we did our best to move the vehicle to a place where it could not be seen from the main road and I began walking southward toward Feni.

When I returned to the destroyed bridge location and moved on a short distance, I saw that dozens of houses had been burned. Many of those remains of the houses were still smoldering. As others gathered about, it seemed that I was a long lost friend, but I did not recognize any of those people.

One young man did ask me, "Sir, were you driving that brown vehicle?" I acknowledged that and he said, "When I saw your vehicle, I began running warning the people that the army was coming, so now I will do that again and tell them everything is okay." I was sorry that I had caused all of the fear but maybe, once they understood I was a friend, maybe that helped some.

Ordinarily, the roads were crowded with people primarily going and coming from market places. But that day, few people were seen as I traveled the remaining thirty miles by walking and riding different rickshaws. The common people had deep fears and they lived near the border of India so the possibility of greater danger was always present.

But when I reached the stream of water my family had crossed on April 15, I knew I might lose my rickshaw because there was no way we could get it across that fast flowing stream of water. But within a short time, a young man came out of a small forest area carrying his rustic rifle.

I did not recognize this freedom fighter but he immediately said, "Oh, sir, I am sorry for all of this trouble to you but I can help." He blew lightly on his whistle and in a few minutes that same banana stalk boat appeared on which my family had crossed earlier. But the boat had been updated with more banana stalks attached.

The friends lifted the rickshaw upon the little "ferry" and in a few minutes we were across that stream of water. Then I heard a final word from the young man with the rifle, "When you return, come through our camp and you will not be delayed." Anything he said was certainly welcomed by me. However, on the return trip I did not enter the camp of the freedom fighters.

But that stream of water, which ordinarily flowed only in the rainy season, and that season was more than a month away, told many Muslim people they had been especially blessed by Allah for that stream would slow the pace of the army. I had no problem with their thinking that. Whether their Allah was the God I knew or not, I found myself hoping and praying again that all people everywhere would come to know the God and Father of Jesus the Messiah. With that thought roaming through my mind, I traveled on toward Feni.

As we approached Feni, I told the rickshaw operator that we were going to travel a small road off to the right and avoid the town area. But as we approached that road, a soldier with a rifle in his hand stopped the rickshaw.

Remember, I was coming to the end of a forty mile trip from Comilla and that road had come within a short distance of India most of the route. So, undoubtedly, that soldier had every right to inquire about us. I told the rickshaw operator not to fear because I could manage the situation. My speaking in Bangla may have been a mistake for the soldier did not understand what I had said so he ordered me out of the rickshaw and the driver out of his seat. The soldier ordered us to sit but before he did that, he searched us and the rickshaw.

After about thirty minutes I noted that the soldier had a telephone. I attempted to get him to call someone who spoke English and I succeeded in that by pointing to the phone and toward Feni. In a few seconds a person answered the phone and the soldier handed it to me. On the line was an army major. I asked him if Mr. Belal, the officer in the Feni area, was present. Then he seemed a little more relaxed and said, "Oh, so you know Mr. Belal. Yes, he is here and you can talk with him."

In another few seconds I was talking with Mr. Belal. However, he didn't say much and of course, we had to speak in English and the major would understand everything we said so I told him of our situation and he said, "The major will take care of everything." In a few more seconds, the major said to me, "Come directly to Mr. Belal's office and I will order the soldier to release you." In just a few minutes, we were at Mr. Belal's office.

Mr. Belal, who had kindly used me to help with upgrading the physical condition of Feni, had little to say. However, the major had much to say. He questioned me about the route I had traveled and why the local people had not harmed me. He asked about when our family was returning to Feni and he did not seem to want to leave that subject. However, after about an hour talking, he asked again about my family and our return to Feni. I rightly or wrongly so answered, "When you and Mr. Belal bring your families here, I will bring mine." Or I said something like that and I guess I said it in fear but I had to say it. The primary point of the major's talk was that everything in Feni was normal.

He did ask me why I had taken the tires and batteries off of our two vehicles and I answered that by saying the vehicles were for helping people and I did not want anyone to use them for killing innocent people. Again, I had to speak how I felt down deeply.

He released me and I rode the same rickshaw to our house. Rather than break the lock when the army took our vehicles, they simple broke down the gate. One section of the gate was lying in the tall grass. The house, though it did not look like it, was still "our home." Other than Mr. Belal, the only person I saw that night was Sultan, our Muslim cook. One look at Sultan told me "everything was not normal." His face and his body were lean. There was not the usual kind expression on his face. I had not had lunch that day but when he offered to prepare some food for me, I refused. But early the next morning Sultan did prepare the best breakfast he could with what he had.

We had left the refrigerator filled with food and of course, all of that was now rotten since the electricity had been off most of the time since our departure. Remember that when we departed Feni we were not cool and collected, but hardly knew what we were doing. I asked Sultan to return to his village and remain near his family. After I had eaten breakfast, the same rickshaw in which I had entered Feni the previous day appeared and off we went again on the bypass of Feni town. As we moved away from the house, I did look back and felt that everything we owned would eventually be stolen or destroyed.

The trip that morning was slow since along the route, we passed over or around the areas of broken bridges and culverts. We passed by the burned villages. I supposed in my mind, I felt that it was quite possible that I would not travel this road again. At the stream of water, the kind freedom fighters seemed to understand that I did not think I should travel through their camp, so they helped us cross again that stream of water on the ferry boat.

My van had been well cared for and as I had traveled south and now back north to that village, I thought several times of the Muslim man who gave permission for me to leave the van in his village. I remembered he was a member of a rigid Islamic political party and probably, a "friend" of army, yet he had not failed his missionary friend. I supposed he knew well that I was not involved in the politics of his country.

At the Noapara market about thirteen miles south of Comilla, I watched as thousands of people crossed the road going from the west to the east into India. The reason for the stop was that our rickshaw tire burst and we were delayed for about an hour having the necessary repairs done.

My eyes were filled with that mass of humanity moving slowly but surely across that road to hopefully, a place where they could live. For how long they were to live beyond their own national boundary, they knew as little as I did. Most of these people were loaded with meager possessions. Some led cows. Some led goats. Others helped push carts pulled by cows. Some were even in rickshaws moving across that national boundary into another country. Little children with heavy loads on their back cried as they struggled along. Generally, however, there was silence.

When our rickshaw was ready to move again, the long massive line halted so the foreigner could move on to his surer destination than theirs. The day was May 7, 1971. It was to be almost eight months later when most, if not all of those people had the opportunity to return to their homes. Most of them returned months and months later with far fewer possessions. Their bodies were even weaker and they left many family members' bodies in graves in India. Most and this included Muslims and Hindus, were to return to the parched earth on which their houses had been located before their departure. They didn't know it then, but at least they were to return to a free land.

It was eight months later that I traveled the Feni-Comilla road again. That area became a continuous battle field. Mrs. Roy and her family again could not have been more gracious to me and I spent the night in the Buckley's house. As I prepared to depart early the next morning, Mrs. Roy had a question for me again.

She said, "I am thinking of sending most of my family into India. What do you think about that?"

My reply was simple as I said, "I cannot even suggest what you should do, but I will support your decision whatever it is." Soon, I was on my way to Dhaka. I soon learned that screaming could be beautiful. Every time I returned from a trip during that war I was greeted with one of those beautiful screams from our children, "Daddy! Daddy! Mother, Daddy has come back." Kathy's high pitched voice was always heard above the others.

It was again good to have the feeling of assurance I have with my family. We went over my trip to Feni in detail. The children were especially concerned about their little friends in Feni, but I could only report that I had no news and they were still in villages or in India.

Tom and I discussed what we should do to hold our work together. We had suddenly gone from seven families to two and we were unfamiliar with many particular projects in which the other five were involved. The military government was pressuring us that all work should continue.

We had to decide how much work we needed to do and we had to consider the livelihood of all those related to our organization. We did accept that not much work of any kind could be done in the present situation.

We also decided that we were going to travel together outside of Dhaka. It seemed the presence of a second person might have value in the event of trouble and we knew that trouble was likely to appear wherever we were. It was interesting that, most of the time, the government did not place any extra traveling limits on foreigners.

In August I was told that I was no longer permitted to go to Feni because it was too near the border of India. Anytime such a restriction was made, it caused us to wonder what would happen next. Was something else in the making?

It was natural that Tom and I travel to Faridpur since I had just returned from Comilla and Feni. The Faridpur people, Christians and Muslims, were pleased to see Tom. Of course they had expected the Thurmans to go back to the United States after going to Dhaka. Faridpur was different from Feni especially since it was far from the border of India, so, it was somewhat more normal. We did consider one thing we possibly could do and that was to take the small truck which Carl Ryther had been using for agriculture work to Dhaka.

The military had used the truck several times but for a few days had not used it. When Tom and I departed for Dhaka, we drove that truck. Apparently, there was no further inquiry from the military concerning the vehicle. Pleasant screams greeted us when we reached the guest house.

Before long we decided that the two of us would again travel to Feni. I had learned that there was an open road from Comilla and the road was inland from the border of India. It was good for friends in Comilla to see Tom, for the presence of any missionary caused some people to think less trouble would happened then. I doubt that was true but if it helped, then that is why we were present.

Going and coming, we passed through Choumuhani, the largest market place in Noakhali District at that time. Business, however, was not our interest as we passed through that market area or what had been a market area. The main area had been burned and now crumbled, rusty appearing tin and ashes characterized the market. Very few people were seen.

Though I had told Sultan on the previous visit to Feni to stay at home or near his family, he was at the house when Tom and I arrived. Though Sultan never mentioned money, I paid him as if he were working full time. That was his livelihood for his family.

We knew it was right to report to the major that we were in Feni overnight so we went to his office. He couldn't have been angrier. Mr. Belal had disappeared. The major said he had heard Mr. Belal had gone back to West Pakistan. Of course, I was glad for him because he surely did not fit into the military situation which involved the killing of so many local people.

Though Tom and I stayed in my house overnight, there was little reason for lingering. Feni was a deserted town so what could we do? The answer was probably we couldn't do anything for anyone.

But at the same time, I knew that word of our presence would travel to many village areas and so people would know I was still around and was ready to do whatever would truly help them. However, again I wondered what that helpful thing could be.

We did not attempt to travel the border road but drove west to Choumuhani and then directly north on the newly opened road. When we reached the area west of Noapara where I had witnessed the exodus of people on the previous trip to Feni, it was easy to understand why so many had chosen to go into India.

When the army had moved into that area in opening the new road, they burned thousands of small houses. Many of those houses were only one room, two at the most. Many had dirt floors, thatch roofs and bamboo sides, so they burned easily and quickly. Those houses which were larger and owned by wealthier people were now burning as we moved along that "normal" route.

A three-wheeled motor scooter, or baby taxi, had broken down on the road. It was just too rough for that loaded little vehicle to make it so the passengers were searching for a ride. Tom and I welcomed them into our microbus with three big seats. Men filled the back two seats and the leader of the group sat in front with Tom and me. That leader was proud of himself. He lost no time in giving his identification. He was a member of the Central Peace Committee. My first reaction was to spit in his face, but you know international missionaries can't do things like that.

These Peace Committees were being established throughout East Pakistan by the military government and I had learned the members of those Committees were radical Muslims who favored the military government.

But I also knew that some people were forced to be members and those forced were faithful to the Bangla people. Those who boasted about their role were pro-military all the way, as was our front seat rider. However, I can say that he paid for his travel to Dhaka with us, not in money but having to listen to two foreigners, who deeply felt that the present treatment of tens of thousands of people was definitely wrong.

I despised this man's boasting but what could I do? If we put him out of our vehicle, that would have been, most likely, more than he would have tolerated. So, here I was, with a traitor to his own people, riding in a vehicle which was assigned to me.

But if Tom and I were compromising, we tried to make up for that compromising. As we moved along that rough road we saw more houses burning as if they had just been ignited. Pathetic poor Banglas ran out to the road and when they did that we always stopped the van. The two light colored faces caused them to open their hearts and mouths to us. We listened with the deepest care but again, what could we do? When they cried out, "They are killing our people," we knew who was killing them but we always asked, "But who is killing your people?" With loud voices, they replied, "The army, the army!" They pleaded, "Please tell the world what is happening." As best I could I had only one answer to that. The answer, "I will do all I can to tell what is happening."

The gentleman riding with us squirmed when we replied favorably to these pathetic people along our route. Tom never hesitated to speak as loudly as I did. Our passenger was paying for his ride.

We had to take a short rest in Comilla. Tom's and my emotions were running high. Maybe talking with some of the Christians could calm us down somewhat.

While we were visiting with friends, the Peace Committee member informed us that he was going to have a short visit with some local members of that Committee. He did want to ride on to Dhaka with us so maybe that helped us not to be overly concerned about what word he might pass on to the Committee members.

After the rest stop, we began moving on toward Dhaka. About twenty-five miles from Comilla, I saw, for the first time in all the traveling I had done recently, the military firing mortars into villages. The thing that troubled me most was there was no firing coming from the village to the army. Probably, some traitor had informed the army that there were freedom fighters in that village or at least that is what I accepted.

While we were waiting under the order of an officer, he asked for our identifications. Every person in our vehicle presented an identification card with a photograph attached so eventually, after a lecture to Tom and me, the officer decided to release us. But first he informed us that we had no right to travel because we might get hurt.

As we drove on, village people from other nearby areas came running out to the road so we stopped. What could we do? We could speak a word of kindness in a day in which there was little kindness to be noticed. That also gave us another opportunity to collect the "fare" from our passenger.

When he got out of the vehicle in Dhaka, I gave him one of my business cards and said, "If you need me, this tells you where you can locate me." I knew the card would not necessarily bring any harm to Tom and me. In fact, our boldness probably worked against him saying or doing anything about the journey. I never saw that person again, but I read about him.

He was "elected" to replace a member of the National Assembly which had never met. The news article said that the person he replaced had gone to India. I also learned several months later that when Bangladesh was free, he fled and went abroad to live.

Again, those beautiful screams from our children greeted Tom and me. If I could have seen that passenger and talked with him, I, without hesitating, could tell him about how any one of us can overcome hatred. As time moved on and people died, I never accepted that without deep sadness, but at the same time, I did not hate. My God loved others and I clearly understood that I was to love Him and my neighbors.

CHAPTER ELEVEN
Assurance in the Midst of Chaos

Since 1972, following the Bangladesh struggle for freedom, many people, mostly friends, have asked me why I bore others by telling of my travels during 1971. I will now discuss one or two reasons.

Most people will surely understand why I went to Faridpur to tell the Rythers the news about their daughter. Because that was an "inland" road, these people wonder if that had been a border road or one primarily occupied by the military or their helpers if I would have made that trip. Absolutely! While it was much easier having a good friend, Phil Parshall, as a traveling companion, my going to Faridpur and I am sure Phil's reason for going with me was to help the Ryther family.

In addition, my having said to friends in both Feni and Comilla that I would return when we first departed that area, meant that every time I traveled, friends were encouraged. So, in addition to keeping my promise, the encouragement friends received was a powerful inward force for me to travel in dangerous areas.

Also, in our first nine years as international missionaries, my family had lived in Dhaka, Comilla, Faridpur, and Feni. I knew I was attached to all of these places and to hinder relationships in any way was simply something I could not do. I believed my God had led my family to this part of His world and He was the primary cause for our remaining there even at a dangerous time for the six of us.

For sure, every time I made one of those trips, I knew the news about my travel reached many people and they would know that some missionaries were permitted by the government to remain in their land. They knew that every opportunity which came to us, we would use for doing our best to lessen the brutality which was happening inland and on border areas.

The first time I traveled to Feni following the freedom movement, I was treated badly by local government. They acted as if I were an agent of the Pakistani government, but by the second trip

I made to Feni, the news that my family and I had been faithful to the local people had spread rapidly.

Most of the time I went through Comilla and on to Feni, and saw only a very few people, but they told me of many others who regularly asked about my family. Though my commitment to my God may have wavered many times, I look back to that land today and only thank Him that He has permitted me to be a part of the "good" which is happening there right up until I write or until you read what I am writing. Remember, and I said this earlier, "God does not waste any witness in word or deed."

Finally, my family must have been a strong family. We loved the Thurmans and at least some of us ate every meal together over a period of three months. Our beloved "Boss" at that time, Dr. J. D. Hughey, warned us verbally about our attempting to live together. We appreciated his saying that, and maybe that helped in our relationships, nevertheless, I do not recall, even one time when relationships between Tom and me were marred.

It is true that I consider myself more aggressive than Tom and maybe, at times, I was abusive, but not one of those times has ever come to my mind. Though the Thurmans returned to Faridpur for a few weeks, we were again back together for another full month.

After the time Tom and I traveled together to Feni, we never did that again. The primary reason was we were the only two men in our organization at that time, so if something happened to one of us, the other one could manage with our two families.

Perhaps no one knew better than I that traveling was dangerous. I loved my family and knew that true love reaches out to others. All the good people, both Christians and Muslims, knew well that my family stood with me. They were courageous, as were the Thurman family.

Tom and Gloria decided to make a short visit back to Faridpur and to leave their sons with us. They traveled by public conveyance so that slowed their journey. When they were returning to Dhaka, night time caught them about five miles from the Padma River and about forty miles from Dhaka and their sons.

They had to spend the night in a building partly occupied by the army. They rested little that night. The next day they moved on toward their sons but had to leave the main road because of plane attacks in the area. Finally they entered the city by crossing the fields so they were able to avoid the direct fighting. When they reached the guest house, their appearance revealed they had made a difficult journey.

Later, Gloria remarked that they would not leave the boys again. In a sense I agreed with that. I wanted my family to be together and when I traveled, often I felt my family's presence. I passed many hours thinking about them in both easy places and in difficult places. Some people probably do not understand that, but it meant much to me. I do admit that I attempted to keep Betty up to date on family matters such as finances, because there was seemingly more danger to me when I traveled than when I was "at home" with Betty and our children.

As I again traveled the inland road from Comilla to Feni, I had a new experience. I was traveling alone and suddenly came upon a massive hole in the road. I got out of the van and filled the hole with a few bricks so I could pass over that area. When I climbed down from the vehicle, I noted that many people ran deeper into the country-side.

As I moved slowly on, a young man came upon the road. I stopped and he asked, "Are you the one who stopped at that big hole?" I was, so we began talking. Then he told me that hole was there because local people had bombed a military jeep. I walked back a short distance and looked carefully for pieces of the jeep or human remains. I saw no human remains and the only parts of the jeep were small pieces. Those soldiers never knew what hit them.

I gave a solemn salaam to the crowd which had now gathered and traveled on down that "safe" road. I trembled in fear as I slowly moved south. People were dying. Many people were dying. Was I ready to die? Was a trip such as the one I was making the right way to use the time that Almighty God had given me? Knowing at times that even my vehicle might strike a mine, I pondered the situation.

Soon I reached the location where there had been so much destruction that Tom and I had witnessed on the previous journey. Few people were seen in what had been that huge market place. The scorched earth seemed to cry out for help. Someone, I thought, needs to be telling the world about what has happened here and that someone needed to be one who had seen and not just heard about what was happening. Maybe I should be that person? However, I believed it was "my Father's" will to do and be what my family and I were involved in at that time.

Upon my arrival, Feni appeared desolate. Then, suddenly standing before me was Sultan. He could not have been more faithful. He began talking by quoting the major. "The major often comes by asking where you are and what you are doing. I only tell him I don't know but that you are a good man and that you will not harm anyone. But what I say seems to never satisfy him." I remained overnight but there was little I could do in such a desolate place. I departed early the next morning as the darkness lifted.

The rainy season was beginning which meant the dirt roads were more difficult to travel. Soon after I reached the inland earthen road I came upon a difficult situation because a large army truck had sunk down into the mud since the rain had soaked the earth. It took about two hours to get beyond that point.

But while there, I learned a lot. Since there didn't seem to be anyone among the military personnel who could speak much English, I knew it was going to be difficult to communicate. But I did make some progress by asking the soldiers where their guns were from. I got an immediate answer. "The new ones are Chinese but they are not good." Then, someone else said, "The old ones are English but they are much better than the new Chinese ones." I had especially wanted to know if they were using modern weapons from my country. I felt better because apparently they had no small arms from the United States.

When I was free to move ahead, I discovered my vehicle was stalled in the mud. I motioned for the soldiers to push but all they did was call out to local men standing nearby, screaming, "Push the white man's car. He is your friend." These men did not understand English, but they knew enough to understand they were to push my vehicle and they came forward to push without hesitating. In Bangla I said, "Truly I am your friend." A soft smile of friendship broke through their fear-filled faces. They knew the foreign man loved them and that the soldiers hated them. I felt that the soldiers knew I was a friend of the local people and to me that was all-important.

But also as time passed I discovered that many army officers expected me to be kind to the local people. Remember, in West Pakistan there were many missionaries at that time. Who knows? Maybe they had passed that on to others. In the early months of that struggle for freedom, I rarely saw any foreigners other than missionaries. If I had met one in the places I visited, I probably, believe it or not, would have kept my lips tight for I would think they can only be intelligence or reporters.

In Comilla, I loaded the vehicle. One passenger was Father Young who I assumed had been visiting our family friend, Father Dan. Then there were two Catholic sisters who I took directly to the international airport. Then, there were two young people from Comilla Baptist families.

At the army check-post the guard asked, "Are these members of your family?"

Rather than confuse the issue I replied, "Yes, they are my family members." To me they were family members. We all belonged to God as His human creation. But more than that, we were His because of His sending His Son to die for us. When we accepted that, we became a part of the family of God. So, in that battered vehicle, we moved on toward Dhaka.

As always, when I arrived, the loud family screams were music to my ears. Those sounds were the kind I always loved hearing.

The city was changing rapidly now. There were new sounds. Some were welcomed but others were not so pleasant. It was good to see the buses moving back and forth on Mirpur Road. Gradually, even the number of rickshaws seemed to be on the increase.

The unpleasant sounds were bombs exploding electric transmission stations. Though we were often without electricity, we knew this was part of the freedom struggle so we made few comments.

In the midst of those unpleasant sounds, Tom always came through with something entertaining. Quite often at night when our two families were sitting together talking everyday about things, there was an almost overwhelming blast. Of course, with that blast, the lights departed. Tom would speak quietly saying, "Ladies, hold on to your purses."

Just as much help in times like those was when we were watching the evening TV news. The reporter often talked about such things as everything being normal and other such propaganda. Tom was usually sitting in the rocking chair and as the news moved along, he tended to rock more rapidly and kept making statements such as "Well, I didn't see it like that," or, "Oh, you don't say." But best of all was his reply, "Well, how could you come to that conclusion?" Yet, maybe even better was, "Oh, I forgot, everything is normal."

Then, in the earlier days of the freedom struggle and our time together, the Thurmans made preparation for going up to the next level where they slept. Tom often remarked, "Since all is normal, we need not fear. Sleep in peace."

Often, after the Thurmans went upstairs for sleep there was a tremendous explosion. Tom always came down and knocked on our bedroom door. Then, he asked, "Did you hear anything?" In the midst of all the chaos, with the Thurmans present, my family slept better.

A new para-military group came into being. They were called, "razakars." They were collaborators in the total fight by the Pakistan army against the people of East Pakistan. On one occasion, there were five hundred of them camped across the road from our house in Feni.

For a few days an American "engineer" stayed in our house with permission. One day when he returned to the house, he learned that the razakars had broken into the house and taken some of our things. This man did not tell me of that event but the person who did tell me exaggerated somewhat. The story was that man walked into the camp and kicked and screamed in English and of course, no one understood his language but much was understood from his actions. In a short period of time everything was returned to our front porch.

How could that engineer do any work at such a time? I never asked him what he really did. Had I truly known, I suppose he and I would not have agreed on what was happening in the land of the Bangla people.

As people began to use Feni as a market place again and as everything began to be "normal," a former politician came to Feni. The local friends of the army decided to prepare a dinner for him. They needed dishes and took them from our house over the objection of Sultan. But can you believe it? They returned those dishes.

The Muslim "Peace Committee" chairman in Feni was ready for me on one of my trips to Feni. I suspected the major had set him up to get my family back to Feni, so I at least pretended to listen to him. He asked, "When is your family coming back to Feni?"

I quickly replied, "Never if it remains like it now is."

As we talked I knew he was expressing the major's ideas and not his own for he said, "The next time you come to Feni, please take my family to Dhaka." The next time I went to Feni I asked about him and the only reply I got was he had quickly departed Feni but it was not known where he was. However, I knew he could never live in Feni again. He had become a traitor to his people.

The Bangla people's actions and words seemed to always encourage us and thank us for staying with them. But there were some foreigners whose families had left East Pakistan in March who seemed to enjoy telling me what we should do as a family. Some went so far as to say, "You may not even know what is happening to your children." Betty and I did understand enough to inquire from responsible people about our children and what we could do to help them in this particular situation.

One of those who became very helpful was Rev. Leslie Wenger, who was pastor of the International Christian Church when we arrived in Dhaka. "You need to help Wade for at his age he may not express himself and he may have little understanding of what is happening." We did that but as we watched Wade more carefully we noted that he went around singing the Bangladesh freedom song. But he always sang it quietly as if he knew it was not the proper thing to do in the presence of some people. One day I cautioned Wade about the singing and he switched to humming the tune. He was okay but was to have some tough times later as all of us did and he probably understood more than we have ever imagined.

Children talk together. When they have decent parents and good friends, as our God's little ones, they do well in difficult situations. While we were in Dhaka I do not know of any Bangla person who was unkind to Wade. Also, he and Philip Thurman became deep friends and that helped much.

There was no need to be troubled about Keith for we knew just about everything he thought. He wanted to travel with me but I just couldn't do that. While there was danger in many places, there was more when you traveled, especially in a border area.

I hope this doesn't sound too arrogant but there was only one reason we remained in that war-torn land and that was because this was God's mission for our family. Our children had accepted friendship with Bangla children without any hesitation. They prayed for them regularly. Wade's prayer was often the same words because it meant so much to him to say what he did say, "Dear God, bless the Bangla people. Help them. Don't let them suffer." That to this Christian man is what life is all about.

The guest house was open. Some people whom we did not know came by. One day, the director of an international organization brought a Hindu woman and her daughter by the guest house. The kind woman, Mrs. Guha, and her husband had been one of the targeted people during the early days of the army's venture to change the culture of the Bangla people. Professor Guha was killed by the army.

Thirty-one years later in 2002, a Christian woman remembered Mrs. Guha and her daughter being with Betty back in 1971, so she suggested I call her when I was in Dhaka in 2002. I did that. Of course, she remembered that day at the guest house. But rather than expect me as an old man to visit her, she rode across most of Dhaka city to the new guest house and visited with me. She was at that time, Dr. Megna Guhathakurta, Professor in the Department of International Relations, Dhaka University.

Seeing Mrs. Guha and her daughter that day reminded me that the last time I had seen Hindus was when they, along with thousands of Muslim people, had crossed the Comilla-Feni road into India while I made one of those forty mile journeys by rickshaw.

Often, the local people seemed to just kind of "walk in." They seemed to come without any purpose and they spoke openly of the hatred they had harbored in their souls. Fear was deep and the future was dark to most of them. They sat for a long time and they talked rapidly. Then, all of a sudden, they got up and said, "I must go." We never saw many of them again.

CHAPTER TWELVE
Travel to Pabna and the Feni Tough Captain

Ray Schaeffer of the Australian Baptist Mission was staying overnight at the guest house. Though we had little room due to our two families living there, we accommodated guests whenever possible.

While at the guest house, Ray asked me if I was available to travel with him to Pabna. I had been there a few times and knew the route quite well. From Dhaka, the journey was west to the Pabma River and then north up that river for many miles. The rest of the journey was by road for about thirty-five miles.

The military had taken one of the mission vehicles and he wanted to reclaim that vehicle. With Tom's and my experience behind us, I, too, wanted him to get that vehicle.

So, we made the journey with the understanding that I was to drive the reclaimed vehicle back to Dhaka while he was to lead me with his car. All went well until we got within about ten miles of Pabna. Then, our eyes were filled with more destruction of village after village.

I found myself thanking God that the missionaries with families and the Pabna Christians, or at least many of them, had been able to avoid death. I did my best to keep quiet for I knew this was Ray's thing or his visit. I was a helper on that journey. We had a special worship led by Ray on the porch of a missionary residence.

That residence had been depleted of furnishings and we knew, without having to ask, who had done that devastation. But that worship time was probably of more help to the local people than it was to me. My mind roamed and I thought of place after place where Christians had been terribly abused, but most were still alive. Ray was calm and I knew our God was directing him as he led in worship of the Living God.

I surely did not blame the Pabna missionaries for leaving East Pakistan. They and their families had seen enough to cause anyone to support them. Also, they could tell others about what was happening and they would be believed.

We had a long talk with a prominent Christian business man and that was most helpful. His story was that his family had fled into the interior as the army attacked. It was as if they stayed far enough ahead of the guns being fired, that most of the time, bullets fell harmlessly to the earth.

But this gentleman had more to say. His two older sons were now with the freedom fighters and his young son sat silently nearby as we talked. Later, the gentleman said, "I fear my youngest son will join his two older brothers." Later I understood that younger son did suddenly disappear to join his older brothers.

Ray and I did not get the vehicle from the military. But we had been well rewarded for our trip. We had visited with friends whom we dearly loved. We had worshipped with them and now we could pray better for them. They knew there was more involved than a vehicle being reclaimed. Though Ray has been in heaven for many years, I often remember him and his kind spirit. He truly loved Muslim people, also.

It was apparent to me and probably more apparent to others, including my family, I had become a person who hated. I had not known much of that in life since becoming a believer in Jesus, or Isa,, as my Messiah, or Masih,, when I was only nine years of age. Friends and especially older friends might today say Jim didn't act too pious in the years they had known him. But from that time at age nine years, I knew Jesus was my Savior and I wanted everybody to know Him and knowing Him was to know the Living God.

As time passed and the city in which we lived seemed at times to be more "normal," the loud sounds, especially at night, told us even darker days were before us. But we were learning and knowing our God better as the days passed. In Feni, reading Bible stories nightly to our children was a way of life for us. In Dhaka, I tried to do no less but often with no lights at night, we had to struggle in making sure we did the thing that helped all of us more, the reading of God's Holy Word, the Bible.

Since times were supposedly becoming more normal, on one of my trips to Feni I visited a place on the eastern side of town which was reported to be a reception center for local people who had returned from India. One Muslim friend, who wanted me to examine the center said and he believed it, "Five hundred Bangla people had been taken there as reported refugees but not one of them had ever been to India." As he talked, he became angrier.

My friend also said, "At one time some refugees did return from India and included in that group was a Hindu woman. That woman was kept overnight. During the night she was raped several times and her screams were heard all night." I chose to believe that friend and this only increased my anger.

A young Muslim army captain in Feni caused my hatred to grow even more. I quickly noted that he was highly intelligent. He spoke several languages and one of those was the Bangla language, or Bengali. He was strikingly handsome. I went to him because one of the Christian families, who had returned to Feni, asked me to go. Soldiers, any time they chose, walked through their house as if it were a camp. He denied that his soldiers did anything like what I had said.

The more we talked, the angrier he became and the more we talked, the more my hatred of people like him increased. I told him about the two families who were Christian. I truly wanted to help them. But in that I may have failed. When I told him one family was in India, he asked, "Why did they run away? Did they fear us?"

I replied, "Yes, they feared you."

Then, apparently remembering that I had told him about his soldiers walking through the house of the Christian family and taking whatever they pleased, he retorted, "Not my soldiers."

I had to answer, "Yes, your soldiers, like the ones standing here with you." This captain was in charge of a group of soldiers who had been recruited from the Pakistan-Afghanistan border areas. They were tough and had even grown up with a rifle in their hands. In route to East Pakistan they had been filled with propaganda and that was primarily that the people of that area were all Hindus.

I did not tell this officer what had happened to our center in Feni town. There had been dozens of Bibles ripped apart, torn into pieces and thrown on the floor to be trampled on by anyone who entered. I saw the horrible condition of that large room which had been so sacred to me but which had been so violently desecrated. The young man who told me who did this awful thing was a young Muslim whose family I highly respected.

Just before the time for my departure from the captain's office, he said to me, "I have two friends in the Dhaka military hospital who have been badly wounded. I want you to visit them and bring me a report on your return trip to Feni." It sounded like a command and probably was no less than that, so I determined I would visit his friends in the hospital.

My companion for the visit was our older son, Keith, who was probably seven years old at that time. I knew Keith had wanted to travel with me on many occasions and I had always said no to him. But now I brought him, and I may have cheated a little for I knew that with a little son by my side, entrance to the military hospital would be easier, which it was. The guard only looked inside the vehicle momentarily before giving us the go ahead sign.

Inside the hospital, we were welcomed. Keith's presence by my side helped in everything done and said on that visit. The two officers had been wounded near Feni. A major had severe flesh wounds. He said to us, "No more of this war for me. I will be flown home in a few days. After recovery, I will probably be discharged. I am glad to be getting out of here." I felt he was saying that what was happening here was not right. He obviously seemed to be a kind person.

But the captain in a bed next to the major had nothing to say. He was badly injured with many wounds and a broken neck. Though he said nothing, he smiled when he looked at Keith.

Just before Keith and I walked out of this room, the major said, "Keith, when you grow up, be an engineer or a doctor or even a missionary like your father. Don't become a soldier." As Keith and I walked out to the vehicle, we were both aware of the fact that not all soldiers hated the Bangla people. They were even opposed to what was happening in that land but there was little they could do about it. They were only obeying orders.

On a return trip to Feni, I learned the captain had been promoted and transferred. I hope I would have had the courage to tell him about what his friends had said and especially what he had said to Keith. Those two officers told me, without verbally saying it, "War is bad and I am glad to be getting out of it." How could I hate them? I didn't. But I did have deep feelings about what I was so often seeing and hearing.

On the same journey when I was ready to report to the captain, I met the officer who was his replacement. He was in charge of a special forces group and had been trained in Key West, Florida. He talked freely and so did I.

I asked him if he had a family in West Pakistan. He did not but he wanted to return there and be married. I felt free to say, "I also want you to return and be married." Perhaps I irritated him just a little so he replied, "Oh, you missionaries are too holy." But he added, "I also am opposed to what is happening here." We talked further and he told me many things which were happening. I have always supposed he was attempting to tell me this war might end before too long.

Though I knew well that there were many Christians who were even officers in the Pakistan army, I did not meet one of those in that nine month's struggle of killings and other destruction. I often wondered if the fact that I did not meet a Christian soldier from West Pakistan was planned by the military. Probably not, for many leaders at times were prominent Christians. I remembered that when we lived in Comilla on our first term in East Pakistan, a young man whose father I knew as a pastor of a Baptist church in Georgia came to visit us for several days. That Christian young American was serving as an assistant to the highest court official in all of Pakistan at that time. The court official was a Christian. That young man was receiving special training as a young lawyer in another country. I thought that was a very good thing. We need to know each other better.

Though thousands or maybe tens of thousands of local people were dying, Pakistani soldiers were also dying. Grave markers lined the banks of two ponds in Feni. That special forces officer in

Feni had pulled away some of my hatred. I felt a little better about myself as a Christian man.

But what about so many of our friends? One we learned about by watching the little black and white television. One night, while our children were watching television, they called out to me to come quickly.

Carefully I watched the man making a report. It was our professor friend from Feni who had been elected to the National Assembly in that free election before all of the violence had broken out on March 25, 1971. He was reporting on the life of a former leader of the party of which our friend had been an elected member. But now the professor seemed to be accusing others in that same party for bringing on the current trouble.

The professor reportedly had been asked by others if he had visited the McKinleys. Of course, he had not visited us but after the war ended and Bangladesh was free, one time he came by the guest house and spoke only a few words before moving on. Apparently, he had been released, as many former enemies of the freedom struggle had been released, in an effort to help the new nation move on to a better life. Of course, I had no comments about such action. I did want Bangladesh to guarantee freedom for all of her faithful people.

Of two other local men whom I had deeply respected before this war of liberation had begun, one we learned about on a secret radio station. Mr. Alam had crossed into India early in the struggle and was now the Foreign Secretary of the Bangladesh government in exile near Kolkatta, India, or at that time, Calcutta, India.

The other close friend among Muslims was Rab Chaudhury. He had held a low position in the acting government even before the outbreak of the war. I saw him often and knew he was fully trustworthy.

Rab Chaudhury had shown his deep appreciation of my family by bringing to the guest house Loren Jenkins of *Newsweek* Magazine and Dan Coggin of *Time*. Many others followed them but all had primarily the same behavior toward us as a missionary family. They never asked the kind of questions which might lead to trouble for us or other missionaries.

One of the international reporters, whom I learned I could trust totally, was Sidney Schaneburg of *The New York Times*. Sidney had first met Tom and through Tom I got to know him. I did do everything I could to help him within my personal limitations.

For example, I gave Sidney an East Pakistan map which was available in any bookstore. With that map, I was able to tell him where to go to get his own stories. I think he always appreciated our faithfulness in not being, or attempting to be, reporters. He came to our house in the evening and the conversation was so interesting that we forgot about the regular curfew. So it was my privilege to show him how I could take him past the police checks during the curfew and never face any particular difficulty.

On one of his visits to Faridpur he tried to interview an army officer and he must have lost his cool for on return to Dhaka, he was escorted to the airport and we did not see him again until after the war. He had been too defensive of the local people for the officer to tolerate. A few months after Sidney was escorted to the airport, another reporter came by the guest house with the map which I had given Sidney earlier. He proved his honesty in more ways than one but I was especially glad the airport security did not check that map for it had my name on it.

Was East Pakistan or "Bangladesh in Bondage" a fit place for any family with children to live? The question often arose in conversation with different people. Our organization had two families with visas granted earlier and they apparently were willing to return. But, even though they had visas they could be turned back at the airport. The Thurmans and the McKinleys, all ten of us, wanted those two families to return so I had only one choice. I had to talk with the general who was supposedly in charge of non-military affairs. I made an appointment and went for my visit with him. It was amazing. As if it were normal, foreigners and missionaries were included in that wide-coverage. He gave me an official note so that if on their arrival at the airport, they had any difficulty, then that order was sufficient to give them clearance.

Our "Boss," Dr. J. D. Hughey came for a long visit. We soon understood that he was there to consider the return of those two families. He was with us for about one week. Near the end of his visit, Dr. Hughey, the Thurmans and my family were having dinner on the back porch. A blast went off that was so forceful that for seconds the glasses shook and so did the tableware lying on the plates. Before the shaking ended, our Kathy blurted out, "Dr. Hughey, are you still going to let the Bennetts and the Teels return?"

He gave a beautiful answer to Kathy by saying, "I think so, Kathy. You and the other children seem to be doing very well."

That explosion had taken place within a block or so of the guest house. We had no reason to ever believe that the freedom fighters would ever harm us in any way. A few nights later, just before Dr. Hughey departed, all of our two families, except little David, were eating at a restaurant about three blocks from the guest house.

A horrible explosion shook the building in which we were eating. Some people ducked under the tables. But Tom Thurman ran out of the building and in a few minutes he returned with David in his arms. After the other five children petted David we ate our food in relative peace. If you could not accept what had happened as a part of life, then you had no place in Dhaka.

The arrival of the Bennetts was a great encouragement to all of us and in a special way to the children. My family's greatest benefit was the return of Debbie Bennett. Debbie's age was between Cherie and Kathy. When school began, Marj Bennett taught Debbie and Cherie, and Mrs. Wilkens, who had remained with her husband from the very beginning of all this man-made chaos, taught Kathy. That left Betty with only Keith and Wade to teach. School moved along well with these three qualified teachers and only five students.

Having the Bennetts living next door with an open connection to the guest house made it even better for us. With our eleven inch black and white television, we had it made. Our guests one night included the Bennetts, the Phil Parshalls, and that included their daughter, Lyndi. The Thurmans and our family had another ten members so we were ready to watch General Yahya Khan, the military president of Pakistan. The broadcast came from West Pakistan, and had been advertised as an update on what was happening in East Pakistan.

The program was to be an interview of President General Yahya Khan by foreign reporters. The children were playing in the yard as the program began. President Khan was still the belligerent man he had been on March 25 when his army turned on the people of East Pakistan. He was either a first class liar or else he did not know what had been and what was happening in East Pakistan. His opening remarks centered around the "normal" situation in our part of Pakistan. According to him, his soldiers had everything under control. He also said the trouble in the eastern part of his country had been created by a handful of people who wanted to destroy the nation.

Even as he spoke, perspiration flowed down his face as informed reporters asked probing questions. While it may have been the bright lights of the television technicians' equipment, some of us knew better than that. His cover-up did not come across very convincingly. As I said many years ago, any little child living in East Pakistan at that time could have refuted every statement the President made. Darkness was just beginning to reveal itself so Betty went outside to call the children inside. Little feet, touching the floor lightly so as not to disturb the television viewing, entered the room.

Just as those eight children entered the room, gunfire blasted out in what seemed every direction. The President rattled on as we all fell to the floor. Was "everything normal in East Pakistan?" I am sorry to need to refute the words of the President but he had missed the mark of truth by hundreds of miles.

My first reaction was to call out, "Let's close the doors so no one can enter the house." Some of us crawled to the doors, pulled them to and locked them. The firing seemed last very long. Uncle Phil, as our children always called him, said to Lyndi, his daughter, "Don't be afraid, it is just like a Wild West show." With Phillip in his arms, Tom climbed up the steps to avoid being in front of a door where bullets might come through and strike them. But he was hardly seated when he came scrambling back down. Bullets had struck that ten inch thick wall and caused it to shake.

At a service station just behind the guest house, glass could be heard crumbling. The firing of the guns was becoming more rapid and forceful. Tom called out, "Everything is normal in East Pakistan."

Wade was experiencing a tough time. I had him pinned under my body. He twisted his head around and said, "Daddy, let's go to America." Fewer shots were now being heard. A few minutes later all was deathly quiet. We carefully opened a door and looked outside. Then, slowly, some of us walked outside.

The para-military forces had set up a road block on Mirpur Road, just by the side of the guest house. We later learned that a group of freedom fighters had run upon the road block but didn't have time to turn around. This had started the short-lived battle. The news was that the freedom fighters had been killed. Then, later on the Free Bangladesh radio, we heard a young man say, "I am one of those who supposedly was killed a few nights ago on Mirpur Road."

Three young men were hiding inside our yard. They were not armed, at least when Troy and I talked with them. I said to them, "Please, just as soon as possible, climb over the wall and slip away." They agreed when I added, "The army may come into the yard at any time and then all of us will be in deep trouble." They departed immediately.

On the opposite side of the road the para-military crouched down with rifles drawn. Then I noted that others were just outside of the wall separating the guest house from Mirpur Road. Some were behind trees and some were down low against our wall but at least they were also outside the wall.

Television was no longer interesting. As soon as it appeared relatively safe, the Parshalls drove out the gate and headed to their home. The Bennetts went to their house next door. We and the Thurmans prepared for bed.

After Keith and Wade were in bed, I slipped very quietly outside. The men with their rifles were hovering near the ground outside the wall. I went back inside and put the boys on the floor where they slept that night. Often, as the years have passed, I have pondered how the children could sleep seemingly so easily and quickly after such circumstances. I hope it was that they felt safe with their parents.

The next morning we saw the clearly marked bullet marks on the house. About where Tom had been sitting the previous night, a large chip of plaster had been blown away. But a long remembered mark was in the kitchen upstairs. A bullet had gone through the three inch window frame, then struck the wall on the opposite side of the kitchen and rolled back just under where it had entered. I still have that bullet.

The population of the city continued to grow as did the number of roadblocks. Houses were being searched. This was an effort to locate arms and explosives. However, it must have failed since the number of explosives seemed to increase. The task had to be insurmountable for many if not most workers in government offices were, at least in heart, freedom fighters.

Usually foreigner's houses and cars were not searched. But when I went to Comilla and on to Feni, my vehicle was usually searched. Sometimes even the smallest bag was gone through. In a way I liked that, which to me meant that those who traveled might be helpers to freedom fighters. But I do state over and over that I never aided anyone who might kill anyone else.

As the population of Dhaka increased rapidly during September and October, that meant more roadblocks and more house searches. It must have been difficult to control a people where probably at least ninety percent favored the freedom movement. As time went by, in my conversations with army officers, they over and over stated that West Pakistan had no right to control East Pakistan.

Betty and I discussed our family driving to Comilla for the day. Mrs. Roy's cooking was the kind which was sure to please our children since they loved curry and rice so much. So, early one morning we made our way there without difficulty. We probably reached there by ten o'clock in the morning. Soon after sharing in Mrs. Roy's perfectly prepared feast, we knew we must start back to the guest house.

In route we encountered a deep problem. At one of the ferries there was a long line of military vehicles waiting. That meant we would not be able to reach the guest house before dark. Our day of relaxing suddenly ended and our courage lessened. I was hard on myself because I knew that when darkness came there was the danger of an attack on the military vehicles. I did not need to warn the children of that danger. They knew it well. After we had waited for about an hour, suddenly, a soldier motioned for us to move onto the ferry. There was a small vacant space and all of the military vehicles were too large for that space. That was our last family travel outside the city, by road, in East Pakistan.

CHAPTER THIRTEEN
A New Muslim Friend

Traveling became an ever more difficult task. Though it seemed at times that the military was in complete control in many areas, there was more destruction on the roads, more blasts or explosions at night and more people coming by the guest house to talk about what they knew. Most of the time, even though we never knew whether or not some of those people were for the local people or the Pakistani government, we never hindered their talk. Sometimes I wondered whether a person might have been sent to inquire about our involvement. Sometimes it took a great effort to understand why some of those people came by the guest house.

In Feni, after Mr. Belal had vacated his post as subdivisional officer and returned to West Pakistan, there was no civilian officer for a time. So I always knew that the military officer would make everything sound as if it were normal even when you felt blasts and saw the results of explosions in all kinds of places.

But on one of my last trips to Feni in what was still East Pakistan, I met the new civilian officer who was in charge. However, it did not appear there were as many military located there as had been. So I went to the office of the person in charge. I guarded every word I spoke because I had enough difficulties without adding to those by saying too much.

The road from Dhaka to Comilla had previously been without any problems. However, on this trip, just after I had crossed a part of two rivers by ferry, I came upon a massive hole in the road. The road had been built up about twenty feet above the level of the adjoining fields. But about six feet deep area of that entire road had been blown away and the pieces of a military vehicle were lying scattered over remaining parts of the road and the open fields on both sides of the road.

The blast had been so forceful that I simply drove down into that hole and up on the other side. But soon I ran upon an area where a public bus had lost an entire front end and was left in the middle of the road. I was able to get around the remains of the bus and drove on toward Comilla.

After driving maybe thirty or forty miles, I stopped the vehicle and sat thinking and rubbing my face which felt so tight. That massaging helped but my face felt as if it were one hardened muscle. But that time in Feni was well spent. I talked carefully with Sultan and again told him that our house and our entire belongings were not important enough for him to defend.

I did not want anything to happen to this Muslim gentleman. But Sultan had something special he wanted to say, "We have a new subdivisional officer and he wants you to see him." He then spoke of this man as being a very nice person.

Before darkness, I went to visit Mr. Akund, that officer. Though I am sure he did not talk as loosely as I did, nevertheless, I felt like I had a new friend. Mr. Akund asked me, "When are you returning to Dhaka?"

I replied, "I am not sure but I have heard that three more bridges have been destroyed between Daudkandi and Dhaka." I should not have mentioned that but somewhere, someone had mentioned that soon after I reached Feni.

I had hardly gotten those words out of my mouth when Mr. Akund said, "How did you hear that?" I knew the location of those bridges was more than seventy miles away.

I mumbled, "Perhaps it is just another of the many rumors."

Mr. Akund immediately made a few phone calls and then replied, "Perhaps it is just a rumor." But he also added, "You must be careful about repeating rumors." I did not know it then, but actually, as I learned later, he was attempting to protect me from rumors. At least I became more careful in my conversation with this seemingly kind gentleman.

Then, Mr. Akund asked me again, "When do you think you will be returning to Dhaka?"

I answered, "I will be starting this afternoon. I will spend the night in Comilla and then move on early in the morning."

After that I received a very pleasant request from him. "May I accompany you to Dhaka?"

Without hesitation, I relied, "Oh, yes, I would be glad to have you as a traveling companion."

That afternoon Mr. Akund and I traveled along what came to be for me a very sad road. There seemed to be many more houses which had been burned every time I passed that area, whether going south toward Feni or north toward Comilla.

Few comments were made as we kept our eyes open on the dangerous road. Just before we reached Comilla, I asked my companion where he intended to spend the night. I knew that there were government rest houses in all of the larger towns. He answered slowly, "I have been thinking about that. I do not want to stay with the military people so that doesn't leave me with many alternatives."

Without hesitation I asked him, "Why don't you stay with me?"

He answered, "Oh, that would be very good, may I?"

I added, "I do not have a place to prepare food so I will eat with a Christian family." Continuing, I said, "But I know they will consider it an honor to feed you also."

Mr. Akund took a short visit by himself and he did not mention to me where he was going. After a short time he returned to the Buckley's house where I was staying and as he came in the door he said, "You were right. They destroyed three bridges last night and we want to be able to travel all the way to Dhaka on the main road."

Mr. Akund responded to the good food and the gracious hospitality of the Roys. Soon darkness approached, so we climbed over a back fence and slept in the Buckley's house. Early morning came almost too suddenly. I did my best to put the vehicle in a place where it was not easily seen. We ate a snack and departed to the bus stand. Though the bus moved out on time, there were very few passengers.

Our first stop was five miles out of Comilla at the army base. All of us as passengers were checked closely on both the east and west side of the base. But after we passed through the base and reached the west side, the search was much more thorough.

The soldier who was doing my search looked carefully at my passport's photograph. He held the passport in my direction and

I understood he was comparing it with my appearance. I had lost much weight and probably had changed somewhat in appearance. But I could only think good of the soldier. At least, he was faithfully doing his job.

However, my traveling companion was having more difficulty. I thought that perhaps I should say that we were traveling together and I could attest to who he was but decided it was better if I said nothing to interfere. After some time, our bus was permitted to proceed.

But immediately I told Mr. Akund, "At any time if you need my help, just let me know." Then, I asked him, "Don't you have a proper identification?"

He immediately began saying, "I have a well documented identification." He pulled out his wallet and showed the identification to me. Then he said, "I absolutely refuse to show any identification to a West Pakistani foreigner. I am a Bangali. This is our country. Why should I prove who I am?" My mind was suddenly at ease. I no longer needed to fear him or what he might pass on to someone else. I only hoped, as we traveled that he was not too belligerent, and let me play that part.

Most of the time on the rest of that thirty mile journey from Comilla to the place we departed the bus, we had many check points but most of the time they were brief. At one of those points where our bus was halted, a young para-military man climbed into the bus. I was seated about two seats from the entrance and as that para-military "boy" slammed the butt of his gun down on the bus floor, tenseness prevailed in that bus.

I decided I had a good opportunity to do something. So, with the severest facial expression I could manufacture, I looked him directly in the face and never turned my eyes away until he did an about-face and stepped down from the bus.

I only guessed at what the passengers were probably thinking... he will return with more men and their foreign friend will be in trouble. However, that didn't happen. The young man slapped the bus on the side and we moved on but with silence inside our bus.

All of a sudden there was jubilation inside the bus. One man walked up front to me and touched me on the back and returned to his seat without saying one word. Others called out, "Thank you, Sir. Thank you."

Again, lest you as readers forget, many times West Pakistani soldiers could not have been more decent in their treatment of me but they were apparently more severe on the local people. The para-military were also local people who were taking the side of the army and I do not think they were ever relaxed in doing what was apparently their job.

Our bus stopped at the last checkpoint on that road. As we stepped down, the guard said, "Only the military can enter this area." So, we were not able to proceed on the road. The destruction of those three bridges was causing the new confusion. Jason, one of my good friends in Comilla was traveling with Mr. Akund and me so immediately we employed a near-by boat. Travel across the fields was no problem since we were entering the monsoon season and water was standing across those fields.

The three of us relaxed in the boat. Our journey would be for about fifteen miles. Our boatman told us each time when we reached the area where one of the bridges had been destroyed. We waved at village people who lived on the high area above the water. Sometimes, they waved back to us. We made the journey on the other side of all the damaged and destroyed bridges without difficulty.

I admit I was tired. The tenseness not only of my body, but the tenseness of the times, was enough to tire anyone. We located a little three wheeled baby taxi and climbed in and down the road we went. But two hours in that boat and being cramped into the small vehicle were not the ingredients that make a journey restful.

After a little time, we reached another road check. It, again, was the para-military. Please remember, I spoke their language. I said to those men, "You are Bangla people. Why do you search other Bangla people?" They were silent. We traveled on to our final destination.

As we traveled on, Jason said, "Thanks, Mr. McKinley, but please be careful."

Mr. Akund added, "These collaborators have no courage. Don't ever be afraid of them, but carefully watch them. Don't press your luck too far."

I suppose that I thought I was helping the suffering people by reacting to some situations. Also, I suppose had I understood what was to happen in the days before us, I would have asked Betty and the children to leave that land and I was ready to go with them. But please remember that often when we as God's people are the lowest, He reaches down the farthest and lifts us upward.

On the east side of the city Mr. Akund got down from the baby-taxi. We went on without delay. Then, as I entered the guest house, the phone rang. It was Mr. Akund. He only wanted to know that we had reached the house without further difficulty.

One of my greatest joys during the time of war in East Pakistan was our Bangla pastor. Pastor Simon asked me to let him know when I was to make the next trip out of Dhaka for he wanted to go with me. That was great. I knew he was a true Bangla man and he was so good compared to lots of people whom I knew well. I hoped that some his goodness from Almighty God might rub off on me.

Pastor Simon went only to Comilla. However, on our return trip to Dhaka we had two memorable events to experience. There was a one-lane, hard surface road which turned right from our direction and went north into the northeastern part of East Pakistan.

One of us had heard there had been considerable damage to electrical connections just north of the army base. So, Pastor Simon said, "Let's go see what really happened." Well, we were, of course, stopped even before we got past the base. I spoke rapidly in English and Bangla to the guard. In exasperation, he motioned us onward. In just a few minutes, sure enough the road was blocked. As Pastor talked, I turned the vehicle around so that we would be able to get back on the main road immediately. The huge electrical pylon was lying across the road. The adjacent substation was in shambles. As we drove Pastor Simon said something like, "Well, maybe someday we will be free. Maybe all of the stories are not just rumors."

I had a fear that the more physical destruction, the longer it would take to bring true hope to the local people. I always remembered what I had felt when I heard my good friend in Feni, in the early years of all this trouble, say, "If you have difficulty finding dynamite, I can supply it." Meaning, they were going to destroy a bridge which my family and I had crossed many times.

Often it is said, "War is hell." My being a Bible believer has always caused me to say, "Better said is, war is just a little corner of hell." Suffering is bad and especially bad when you do little of it and watch as others endure so much.

About an hour after Pastor Simon and I had seen the damage to the electrical installations, we reached Daudkandi. Two rivers converged there and that made the ferry ride quite lengthy. As usual, we had to wait for the ferry to come from the other side. I purchased our ticket and began walking back to our vehicle.

As I was walking, a West Pakistani soldier walked toward me and I thought nothing about that. But apparently I made the mistake of placing my money, not down in the front pocket, but in my shirt pocket. The soldier had a rifle in one hand and with the other hand, he reached for that money. He didn't get that money for I fought back and in our pushing and shoving, other soldiers ran quickly and pulled him away from me.

Except for the ferry workers and the ticket salesman, all of the other people were soldiers. One of the soldiers spoke English and spoke kindly to me by saying, "Please pardon him. We are sorry for what he attempted to do."

Though that experience took place years ago, I remember well the kindness of the soldier who rescued me from one of his colleagues. I often think, "That was a simple thing. No one was physically hurt and it was a time of brutal war."

As I climbed into the van, Pastor Simon said, "I am very much afraid but thank you for what you did. You are trying to help us." It all seemed so foolish. For a very small amount of money, I put myself in a dangerous position. I was certainly not a person who believed fighting was the answer to any country's problems. I had been forceful, but had it been an open fight, I was far too weak to take on a military person.

But as my pastor and I traveled on, I well remembered that destruction, killing human beings and all such behavior, takes its toll on many people. Surely, I could rise above all of that and remain faithful to my God and not be a fighting person, especially as an international missionary and the husband of a precious wife with four wonderful children.

Any common sense warned me that these soldiers were away from home. They were paid very little salary and probably knew they had more difficult days ahead. They had not been the ones who made the decisions to subdue the Bangla people. To be realistic, I often recalled that my beloved home country was primarily committed to the support of West Pakistan. The soldiers, of course, knew nothing about support or lack of support from other countries.

I was well reminded by the incident of waiting for the ferry that I loved the local people, Muslims, Hindus, and Christians, and I knew that most of them were extremely poor. I had grown up as a poor boy but the poverty I had known wasn't comparable to what these Bangla people and that soldier lived in daily.

If I was way down low spiritually, then we as a family got a tremendous lift from Lord God Almighty when another of our families returned to East Pakistan. The Teels had two children with them. Two more were studying in Bangkok, Thailand. Marsha Teel provided more companionship to Cherie and Kathy, our daughters. Stephan Teel was another friend for Keith and Wade.

But in the midst of our rejoicing, word came from Thailand to the Teels that their two daughters needed help in their schooling. So, before long we dipped down more lowly as a family. We were well into our fourth year of being in East Pakistan. Although at the time of that terrible tidal wave, we had been on a wonderful vacation, much of our strength, physical, mental and spiritual had been depleted. Mrs. Teel, Maxine, and her son and daughter, Marsha and Stephan, moved to Thailand so we made new adjustments.

It is probably correct to say that our children became even closer to Debbie Bennett, next door, and to Philip and David Thurman. You might ask, how could they become closer? Again, after these many years and many of life's changes, "our four" and "these three" are still devoted friends.

From childhood, I remembered well the saying, "It takes a heap of living in a house to make it home." Our house in Feni gradually seemed less our home. In August, I was informed that I should discontinue my going to Feni. The next time I went there was more than four months late, and I was permitted by the security police to drive within ten miles of Feni so I was able to keep some contact with Sultan and James Halder, one of our Feni co-workers.

A visit through Comilla and on to the Noakhali District in late August was almost unbelievable. I had experienced nothing during the past seven or eight months to compare with that visit.

CHAPTER FOURTEEN
Two Young Men and a Muslim Village

"Different" is probably an understatement of our late August travel to Comilla and on to Noakhali, but it is surely stamped upon eternity. I never truly regretted any time I devoted to going back to Feni. Probably more people in that area knew us than in all the other three places we had lived in East Pakistan as missionaries. I tried to understand just who had made the decision to restrict my traveling, but I was only slightly restricted, and my travel continued to be helpful to me if not to those I visited.

However, I know there are some people living today who deeply appreciated the times I came for an update about how they were doing and how others, known and unknown to me, were doing.

So it was time for me to travel again. This time, I had to make it on my own because of the great number of bridges being destroyed between Dhaka and Daudkani. My colleague, Troy Bennett, took me as far as his vehicle was permitted. A ferry was waiting at that river crossing but I discovered that it was for military only. After about an hour, the military released the ferry so we walking people were able to get across the river.

On the other side of the river, there was absolutely no public passenger service available, not even a rickshaw. The word from almost everyone was that the military were doing a special campaign following the last destruction of three bridges.

The things I had in a small handbag were not too heavy but they seemed to become heavier as I moved along on that ten mile journey. There were probably a dozen people walking and among them were two young men. I was not comfortable with them because I felt they were collaborators with the army or else they were in a dangerous situation because of the military campaign in that greater area.

But those two young men were working on that situation, I discovered. Soon, they said to me, "Sir, your bag is too heavy for you. Let us carry it." I didn't hesitate. There was nothing in the bag to cause problems for me if they were in partnership with the army, and also I walked much easier without it.

The three of us reached the last river just before darkness. The young men arranged for a small boat to take us across that river. As we reached the other side, we discovered the army was making preparations for the night. One of my companions said, "Sir, don't leave us. We are very much afraid of the soldiers. If they take us after night, you know what they will do to us."

Though we were on an open road of about thirty miles, there was not one public conveyance. So I said to the young men, "Do not look around. Keep your eyes straight ahead on the road. We will walk normally and as quickly as possible to get out of this place." I deeply felt the two young men would not be taken from me. I guess I felt like they needed me and I needed them. My question was, "Where am I going to spend the night?"

We were rapidly moving away from the location of the army and I felt somewhat better. Then one of the young men asked me, "Sir, where are you going to stay tonight?"

I simply replied, though I did not really know anyone in that area, "I will stay in some village somewhere."

We knew we would be checked often as we traveled and came upon roadblocks; that probably would be far more difficult for my companions than it was to be for me. But one of them suggested that we do our best to find someone who had a rickshaw. That was logical because many villages have several rickshaws and if I could get them past the para-military check points, they could make some fast money.

Before long, we located a rickshaw. We had traveled only a short distance, and we were now in the darkness of early night. That rickshaw operator told us about a checkpoint just a short distance ahead. I immediately told him what we wanted him to do.

The top of our rickshaw was down and it had to remain that way for the three of us to travel together. There simply was not enough space to let the top up. So I told the rickshaw driver, "When we get within a short distance of the guards, I will point my flashlight in my face and hold it there. My two friends will sit back as far as they can so the light does not shine on them."

Then I added, "You do not stop the rickshaw for any reason." The plan worked. I had never been in such a situation before, but maybe I could think of something to save the life of my two new friends. So when I noted the guard motion for the rickshaw to continue, I quietly said to the driver, "Go as fast as possible and if they call out or do anything, do not stop." I think that driver felt good about the early part of our trip.

When we got out of what I thought was rifle range we stopped. Of course, the four of us were nervous. One of the young men asked, "Will this work again?"

I only answered, "We will give it a try." As we moved on, it seemed every little bridge had a guard but we only slowed down a little as I shined the light in my face.

I knew only the para-military were involved in what had happened relating to the bridges being destroyed. The entire area was different—wherever we were, whatever the situation, people were more nervous.

I well knew that if the regular army had been manning the checkpoints, I might have lost my friends that night. It always appeared the para-military were not sure of themselves and I took advantage of that. There was no doubt that they wondered about the future and how this was all going to end.

But it would be very wrong for me to write it off that simply. Someone who knows more about everything was again managing. I deeply believed in Him and the mission on which He had sent not only me, but also my family. I received added confidence in Him when I felt I had the responsibility of the lives of two young men in my hands.

As we moved along, we discussed a nearby place where we might be able to spend the night. This village was not far from their home village. Soon we were moving down a narrow dirt road which ended at a large body of water. One of my friends said, "I will take a boat across and inquire if it is okay for you to spend the night."

In a few minutes, my friend returned with a large smile or at least it looked that way with the light we had. He said, "It is okay. They welcome you." In a short time we had crossed the body of water and climbed up a short hill where probably about a dozen houses were located.

An elderly gentleman could not have been more polite as he welcomed me. This gentleman's beard was white and flowed down under his chin and some distance further. He was dressed in a white cotton cap, white cotton shirt and white cotton trousers. The yard was clean and there were several lighted lanterns.

The time was about eleven o'clock and that meant I had been traveling for about fifteen hours so I was tired. For much of that traveling time, I had been very nervous, especially at the first check point in our rickshaw journey. But these people were not considering sleep. We had to talk and I seemed to rest as we talked. They asked many questions about Betty and our children. Then I remembered that about five months earlier, we had all traveled their nearby road as we moved from Feni to Dhaka.

At times some of the younger men would laugh and say, "It is great to have you in our village for the night. Many of us have never seen a white man before and we are so pleased you are with us and we will tell all of our friends about this night." It was a great time for me and I think for these gracious Muslim village people.

I was hungry and especially noted that when they served good curry and rice. I had my lunch of primarily fried chicken which the little children ate gladly. You did not need to doubt it. We had suddenly become friends. After eating, we talked a little about what might happen during the night. They carefully told me about nearby villages where every house had been burned by the army. Probably they understood that it might be better to have me with them for the night, or at least I accepted this as their spoken attitude.

At about midnight, the elderly gentleman took me into one of the houses and showed me where I was to sleep along with the two young men. The bamboo structure was one large room with a frame, about six feet high, separating the room into two sections.

The men were on one side and the women on the other side. The bed was a simple wooden frame with a piece of cloth covering it. A large cane mat was nearby on the floor. Several little boys lay down on that mat. Most of them were soon fast asleep. The elderly man soon joined them.

I heard the women in the adjoining section call the elderly man. The conversation was about me and what I heard was pleasant. The female voices indicated concern, maybe even deep concern as they asked, "Isn't it dangerous for us to have that man with us? What if the army comes to our village?"

I deeply felt that the elderly man would give an answer which would please me and he did for he said, "If the army comes he may be able to help us." If my presence that night meant the slightest amount of security to these people, then I had been more than overpaid for the journey.

But the women had another question. They asked, "But what if the freedom fighters come?"

There was a pause but no fear on my part as I wondered how he was to answer the women. He said, "If the freedom fighters come, it will not mean any danger to us for he is one of us."

My listening to their conversation did not cause any guilt on my part. But I did feel as good as I had felt at any time during the thirteen years we had lived as a family in East Pakistan. So many times I had wanted very much to be wanted by the non-Christians in the land that had come to mean so much to Betty, our children, and myself. However, it had always seemed there were miles separating us. But at least for one night I had heard, "He is one of us," and that was enough to cover any amount of trouble I might have during this time away from Betty and our children.

The two young friends joined me on the wooden frame. That bed was impossible for my lean body. My bones seemed to rub holes in the plank. After the elderly gentleman had lain down on the mat with the little boys, the slight light from the kerosene lantern seemed to indicate that everyone except me was asleep.

This was a different kind of night. It was a night for me to become better acquainted with my God who knows how to do all things very well, regardless of the situation. I had been so blessed by Him. Though missionary salaries, compared to those of other educated people, are the low, my one month's salary surely was enough to pay for a house like the one in which twelve of us were staying that night and all except me were sleeping peacefully. I liked that very much.

My family had, during the past recent months known fear, but our fear was small compared to theirs. The army often moved in at night and left entire villages burning. The people with whom I was given a place of rest for the night knew those deep fears. I chose to think my presence helped them to sleep better that night.

At times, the night seemed very long. It was especially long when I thought of the fact that the army might make its attack on this village. I became cold but all I could do was pull my sweater a little closer to my body.

The light of the day was beautiful. It was as if that light brought security with it. At least the kind people of that village knew where to run in the daytime in the event of an attack. The six little boys and the elderly grandfather began to stir. The legs and arms of the little boys seemed so entangled they looked like an octopus. When the grandfather sat up, we all began to arise and go outside.

We sat on logs outside the little house. There were probably about twenty men and boys talking freely. One of the boys said, "We just can't believe it. You spent the night with us, didn't you?"

I answered, "Yes, I believe I spent the night with you." They laughed a little at my remark.

For breakfast, we ate popped rice and drank hot tea. The rice was dry but the tea helped melt it. But most of all, the hot tea warmed my body.

In a short time, many area village people joined us. They were also full of questions about my presence. Some thought I was a reporter. Others thought I was with the freedom fighters and I didn't want them to think that. So I again explained who I was and where my home in Feni was located.

The elderly gentleman and local village leader said, "Last night you told us about your work and your family. But we do not understand why you stay in our country at such a horrible time. I know it must be your religion. Will you tell us something about it?"

Just before sleep came to the village the previous night, this gentleman had said to the women, "He is one of us." Now he, a Muslim gentleman, was asking me, an international missionary, to tell them about my religion. I spoke clearly about Jesus as my Savior and Lord and briefly about His coming to earth, His death and His resurrection. At a time like this I never even thought that anyone who knows anything about the Quran, the Muslim holy book, knows that it denies that Jesus died on the cross. I was doing what I had been asked to do by the in-charge person and I deeply believed that the over all In-Charge Person helped me as I spoke.

But another older man in the group, who had come from another village, spoke loudly in saying, "We do not want to hear this." I did not reply but the leader did say clearly, "I asked this man to speak, we will hear him."

When I finished, there was a complete silence. I knew for most of those listening, which included the women who were nearby but out of sight of the men, that they had heard the name of Isa (Jesus) before. However, most likely they had never heard that He had died on the cross before. But now they had heard, and heard from a man who, at least, tried to speak kindly to people whose greatest need at that time may have been kindness expressed in telling a little of the great story of history.

A few minutes later as I prepared to depart, the two young friends of the previous day and night also prepared to depart. I saluted them with a salaam as they walked away. I expressed my thanks to the elderly gentleman and made my way to the little boat to cross the water nearby. I walked about one mile to the main road and there sat a baby-taxi waiting for someone to give him a good fare. He had one who would give that good fare and some extra.

As we moved along toward Comilla, I asked the driver to go slowly so that I could see as much as possible. As the little vehicle bounced along the road, I saw what I did not like to see. I saw smoke swirling into the sky from hundreds of little houses as they were becoming ashes. I didn't like looking but I deeply felt that I must look and try to understand that violence often is directed to the most innocent people. The houses of the poorest burned down to the earth and those people will be poorer, I thought.

But even as we drove through such horror, I well remembered the previous night and especially, I remembered that early morning when I had been so privileged to share the possibility of a better life for those people with whom I had spent the quiet night. It was good to be an international missionary, to be with such people through the night, and to move on to what I did not know.

But I did know Him who directed my path. He surely knows how to do it and I knew He was much experienced in doing no less for His people across the world.

Two days later I returned to Dhaka and received the same royal welcome, "Mother, Daddy is back." The strength of Betty, Cherie, Kathy, Keith, and Wade meant much to me. I do not think they ever asked me not to travel. It seemed to me that they felt as if they traveled with me and that meant I was privileged to walk with my God and walk among people for whom He had given His best, or of Himself, His Son.

Birthdays in 1971 ended with Cherie becoming thirteen, Kathy twelve, Keith seven, and Wade five. As much as foreign children can be rooted in the local soil I felt they were that deeply rooted. People through the years have asked sometimes, harshly, "What right did you have to keep your family in such a place of danger?"

When I felt naughty enough, I answered, "I didn't keep them there, God did."

In September, when Cherie was studying along with Debbie Bennett, and Debbie's mother, Marjorie teaching them, Cherie wrote a poem as part of her school-work. That poem covered the air attack on our town of Feni and nearby villages on April 6, 1971, about five months earlier.

Roaring out of the Bengal sunset they came,
Two black dots on a warm summer evening.
Some children stop their playing to set clear
eyes upon them,
In awe watching the pair, soaring over rice fields
and straw huts,
Like finches looking for some place to rest
their wings.

But suddenly, as they spot the tiny town,
Their nature changes, and now, like vultures,
They screech and dip down upon it.
A piercing wail rings out and then,
BOOM!... BOOM!... BOOM!
The children scatter like frightened ants into their
houses,
Amid the constant shattering and blasts.
Flinging themselves upon the floor,
They lay frozen in fear,
Their faces ghastly, their blood cold, their
heads buzzing with the question, "Why?"
While outside the vultures peck at their prize.
A mother tries to comfort a child with shaking hands.
The only comforting sound is the thunk,
thunk, thunk of the father's feet,
Pacing the floor.
Again and again the planes dip,
BOOM!... BOOM!...BOOM!
Then in the same mysterious way they appeared,
They are gone.
All is quiet, the world seems dead.
But... off in the distance comes the clattering
of wheels on the old road,
And the jingling of bells.
Like water from a broken dam,
The living gush into the countryside,
Trying to escape from the smell of death and blood.
Some crying, some with faces of white stone,
They all plod along together.
Not saying a word,
Not having to, because their grief is written on their faces.
Slowly, they filter away.

The night comes, the stars twinkle,

A cool breeze blows from the south.

The only irritating sound is the crickets which

seem to say...

LOVE YOUR ENEMIES...

LOVE YOUR ENEMIES...

LOVE YOUR ENEMIES...

Cherie's poem helped Dad in his struggle with hate against those who seemingly have no purpose in life but to kill, to cripple, to burn, to devastate.

Surely you understand why this writer has great difficulty today when a section of Islamic people kill more of their own than they do others. (Yesterday, at least fifty-six people were killed by Islamic terrorists and possibly all but one were Muslim people.)

LOVE YOUR ENEMIES...

CHAPTER FIFTEEN
A Pleasant but Partly Difficult Trip
to the Tidal Wave Disaster Area

The opportunity to give a verbal witness in the Muslim village was one of my life's greatest joys. I always think, "What could be better than to be honored by having the opportunity to speak for my God who has so beautifully revealed Himself through Jesus the Christ?" My last traveling in about the middle of November may have given me just as important an opportunity as my previous journey had given me.

This time I was attempting to enter the badly affected tidal wave area. I very much wanted to see if there had been any progression of the building of houses for a large group of people, mostly Hindus. The money for this project had been given to me by several persons and organizations. A report on this was sure to be helpful to those who had given that money but not nearly so much help to them as to those receiving the little houses.

So why not take an almost direct route into that area from the main headquarters of Noakhali District? I knew my friends at the Catholic Mission southwest of Maijdi, the district headquarters, were able to care well for my vehicle. When I departed Dhaka, my intention was to reach within at least ten miles of the ocean water that had caused so much suffering.

I knew that this journey might not be simple but that it was entirely possible. The old map which I had showed a road, but I knew that after leaving the Catholic Mission, the entire route was to be nothing but earth. The rainy season had ended so that meant the dirt road was to be dry. What else could I ask for?

As I traveled through the army base west of Comilla and then Comilla town, I noted vast mounds of earth which seemed to almost surround that entire area. I was later told that earthen mound was to slow down or stop the tanks of India, if India decided to openly enter the struggle against Pakistan. Since I knew nothing about war and didn't want to know too much about what was happening, I waited until later to tell friends what I had seen.

Across that army base dozens of trucks and jeeps were towing field guns of many types and sizes. As I moved through that area I did understand enough to know that I was going to move as fast as possible and get back to Dhaka soon. Laksam, the railway center about fifteen miles south of Comilla, was surrounded by small bunkers but as I moved on without any hindrance from the army, I noted that those bunkers had been abandoned.

However, since my last trip along the same route, I noted newly cut trenches all around the railway station area. Even with my little knowledge of military actions and preparation, I guessed open war was eminent.

My friends at the Mission knew that I needed to move on quickly for night was to be on its way in about five hours. I had no idea how many miles I had to travel before the sun went down.

Immediately, I was able to hire a baby-taxi and it may not have been in keeping with my nature as a Christian helper, but I was to be the only passenger in that little vehicle. I requested the driver to go as rapidly as his machine could manage and he honored that and at times, I thought he had more than honored my request. That was especially true when my head struck the iron rods several times. I suppose those rods were to keep the cover on the baby-taxi in place and were necessary.

The ride was not too bad for a hardheaded person like myself. But the longer we drove, the more bumps were in the road. Finally, I decided it was better for me get out and walk. So, I paid the driver well and gave him a salaam and he immediately turned back toward the Maijdi area.

The walk, of course, was good for me and after about two miles, I reached a small river. The ocean tide was just beginning to make its way up the river channel. A few men sat quietly on the river bank. They seemed to ignore me but were courteous, as they usually are. One finally said to me, "There will be a boat in a short time to take us across."

Though I was extremely tired, I felt I should attempt a conversation with those men so I tried to let them know who I was. I was sure they would understand when I said, "Following the tidal wave last year, I sunk many tube wells in this area." They said very little other than that they did not recognize me nor had they heard about the wells. It became clear to me that they considered themselves freedom fighters from another area and that they were there to keep order.

My destination, Char Alexander, was about ten miles away. I knew if they were from that area, then, as we talked, I would be able to fully understand exactly what they were doing. So I asked, "Are there any freedom fighters in this area?"

The one who seemed the eldest among them asked, "Are you afraid of the freedom fighters?" I replied that I was not afraid, but if there were freedom fighters from the immediate area, perhaps I might recognize them.

I did my best to be patient and then the response came. The elderly gentleman said, "Sir, we are all freedom fighters." The conversation became even warmer when I asked about Captain Aziz. Aziz had been very helpful when we sunk tube wells and especially when we distributed blankets. Their faces brightened and one of them said, "We don't know him but every body in this area knows about how much he helps in our struggle for freedom."

We were becoming closer and I admit I like people wherever they are if they are sincere and support others who have great needs of many kinds. I knew all was well when one of their group said as a large boat passed, "Part of our responsibility is to protect people like those in the boat."

Naturally, for me, I had to know more so I asked, "Then, who are those people?"

The answer made my day. "They are Hindus, and we have suggested they move to another location for the para-military or razakars may be after them."

The men with whom I had finally reached a good conversation were all Muslims. They were protecting Hindus from the military. I knew I was their friend and I knew they could be good Muslims and yet, protect the Hindus from death. As the boat moved slowly past us, I saw what was one of the most destitute looking groups I had seen since the tidal wave more than ten months earlier.

But sitting there on the river bank in this lowly area, I could only ask Almighty God to bring peace to this area and to help all people, Muslims and Hindus, know God as I knew Him. A small boat arrived and many people crossed the river. As we disembarked, the mud was difficult. The soil, for some reason, was not sandy, hence the mud stuck to my bare feet. On the other side of the river, people who had crossed in our boat and others seemed to spread into almost every direction. Night was approaching and they, in such times, did not like the darkness.

After walking about three miles with some of the people who had crossed the river in one of the boats, I located an empty rickshaw. I had about seven more miles to travel and I very much wanted to arrive in Char Alexander before the deep darkness arrived. Of course, I did not hesitate to request the driver to go as fast as possible. We must have made that trip in just a little more than one hour.

Char Alexander was the place where Mr. Alam had stayed many nights. He was now serving in the Kolkata, India, area as Foreign Secretary of the Bangladesh government in exile.

I went as quickly as possible to Mr. Nouman's house. My welcome could not have been better. Nouman said to me, "I want you to look now for it will soon be too dark to see what I want to explain to you." Then, he pointed to a massive food storage building with a flat roof. He remarked that the building was empty of food but then pointed out that the men on top of the building were razakars and under the direction of the Union Council of that area.

Nouman knew that I understood well about that leader of those dangerous people. He had given nothing but trouble to us when we sunk tube wells and distributed blankets. But just before we entered his house he said, "Let's stand here until those razakars pull up their ladders." They may have had the best of arms, but they also knew how to sleep in peace on top of that huge building. "Now is the time," Nouman said. The razakars pulled two long ladders to the top of the building. Now, they could sleep in peace for no one could get to them during the night.

We went inside and discussed the building of houses for which I was using money given by friends to help. We made plans to visit many of the new houses the next morning. That made my sleep come more easily. The wooden frame bed had several blankets and quilts which served as my mattress so I was soon fast asleep. Noise outside in the nearby market awakened me the next morning.

Nouman and I walked and rode rickshaws most of the morning, looking at the new houses. I became very much interested in the people I saw, most of whom were occupying the new houses. I had understood that most of them were Hindus but they appeared to be Muslims. So I asked Nouman about this, thinking surely he would never do wrong and trick me in any way. He laughed and said, "Oh, I am sorry. The Hindu men are all now wearing beards. The dumb razakars who sleep on top of the building are not from this area and they do not understand anything."

Also, I learned from Nouman that some of the houses which had been built following the tidal wave had been burned in a nearby area by the military. I had trouble with that awful added suffering but those were the days you learned how to somewhat tolerate very bad actions by many people. Nouman volunteered he was keeping careful records of expenditures for the new houses and the next time I came that he was planning to give me that final report.

Nouman showed me some lumber he was purchasing for the remaining houses to be constructed and that at the time, the price was much lower since there was little marketing being done. So, again, at least a little good was happening.

The razakars saw me several times but never inquired directly about what I was doing in that area. I am sure that as soon as I departed they searched for details. For some reason, they had not attempted to harm Nouman and his friends. In fact, I learned that even in the afternoons, they often pulled up their ladders and had a long sleep.

My return journey was exactly the same route as when I went into this area from the Catholic Mission. My vehicle had been well cared for so I was soon moving north hoping to reach Comilla where I would spend the night in the Buckley's house and eat with the Roys.

The next morning I was off for Dhaka. All along the route, I kept noting military movements that looked if something drastic was about to happen. Little or no attention was given to me and I liked that. For every mile behind me, I was glad for I did not want to be separated from Betty and the children.

The family greeting was loudly echoed. Though I did not realize it then, that was my last journey in East Pakistan. The next trip to see Feni again was when I would be traveling in free Bangladesh.

Perhaps the thing that helped me most on that last journey was that the Bangla Muslims did not take advantage of the few Hindus left in East Pakistan but went so far as to help those of an altogether different religion. I knew how to try to bring all people together, but from what I had learned in the previous thirteen years was that most people, in most areas of the world, care little about other kinds of people and togetherness is not their concern.

CHAPTER SIXTEEN
Final Days of War for Independence in Bangladesh

Though I had seen what appeared to me to be Pakistan preparation, down deep I felt India would not become actively involved with an invasion by their army. But there was a difference in Dhaka. At night the streets were fearfully quiet. The only noticeable noise was from the military vehicles of Pakistan.

After returning from the tidal wave area of Noakhali District, I heard that all of the ferry boats on that route had been sunk by freedom fighters. This probably was one of the reasons for the quietness in the streets of Dhaka at night. Maybe preparation was being made by Pakistan to face India in battle. We didn't know what that was to mean for us as a family but it certainly did make us more nervous.

John Freeman, a missionary doctor friend serving in Thailand, came to join us at the guest house. I had sent a cable to John asking him not to join us. However, we were grateful for John's presence. The Thurmans had been back in Faridpur for several weeks but they decided to again join us and their presence was also welcomed. Of course, we and the Bennetts had Howard Teel with us. That was all good, for we were able to live in the guest house and the Bennett's adjacent residence. We were together.

Then, also in late November, Bill Marshall, area representative of our organization, came for a visit. So that gave an opportunity for us to have a formal meeting of our missionary group. Bill led us in worship during that meeting and since he had come in from the outside, he may have seen us differently. We all knew we were facing difficult days and perhaps we even understood the days before us might be even more troublesome than those we had faced in the past year or so following both the tidal wave disaster and then the war involving the freedom movement.

During one of our special worship times, Bill gave our children an opportunity to say anything they wanted to say. For a considerable period of time, none of the children spoke but then Keith got up from his chair and walked across the room to Betty. He wanted

Betty's permission to speak. Then, in a broken quivering voice he repeated some of the horror of the plane attacks in Feni back in early April of the same year. Tears flooded his face and ours. Our children, of course, had been deeply troubled by all that had happened and they had seen and heard much.

But through this experience involving one of our younger children, hope came again. As a father, I considered that my children had and were experiencing life with depth of meaning and not just short emotional outbursts. God comes through at some of the most opportune times for His family. He knows when we need massive uplifts and cares for us in His unique way.

Since I was the leader of our missionary group at that time, I was presiding when discussion began regarding the question of whether or not some of us should consider evacuation. If within the group someone might be eligible for that, then probably our family was one of those to be considered. We were well along in our fourth year of service. The Thurmans and my family had gone through the tragedy of the tidal wave and I had been deeply involved in efforts to aid the people of that tidal wave. Along with the Thurmans, we had heard and seen much since the first attack by the Pakistani army on March 25.

Our discussion in that meeting involved the possibility of my family departing for early furlough to the United States. Being the presiding person of the meeting, I was in a difficult position so I said little but felt much. My primary feeling was that at times like the ones in which we lived, any such discussion should not lead to any decision for anyone or any family to remain or to depart. I thought such a decision belonged only to the family itself. We finally ended the formal meeting with no decisions made other than to continue as we had been, fully supporting one another.

While all of us were together in the two houses, foreign news broadcasts revealed that the India military had invaded the border of East Pakistan and that fierce fighting was happening all over those border areas. Many fewer people were seen in the streets and especially on Mirpur Road where we could see anything and everything which happened in our part of the city. We knew that in such situations, water is essential, so we sank our own tube well at the guest house in the event the water supply was hindered.

We bought food of many kinds but where possible we bought canned food at whatever the price was, for we knew it was the easiest prepared kind. We increased our kerosene supply for the lanterns and wood for cooking fuel. First-aid supplies and medicines were also purchased. With John Freeman as our doctor we probably considered that we were prepared.

Bill Marshall had a meeting scheduled in India but he decided he was remaining with us. Though we deeply appreciated his sincere kindness, we wanted him to be with his family hundreds of miles away in Nicosia, Cyprus. Since nothing had happened in Dhaka, Bill departed in the late afternoon of December 2 on a plane of the Pakistan International Airlines for Karachi, West Pakistan.

The flight Bill Marshall took was, not known to us then but later, the last regular passenger flight to ever depart from East Pakistan. At bedtime that night, all was quiet and calm. We heard or saw only a few Pakistan military vehicles on the nearby road. The Bennetts were next door or about twenty-five feet away from the guest house. The Thurmans, Howard Teel, and John Freeman were upstairs in the guest house. My family was in three rooms of the guest house ground level.

It is for sure that our prayer that night, just before sleep came, was as real as it had ever been. We wanted God and we not only wanted Him ... we knew He was present. With that, sleep knocked at the doors and we looked forward to a good night of rest. But that rest was only temporary.

Sometime past midnight we were rudely awakened. It was as if the city were being blasted apart. I ran to bring Cherie and Kathy into our room while Betty was bringing the boys in with us. I said to the children, "Don't be afraid. It is the freedom fighters attacking the Pakistani army and you know the freedom fighters won't hurt us." There was a brief calm and then sirens echoed out across the city.

Suddenly, we heard the roar of jet engines. I was all wrong as I had often been in trying to understand events of war. It was an air raid on the city. Of course, the freedom fighters were hardly involved in that. In a few minutes the sky appeared to be filled with jet planes as they struck military points in areas near the guest house. Those Indian air force planes were making an all-out effort to destroy Pakistan military installations.

We pulled the foam rubber mattresses off the beds and dragged them into the narrow hallway. The Thurmans climbed down to our floor level and were in the hallway almost by the time we arrived there. All of our detailed careful preparation suddenly seemed meager. We needed a bomb shelter. We stayed under the foam mattresses since we expected the plaster to begin falling at any moment.

The Thurmans and my family knew by experience what bullets from jet fighters could do. But this was a far more dangerous time with bombs blasting those military points. The smaller children cried. We parents tried to remain steady. Howard Teel and John Freeman joined us.

Obviously, it was a tough time for all of us. Tom suggested that we sing. We were hardly able to compete with the outside noises but singing helped. "Jesus loves the little children, all the children of the world," eased out of the hallway. Then, "Jesus loves me this I know" sounded out but probably with a little less vigor. We tried, "Holy, Holy, Holy is the Lord God Almighty" and that also helped some but we were overwhelmed by our concerns about what might finally happen that night.

So we prayed and we called the names of people we knew who were praying for us right at that particular time. Extended family member's names were called as were dozens of friends from many countries of the world for we knew they were praying for us. Strength came because we knew that every missionary who had left the country was praying for us. We knew that in Thailand John Freeman's family was praying. We also remembered Howard Teel's family and their friends were praying. Strength continued to build within us and the children grew quieter.

Steve and Becky Bennett were surely praying for their parents and their sister, Debbie, next door to us. But perhaps the greatest help to our children was knowing that Dr. Hughey, our administrator of the International Mission Board in Richmond, Virginia, was praying for them. Our children and the Thurman's children truly loved him. When he had visited us a few months earlier, he had acted so properly by leaving most decisions to us.

We didn't know it then but even though we were about twelve hours in a different time zone, Dr. Hughey had been asked by many of the office staff what he was going to do about his missionaries in East Pakistan. He went home to be by himself. The "big thing" he was doing was praying for us. The children in all of the present chaos knew what he was doing. He, again, was praying.

In the guest house hallway, the tension eased a little. A few smiles were seen as the small flashlight provided some light. All became quiet again. We returned to our rooms expecting to get more sleep. But our expectations of getting more sleep passed by since in a few minutes, we had to race back into the hallway, our place of safety.

Planes again filled the sky over Dhaka. Bombs and rockets burst with noises near to ear-splitting. Anti-aircraft guns blasted away at the planes. Dawn of December 3 found us still in the hallway.

We attempted to eat breakfast on the screened-in porch, but that became impossible. We could not swallow well with planes zooming over our heads and hitting nearby targets. The air attacks continued throughout the day. But there was less fear since we were able to see the planes and that helped us confirm that only military installations were their targets.

The daylight scenes told us more about what happened during the night. In 1971, the nighttime targets could be missed and that was what happened when planes struck a children's home one night. That strike killed many children. Huge craters, splintered buildings and mangled bodies of little children were a reminder of what might happen at night.

As the crow flies, the guest house was more than one mile from the end of the airport runway. We had a clear view of the airplanes and their fighting during the day. On December 4, each attack by the Indian planes brought a response by the Pakistan planes. The sleek faster jets of India were not matched by the older planes of Pakistan. Pakistan's choice planes were on the other side of India in West Pakistan.

But the anti-aircraft guns of Pakistan roared away at the Indian jets. The bursts of the shells filled the sky with huge pockets of black smoke. We saw planes explode in the air and their pieces fall to the earth. Other planes, burning furiously, crashed with earth-shaking thuds and sent up a cloud of smoke.

Shrapnel filled the yards of residences in the airport area. Some of the pieces were small while others were large and crashed on to the nearby automobile's tops. During the day, we watched the chaos around us while standing under the carport. Early that morning of December 4, a representative of the United States Consulate came to the guest house with a message that any US Americans wanting to leave should go to the Intercontinental Hotel that afternoon with one suitcase each.

Responding immediately to the Consulate representative, Betty said, "Put our children and me on the list." I guess I was stunned. I had no idea she would respond so quickly and so convincingly. But she had probably been considering such a decision from the time of our discussion when Bill Marshall was with us in the special meeting. In that meeting it had been stated that if anyone should leave, the McKinleys had that right due to their furlough time and the fact that they had been involved for a part of four years.

But I was silent. Betty didn't need to ask how I felt. Both she and the children knew that. The evacuation planes were delayed in their arrival so they remained at the guest house for another night. The next day, the same word came from the Consulate that the planes were arriving one day later. So Betty and the children prepared to remain another night at the guest house.

That night was most difficult for me. I was aggressive. No one needed to ask how I felt about the awful days of the past eight months for I made sure they understood without asking. But Betty and our children were God's source of strength for me. I wondered what I would do without them.

Betty told the Thurmans of her decision. I went next door and told the Bennetts about my family's intended departure. That night I thought about the children and Betty. I thought about what they had endured in Feni, especially when the Pakistani jets made their two attacks on our town. Cherie's arrival in that land had been when she was ten months old. Kathy and Keith were born there and Wade had arrived from his Philippine's birthplace when he was twenty-one days of age. I considered them "children of the soil."

I had absolutely no doubt that Betty loved the Bangla people. I knew she did not want to leave, but those discussions by our group had led her to think that leaving was the right thing to do. The morning of December 6 was a gloomy time for all of us. At breakfast, we talked very little. The suitcases were packed though since that time, I have often thought those suitcases had little in them, for we had little. However, I was prepared to take them to the hotel, the meeting place for those departing. But in what I suppose was a moment of weakness and the last moment before that departure, I asked Betty to reconsider.

Betty paused briefly and said, "Let me talk with Cherie." But why Cherie? Cherie was our eldest of the four children but Betty and I knew from the day she struggled to keep her two little brothers pinned to the earth while the planes zoomed over their heads spewing bullets by the hundreds and now with planes again zooming day and night, that times had been difficult for her.

While Cherie had Kathy and Debbie Bennett with her now, that Feni experience undoubtedly still weighed heavily upon her and no two young girls could have possibly acted better than she and Kathy did on April 6 when those planes first struck Feni.

Betty and Cherie went into the room and closed the door. Naturally, I was inclined to think that a thirteen year old girl who had experienced so much during the previous eight months would find it difficult to refuse an opportunity to leave such danger.

The bedroom door opened slowly and Cherie came out first. Tears flowed down her face as she tried to speak to her dad. Eventually she was able to say, "Dad, Mom and I have decided that we want to stay with you." As many tears as had flowed down Cherie's face were now flowing down my face. I fully understood that even though there were many people involved in their consideration, I had figured prominently in their decision.

Maybe they thought they needed to be present so they could keep me out of trouble. Regardless, I was never more pleased as a husband and as a father. We again shared the decision with the

Thurmans and the Bennetts. Then I went to purchase more supplies for the dangerous days ahead of us.

We prepared as if we would be in the same difficult times when Christmas arrived so we had to have some good food for that all important time. It was reported that the planes for evacuation actually entered East Pakistan air space but were driven back by India's jet fighters. But we also understood that since Pakistan's planes were much older than those of India, they were fast losing the battle of the skies.

Some of us witnessed an Indian jet fighter going in for a dive over the airport. The plane came out of the dive and like lightening, it shot upward. But as it went upward Pakistani anti-aircraft guns blasted and hit their target. The plane became a ball of smoke and suddenly turned downward.

A few seconds later, before the plane hit the earth, the pilot ejected and we saw him fly upward but then down to the earth with his open parachute. We watched him, a prisoner of war, on television that night. His country, with the help of freedom fighters, may have been winning the war but he had lost.

The delay of the evacuation planes helped us in at least one particular situation. An American family was planning to be evacuated and had some food which they offered to us. Kathy and I rode by the airport and found the food. We discovered that there was a huge quantity of it, much more than what we now had at the guest house.

Kathy and I loaded the food and Kathy had the extra job of watching the airport area for planes. When we were ready to make our way back to the guest house, I turned on the road to the airport. Kathy said, "No, Dad, do not go that way." She had seen too much to drive by that airport on our way home. I simply turned and hoped I could locate another road.

I did locate another main road eventually, but as we drove we saw Pakistani soldiers by the hundreds ready for a land battle. Keith opened the guest house gate. As we got out, Keith said to Kathy, "Did you get the food?"

Kathy answered, "Sure, why do you think we went?" Our kids could be funny even in chaotic conditions.

Since we knew that we were in deep trouble, we did everything we could think of to get some physical protection. John Freeman assumed the responsibility for preparing the guest house as best we could. We lined the outside of the back porch with anything and everything such as book shelves and other pieces of furniture. Those protection articles included the refrigerator and deep freezer. We covered the windows with heavy black paper for the blackouts. We removed the ceiling light fixtures and picture frames from the walls.

The only things left in the room where our entire family had slept were dining tables, a desk, and foam rubber mattresses. At night we separated the narrow dining tables and placed them along the walls which appeared the safest. Kathy chose to sleep under the desk. Cherie slept under a table nearest Kathy. Betty and Wade were next under their table and as was proper to us, Keith and I slept under a table nearest the front door.

The Thurmans moved downstairs and prepared a room for themselves. They lined the outside wall with wooden chests. Then they moved one chest near the table under which they slept as a family of four.

John and Howard moved into a room with the Bennetts and soon Pastor Simon and his family moved into the guest house with us because they lived near the airport and most of their neighbors had left their houses vacant.

Eventually we had forty-five people in our three living places. However, not all of us could get into those apartments so many lived in two garages. It seemed that everyone thought that numbers meant safety so there were no complaints.

We did get another visit from a person with the United States Consulate, but I was not present when he came. But it apparently made little difference though that he warned that the freedom fighters would kill people like us when they came into the town. The fact was that the freedom fighters were all over the city, but we had no fear of them. They may have been young Muslim men fighting for freedom, but most of them knew we were not their enemies.

The curfews enforced by the Pakistani army were difficult times for us. The big difficulty was they sometimes lasted for forty-eight hours. But we managed and if we went outside it was only for a short time and for something special which we thought had to be done such as bringing in water. The tube well we had sunk was surely an asset.

On the evening the curfew was suddenly put into force, I looked out the back side of the house and lights were shining brightly at a service station just over our wall. I called for Keith to go with me so out the front gate we went. Just as we reached the service station, a truckload of soldiers drove up. We ignored them. They drew their guns and walked toward the service station. Keith and I were busy and I suppose they were dumbfounded about who we were and why we were busy putting out the lights. They probably thought that it was a plot staged by someone who worked at the station.

Anyway, Keith and I were busy turning off the lights after we had broken into the main building. We did not know how to turn off some of the lights so we put a table under them and I climbed up and unscrewed the light bulbs. Keith held whatever I had given him and those soldiers watched as if they still had no idea who we were. One outside light was on and we had no idea how to turn it off. I simply began throwing bricks at it and in no time, it broke.

Having completed our job, Keith and I began walking toward the guest house gate carrying the light bulbs and tubes. A few minutes later, we heard the military vehicle drive away from the station. Our job had been done so there were no lights left shining in our area. We wondered what the soldiers were saying as they drove away.

The soldiers did not know that the owner of the station was a prisoner on the army base, for had they known that, they probably would have destroyed the station. We took the bulbs and tubes back to the station the first time it was open and apologized that we had done so much destruction. However, they thanked us and explained they had simply forgotten the lights were on since it was daytime when the curfew was proclaimed and they had quickly made their way to their places of residence.

Of the forty-five people in our compound no one created more enjoyment than John Munshi. John and his family had departed Dhaka several months earlier out of a deep fear. But then John and his brother-in-law decided to return to Dhaka for they had no way to earn a living. John worked at the international airport and had served in the Pakistani army. Having been in the army might have made him appear more dangerous. He also spoke Urdu, the language of the army.

John had first brought some of his children to the guest house. Then, he brought his sons and a few days later, he brought his wife. Then, at last, he drove the vehicle through the gate and said, "Where can we hide this thing? I am remaining with all of you." We did our best to hide his vehicle and ours; we hid them under trees and covered them as best we could.

John's brother-in-law had been taken from the train they had been riding on by the soldiers. John had tried every way to learn about him but failed, until he eventually learned that his brother-in-law had been killed. He could not speak Urdu so there was no way he could communicate with some of the unlearned soldiers.

The telephone occasionally worked but we had very few telephone calls. However, one morning it rang. On the line was my friend, Rab Chaudhury. I could hardly distinguish his voice and he was trying to speak entirely differently from the way he normally did. The primary thing that we settled was that we were to try getting connected once per day. If we could not connect by phone, we were to try my going to his home or his sending a messenger to me. We had talked earlier knowing that he was on a list of those to be taken and probably be killed.

It was always apparent that a ray of hope came to us with every piece of information we received, such as that from Rab. The Avery children had returned from their boarding school and Stuart was unable to take them on to their home in Chandpur. Often, he brought the children to the guest house to be with our seven. So, with our seven, Debbie Bennett, Philip and David Thurman, and Cherie, Kathy, Keith and Wade, Lindy Parshall, and four Averys, we at times had "the twelve" international children who were in Dhaka at that time. Their being together always seemed to give an added ray of hope to our children. This was what I called and continue to call "God's special arrangement" at a time of great need.

Eventually, those evacuation planes came and departed without any difficulty. The Indian and Pakistani air forces ceased their fighting so those planes could come and go. "How Noble!" is all I could say then and now. India, Pakistan and the freedom fighters ceased their killing one another and let the "foreigners" depart. Our twelve didn't act like foreigners, but maybe like internationals who deeply loved the local people and remained with their moms and dads.

During the night following the evacuation of the foreigners, the drone of a plane's engines awakened us from our night's sleep. That drone seemed to increase. Undoubtedly, it was near the guest house. Then, a thud, a massive blast, the shaking of the guest house and the quivering of the earth frightened us tremendously. Within moments, another thud, louder, stronger and nearer the guest house, gave us a ferocious jerk. Bombs had caused a massive hole within a short distance of the guest house.

A fourth attack made us wonder just how much our building could endure. Apparently as the plane pulled out of its dive, it was almost directly over the guest house and then that was the last we heard of it. The plane seemed to move away into the sky. But that was not the last we heard of other planes.

There was a para-military base only a short distance to the south from the guest house. India's planes flew over the Intercontinental Hotel, going east to west, and we could see everything from the back porch of the guest house. That helped us as we watched during the daylight knowing again that the planes were attacking military installations. But as those planes attacked that para-military base, they also flew directly over a long line of apartments.

A friend, who had visited us along with his brother, lived in one of those apartments. The phone rang and Sudhir was on the phone. His wife was ill and needed to be taken to the hospital. My only reply was, "I am on my way."

But he asked, "How can you get here with the curfew in effect?"

I could only reply, "I don't know but be ready. I am on my way."

I drove to the first police check-point and asked, "Will one of you ride with me so that I can safely travel to a house and then the hospital?"

"Oh, no," came the reply. "You can make it okay." That was all I wanted to hear. I wasn't even stopped as I passed through checkpoint after checkpoint, going from the guest house and back to the guest house.

Sudhir was waiting and his wife was soon with us. She didn't look sick and really wasn't. She was just overwhelmed by those planes flying directly over their apartment. In no time at all, we were on our way to a Christian center about three miles from their apartment. As we traveled, Sudhir said, "I have been told I am on a list to be taken by the para-military and I may need to be moved again."

I had only a brief comment, "Let me know if you need me."

I was back at the apartment house. A Muslim family had asked if I would return after taking Sudhir's family to their place of safety and then take his family to another area. I had said to him, "I will return for you. Kindly be ready to depart immediately." Now they were ready. They loaded their valuables and themselves as planes zoomed over our heads. We drove and drove. We went into areas of the city that I had never seen before. But we had the streets to ourselves except for the check-points who rarely troubled us.

Finally, we drove down a narrow city street. The man in the family, a scientist, watched carefully for a certain house which was our destination. We found it. The gate was locked. I blew the mini van's horn.

Then we saw someone peep out a window. In a few seconds a person came running to open the gate. That family got down, thanked me and as I was turning the van, they called out as they walked toward the house, "Thanks, thanks." As I drove away, I needed no thanks, but "thanks" seemed to echo and that probably helped me more than I will ever be able to understand.

While at that apartment house, a Swedish woman had asked me to try to locate her husband who had been taken by the para-military. He was a scientist with a doctor of science degree.

I went to the Intercontinental Hotel and asked the Red Cross personnel about the scientist. The only reply was that if he had been gone as I had told them for more than twelve hours, then there was no hope of finding him alive. I reported back to that kind woman and later she learned he had been killed. Though he was a Muslim, he was an educated Bangla man with a high degree and those kinds of people, if located, were taken and killed immediately by the para-military forces. Howard Teel later took that woman to the hotel and as soon as the fighting ended she was on her way back to Sweden.

So often, too often, we noted old buses passing down Mirpur Road and noted that those buses moved mostly during curfews with their passengers all blindfolded. We came to know that those men, Muslim men, were on their way to an extermination center.

The long night of December 14 gnawed at us forcefully. The planes of India's air force attacked constantly. Added to this was the roar and blasts from Indian heavy artillery on the outskirts of the city. One blast shook so forcefully that we rose up from under our tables quaking in our boots.

Danger appeared to be near as the night moved on. Our five year old Wade, the youngest, had not talked much about what was happening. But in the middle of the night, his softly spoken little words brought tears gushing down our cheeks when he asked, "Daddy, will we all be killed?"

I had difficulty answering Wade but eventually was able to pull out the words, "Yes, Wade, we may be killed, but that is not the worst thing which can happen to a family. We love one another and we are together. We love the Bangla people and we know they are suffering much." That was about all I could say to my youngest child in a situation that was brought about by my decision. But now, about thirty-four years later, I wonder about what I did and what I said to our children during that time of death and horror. Most of the time, even today, I feel that God led us to do what we did. He led us to that place which was our home. We learned that He arranges what is necessary and teaches us through those experiences which were ours because of Him.

In 1978 I wrote, "Our emotions were overflowing. Love was at work. God was very much alive and not in a superficial way to us but for real. We felt that we somewhat knew Him. We were involved in a great struggle and in that struggle we always found Him."

Bangla freedom fighters and the India military forces had Dhaka surrounded. Radio sources said there were about forty thousand Pakistani soldiers in the city and that they were well fortified. General Niazi was reporting that he and his men would fight to the last man. Ships from the United States were reported to be in the Bay of Bengal for any necessary evacuations.

The Pakistani soldiers were apparently ready for an all-out attack. On the morning of December 15 we heard on the short-wave radio, "The Indian army has the city surrounded. Their planes control the sky. General Niazi continues to say his soldiers will fight to the last man to hold the city."

Such news caused us to tremble. Thousands had left Dhaka in early December, but it was estimated that there were about two hundred thousand civilians left in the city. Yet, in the midst of all of this, we ate regular meals. We talked much and gave opportunity, again and again, for our children to talk.

When we had difficulty wording a verbal prayer, we knew that others, in many parts of God's world, were praying for us.

During the few times of December 15 when the planes were not attacking, there was an absolute silence, except for the shells bursting on the periphery of the city. Very few smiles were seen on anyone's face. That night was quiet except for the planes of India attacking north of the airport.

Rumors from many radio sources reported that Pakistan was about to surrender the city. I suppose that hope, however, was beyond us. The morning of December 16, I climbed the steps leading to the flat roofing of the guest house. I carried a little radio in my hand. On the local station there was only music. The quietness continued to be fearful. I expected an all-out attack on the city but I was wrong as I had often been wrong in the previous months.

The local radio station announced, "General Niazi has been ordered to surrender his forces in East Pakistan to the Indian army." Suddenly, we saw, we experienced the birth of a giant nation. Bangladesh, the eighth largest populated nation in the world, was born.

A short time later, we witnessed the movement of hundreds of Pakistani soldiers moving toward the local army base near the airport. They were on their way to surrender to the Indian military. Even their weapons appeared too heavy for them to carry. They were on their way to surrender to the Indian military. They were assisted by young Bangla men running into the streets and relieving them of the weapons.

But going rapidly in the other direction were dozens of razakars, the local para-military who had cooperated with the Pakistani army. These cowardly young men changed clothing as they ran in an attempt to hide among the population. For years to come, they were to pretend they had never sided with the Pakistani army and they continued to be a political force for the worst possible behavior.

Even the police at the station just south of the guest house abandoned their station. They, or at least many of them, had cooperated with the Pakistani army. But while all of this was happening, the local civilians ran into the streets shouting with joy.

Our children, along with Debbie Bennett and the Bangla children who had lived in our "place of safety" for several days, stood, some of them inside the gate and others outside the gate, to wave at the freedom fighters and the Indian soldiers as they marched properly down Mirpur Road.

Those children drew wild informal applause from the military people walking south down that road because they held in their hands a free Bangladesh flag tied to a long stick. Perhaps most people in the world will never think of children in this way, but one man, the father of four of those children, salutes them with his hand and his heart.

Soldiers of the Indian army were soon at the guest house asking who we were and whether we were okay. Yes, we were okay. I say, we were "okay" if you compared our situation to an hour earlier that day and in examining it thirty-four years later, OKAY was correct.

CHAPTER SEVENTEEN
Unwelcomed in Feni, Our Home

Newspaper reports gave some horrifying news. Some were saying that three million people had been killed. I had heard much about the Comilla army base and that as many as one hundred thousand had been killed there. Other reports said that two hundred thousand young women had been raped and that most of them were pregnant.

Other news sources reported that four hundred bridges and culverts had been badly damaged or destroyed. I accepted that as fact because even in the limited amount of travel I did during those nine months, I had seen many of those destroyed bridges and culverts. Also, many ferry boats had either been badly damaged or destroyed. I believed that to be true since I had seen more than enough of that type of destruction.

The economy of the new nation was to be based on agriculture just as East Pakistan had been. Time would bring about changes but that would be slow, indeed. But in my first trip back "home" to Feni, I could hardly believe that rice fields looked like jungles in the making. Ordinarily, in December, the rice fields would be covered with rice just beginning to ripen. There were others fields which were planted in early September which ordinarily showed a beautiful green color. I began thinking to myself that starvation will be our next massive challenge.

Manufacturing had primarily been owned by wealthy Pakistanis. They were now gone to West Pakistan and most were never to return. So what good were manufacturing facilities if there was no money to pay the workers?

Jute had been the largest earner of foreign exchange but that market, too, was gone. Even before the war had begun, synthetics were becoming more popular on the international market. Though jute may have been an important export, it was to be only a minor product.

Construction of buildings usually began in November. But before that, brick had to be made. However, the making of brick required a large amount of capital. Where that money was to come from, we had no idea. Also, it would be weeks before those who had money could assimilate all of the needed resources to begin the brick manufacturing.

The Bangladesh taka, the new currency, had little value on the world market so most trading had to be done with the promise of payment sometime. But the greater problem was to be that of the refugees. There were probably about ten million of them who had gone into India and had returned with obviously less than they had when they departed.

Then there were probably about two million Hindus who had remained in East Pakistan, many of those in parts of the Noakhali District. Most of those who had houses found them totally destroyed when the war ended. Also, many Muslim homes had been destroyed. They had been destroyed, if vacant, which meant the owners were sympathetic to the freedom struggle.

For an international Christian missionary, living in an Islamic land meant you did your best to keep your mouth zipped when it came to local politics. I admit that I had trouble doing that with all of the killing I had known about during those past nine months. Ordinarily, when we were in the United States for leave, many people asked me about that Pakistan arrangement with the two parts being separated by one thousand miles of India. I usually replied that they seem to manage. I really had not considered it since it was not my responsibility. I was not a local citizen but a guest.

Another deep problem was the presence of a large ethnic group called Biharis. These people had come to East Pakistan primarily in 1947 when the creation of this new nation of Pakistan had taken place. Since Bihar, an Islamic part of India, was near East Pakistan, many of them had come and established their businesses.

They had help because the East Pakistan government, supported by the national government of Pakistan, had supported them in establishing their businesses. Now the support was gone. This support was not just economic, but it had also been political especially during the war when they sided with Pakistan and against the freedom movement.

On December 16, 1971, the day of independence, a Bihari woman who lived across Mirpur Road from the guest house came asking us, "What are you going to do?"

I answered, "We are going to rejoice with the Bangladeshi people in their freedom."

Then she asked, "But aren't you afraid?"

My reply was, "Why should we be afraid?"

Her words flowed quickly, "Of what these people will do to you?" My only available advice to her was that her family remain inside their house as much as possible, and then if there was trouble, to please, somehow, let us know.

The struggle during the war had been Muslim against Muslim. Now, battles actually happened in the days immediately following the freedom day, when freedom fighters fought the Biharis within the area of Dhaka.

Since my family had only about six months left before our regular departure time for return to the States for what is now called, "state-side assignment," I very much wanted to work in Noakhali or more particularly in the greater Feni area. I was pleased that some of our colleagues were to try to help the Bihari people in their struggle to live.

Without a doubt, the greatest problem of all was that of a large nation without their leader. As far as we knew, Sheikh Mujibur Rahman, who had been elected by popular vote as President of Pakistan in 1970, was still in a Pakistani jail on the other side of India. Or had he been killed during the final days of the war? We did not know that answer.

I had a deep longing to get back to Feni and to learn what I might do in programs of rehabilitation. Betty consented that I go because we also had stored Christmas gifts for the children in a large metal drum and we wanted them. So, off I went with little anxiety.

Travel by public conveyance was simple for the first few miles. Fares were high but that was expected. I soon discovered that as I moved southeast, when people recognized me then all was well. But I quickly understood if people only knew I was an American, then they had little or nothing to say to me.

Since this was the third day following the independence of December 16, India was already moving some of her military equipment back toward the border. That pleased me, but it also meant they had all of the ferries reserved for some of the most massive equipment I had ever seen. I knew when I saw some of the field guns being towed by huge truck that if one of those shells had fallen in a residential area, many civilians would have died.

I noted a jeep on one ferry with only the driver and an officer in the back seat. The insignia on the jeep was covered, and as I looked I thought the officer was a major. I decided to ask him if I could accompany him. He seemed to welcome me. Then he introduced himself and I again had blown it; he was a brigadier, or in U.S. terminology, a brigadier general. Anyway, I tried to be more proper and as time moved on, he warmed up to me and I went all the way to Comilla with him. From there he was going to cross the border back to his home country of India.

From Comilla, I hired a rickshaw and moved as rapidly as the driver could pump the pedals. As we rode along, I noted Indian tanks blown to pieces. Local people reported that a large group had fought intensely and many people were killed. That rickshaw ride gave me a clear picture of the country-side and what I saw wasn't pleasant. No crops existed in the fields.

At one village on the eastern side of the road as we moved south, a group of village Muslims screamed out and we stopped. Then they asked me to come into their village. Their houses had all been destroyed. But that was not what they wanted me to see. Probably they thought I was a reporter. They had been digging a foundation for a house and had discovered that in the middle of the court-yard was a massive grave of human bodies. I did my best to console them and give some hope to them in that terrible situation. Years before when the village was first constructed, they had built the area up at least fifteen feet above the land level. Now, a huge area was a graveyard and they had no way of knowing anything about who had been buried there. Some of these people said there were at least fifty bodies but I do not know how they could have come to that number. All I could do was give them a salaam and move on in the rickshaw.

While riding along, I heard a vehicle coming behind me so I prepared myself to ask for a ride, regardless. What a ride it was! Two Indian army majors were in the jeep and one of them was driving. This time there was no rank mistake. When they learned about me they had more questions than I had answers. At least half the time we drove through the fields by the roadside due to the destruction of so many bridges and culverts.

At one place, thousands of refugees were returning home. This was the place where I had seen them go into India in late April. I knew they were returning to the blank earth which had been the foundations of their houses. I could pray as I watched them move slowly toward their new country of Bangladesh. Surely, I thought, my God will arrange for me to help some people like these and to help them in a significant way.

The gracious majors let me down in the middle of Feni so I decided to go directly to the civil service office and inquire about what I might be able to do as soon as possible. The officer was new but very polite to me. But he could only say that I should go to the office of the political leader. He was one of those elected to the national assembly earlier, along with my "friend" who had betrayed his people earlier in the war.

When I walked into his office, I knew I had trouble. I asked him about the situation and he became angrier and angrier. Finally he said, "Get out of Feni and do not return. If you return I will have you arrested." I quickly made my way toward the house and as I walked, I tried to think of what could have happened.

While walking, I remembered someone had told me early in the war that this man's brick house had been torn into pieces by dynamite. I also knew that he had probably inquired about me and someone had said that I had returned to Feni on several occasions. That, to him, meant I had been able to do that without danger to myself. Well, I knew he had missed that one.

But I knew the biggest problem was that my home country had sided with Pakistan during that war. He did not understand that as far as I was concerned, I had not met an American during all of those months who approved of what the Pakistani army was doing.

Our house was filthy. The odor was almost too much to bear. There was no electricity and no food. I slept very little and had to wait for daylight to search for the children's Christmas gifts in that metal drum.

Early the next morning I opened the drum without any difficulty and found all of the gifts for our blessed children. I packed them in a sheet and tied it together carefully. I locked the door and walked through the back streets to the train station.

At the train station, I felt better. I was searching for hope and I found it. The station manager told me the first train to move out of Feni since Bangladesh independence was soon ready to depart north and that was my direction. I bought my ticket and in a short time boarded the train. The engine was a steam engine and all of the cars looked to be very old, most of them baring huge shell holes and bullet marks all over the outside. But we were moving.

The train passengers asked me many questions. I did not recognize any of them but that did not seem to matter. When they learned my family had lived through the entire war in their land, they warmed to me and that helped much.

From Comilla, I rode a bus and though it was not very comfortable most of the people seemed happy and for some reason, they encouraged me. I did tell them that I hoped to help people who had lost their houses and other property but that had not yet been approved. When we arrived at the first ferry crossing, our bus stopped for a return trip to Comilla. I was thinking that I had no choice but to walk much of the remaining trip.

But as we crossed the river or actually parts of two rivers, I noted a special Indian military vehicle. I also noted there were only a driver and an officer, a lieutenant. I did not approach him. He came to me asking questions about who I was and what was I doing on that ferry. I had no idea how much he needed to talk with me. If you could believe it, he let me know that he was a Christian. Then he began to tell me some of his experiences in the last few weeks.

He first spoke highly of the Bangla freedom fighters and that they had led the combined forces into battle on many occasions. I felt good about that. He even explained that some of the freedom fighters had been maybe too aggressive but he said they wanted to win to have a free country and often because of that eagerness, they moved ahead of the stronger forces and many of them had died.

But then, what that seemed to trouble him most, and that he needed to tell me was that some of the large fox holes had Bangla women in them and they had been kept there for several days. With tears in his eyes, and he was a married man, he told of one fox hole where the woman was naked and had been cut down the front part of her body.

In other fox holes, the women were hardly alive. I knew he was talking about war, but that did not make it any easier for me to hear what he badly needed to say. So I did my best to listen carefully to every word Lt. Nobo spoke.

It took about twenty minutes to cross on the ferry and as we were docking he asked me how I was traveling. When I told him he immediately said that I could ride with him. I had noted the front seat had only two seats and I had no idea what was inside the back of that small truck.

He opened the only door to the back part of the truck and I immediately understood that this was a communications vehicle with thousands and thousands of dollars worth of equipment in it. Lt. Nobo climbed into the vehicle, pulled out a folding chair, and asked if that arrangement was okay. Of course it was okay. We crossed four more rivers on ferries and each time he opened my door from the outside and we continued our conversation.

As usual, I was welcomed home. Things were now different. There was only our family in the guest house. John Freeman and Howard Teel had gone back to their families in Bangkok, Thailand.

The streets were noisy. People were demanding to know about Sheikh Mujibur Rahman, their leader. The approximately ninety-three thousand captured Pakistani soldiers were under the control of the Indian army. Rumors were that the primary Pakistani officers had already been flown to India. My trip to Feni did not make me feel any better except that we had Christmas gifts for our children. But two questions haunted me and all the people who were ready to build a new nation out of this war-torn situation. Where was the Bangladeshi president? Was he even still alive?

CHAPTER EIGHTEEN
Struggling in the New Country

There was absolutely no law and order. The freedom fighters were still armed and so were the Biharis. Local news sources reported battles that broke out between the freedom fighters and the Biharis. The Indian army seemed to being doing its best to stop the fighting. Their officers were disciplined and I soon learned they wanted peace, if for no other reason, so they could return to their home country.

Always, however, the question about Sheikh Mujib was asked over and over by even the simplest of people. They knew a leader was, beyond question, a necessity. The villages had to have leaders so how could a nation function without its leader?

Young men, and apparently many of those who had done nothing to win freedom for their new country, roamed the streets acting like freedom fighters. Some even came by the guest house asking if we had shells for their guns. It was ridiculous but such times now existed. Some wanted to use our mini van and other vehicles which had been left with us for "safety." As if we could protect their vehicles.

Our friendships with many people was not known by those that I met while traveling. We were soon known only as Americans whose country had supported the Pakistani army. We struggled with this but as time moved on and news traveled, many people understood that as citizens of our country we might disagree totally with government actions of our country. That philosophy of citizenship probably saved us from the most violent responses from many local people. But they learned and I think many of them began to consider that this was the kind of government they wanted for their new country.

Former police, many of whom had gone into India in the early part of the war, began returning and that helped as they were accepted in the various police stations. Then, slowly, it seemed that those who had previously served in the Pakistani army before the war began organizing to help in the law and order situation. Though all of this helped tremendously, this new nation badly needed their elected leader.

In the midst of all the chaos, there were constant helps to us. One of those had been an Indian army captain who came to the guest house soon after December 16. Captain Jai Ram, a Hindu, could not have been more gracious to us. Perhaps, even more than Betty and our children, I was searching for security for all of my greater family members and for others in similar positions. Captain Jai helped me in this.

There was no doubt Captain Jai was a very intelligent officer. From our earliest acquaintance, his questions led me to believe that he was with army intelligence and I still hold that position. But we didn't know anything he did not know as an army officer so if he was with army intelligence, that did not matter to us. I always thought that when others saw him visit us they understood that we were not supporters of the former Pakistani military.

Anyway, just one story about Captain Jai. One day, when he came by to visit us, he seemed to do nothing but complain about the local people or our friends. I thought nothing about what he said because, even years before as I had read many sources, I knew that an occupying army faced great difficulties such as "are they going to occupy us as did the previous army?" Captain Jai departed that day with the same attitude he had at the beginning of his visit with us.

This army officer had hardly gotten out the front door when Cherie confronted me. "Dad," she said, "you let that Indian army officer sit right here in our house and criticize our friends with whom we have lived for so long and you said nothing." I immediately apologized to Cherie and our other three children and promised I would confront the captain the next time he visited us.

The next time Captain Jai came to the guest house, I told him all that had happened following his previous visit with us. He asked if I was going to permit him to talk with our children and the answer was "yes." When he was seated I called the children.

Captain Jai stood and apologized to Cherie and looked at all the other children as if he had committed a crime against them. I could tell that he knew he was forgiven and Betty also knew that. We had felt often during the past months that forgiveness, practiced and taught by our Lord Jesus, had become a way of life for the six of us. Sometimes we had a delay in practicing that forgiveness but it was present within us.

The next visit by this kind Indian officer was different. He had two younger officers with him and as I invited them to enter our house, he said to the others, "This is the house I told you about so do not criticize the local people for if you do you will be in trouble." We had many visits by this gentleman in the days which followed and all went well each time.

The last visit with Captain Jai gave him the opportunity to ask for a copy of Cherie's poem. We later learned that he had that poem translated into several Indian languages and that it was published all over India. So goes God's forgiveness and our forgiveness, and also maybe some witness for Him and for His glory.

Rab Chaudhury, the Bangladeshi civil service person, came by regularly. He knew that I was his standby in the event he was taken by the Pakistani army during the closing days of the war. But now we were beyond that and our thinking was concerning building the nation. I knew that in time, Rab would receive a much higher position than he had during the past but we were to just wait for that.

Alam Chasi had not yet returned from Kolkata where he had been the foreign secretary of the rebel government of the nation to be Bangladesh. We knew he would let us know soon after his arrival and as Rab's help was, so would be Alam's help to us and other Christian missionaries. Yet, hoping sometimes lost me, at least for a time. Streets were filled with shouting people, many of them armed with crude weapons which could still destroy human life. The cry of sincere people was correct—this nation quickly needed her leader.

All kinds of stories existed such as Pakistan and Bangladesh would form a united government, but that was while they had Sheikh Mujib in one of their prisons in Pakistan. At least, now there was news that he had not been killed. We knew that General Yahya Khan, the military dictator of Pakistan, was now being replaced by Ali Bhutto who had received the second largest number of votes in elections the previous year. Maybe, at least, Bhutto did not have to fake his previous decisions as did General Yahya.

One of a long list of crimes committed by General Yahya was that of appointing General Tikka Khan as chief of staff of the Pakistani army during the war. Often we had heard General Tikha called "The Butcher of Bangladesh." But now both were more or less off the scene. Maybe Bhutto would do better. At least, he had that opportunity.

On January 8, 1972, Sheikh Mujib was released. Who ordered his release, I do not know, but an awful decision was made in Pakistan—Sheikh Mujib was sent to England rather than directly to Bangladesh. Great Britain treated him royally and after a few days the Sheikh arrived in Dhaka, Bangladesh, his land, his country. In Britain, Sheikh Mujib was able to learn for the first time of all the tragedies committed in his country. On January 10, he arrived in Dhaka and what a day of rejoicing!

Perhaps Sheikh Mujib had learned in England that the United States was hesitating to recognize Bangladesh. Many of our friends and many members of the United States Congress were encouraging our president to make that recognition but it came slowly, too slowly for a land that had suffered so much with suffering that had not been their making, but imposed by those on the outside who had dominated them.

Sheikh Mujib's return to his country brought a new sense of responsibility to Bangladesh and I thought that surely most of the world's governments would give him time to understand and for his people to truly accept him as their leader. That seemed to happen in his early days of this massive new nation. I know I felt much better regarding the safety of my family.

I now believed that I could return to Feni without fearing physical harm to myself. Businesses began to open earlier and remain open until early evening. The streets became quieter and traffic flowed more freely as police began to be more regular in their duty.

I felt that I could drive all the way to Feni since I had heard the India military had made it possible by doing minimum repairs to small bridges.

As I drove, I helped as many people as possible and always enjoyed talking with them and hearing them talk with others. You could hear easily that hope was now being built. As I drove, I had time to deeply consider how I was to approach the political leader.

I suppose there was a degree to which I had become arrogant in my feelings about the place of my family in this new country. But that had grown from the time of the awful tidal wave on November 12-13, 1970. This was due to the fact that I had been so involved in the life of local people who needed help which I could arrange for them, that I felt a part of that land. But all of that had been ripped from me by the political leader on my last visit with him in Feni.

Now, as I walked up the steps to his office, I had no idea how he might act to my presence. I well remembered that he had threatened me on that last visit. But I made it up the steps, slowly but surely. I was received graciously by Mr. Ahmed. There was no doubt he had talked with the right people about my family and me. I sat in a chair designated by him. He asked about my family and the local Christians.

When I told Mr. Ahmed that since we had only about six months before our leave in the United States and that Betty had help in Dhaka to teach the children, he encouraged me to bring them back to Feni and that he would guarantee their safety in every way. I am sure he would have and could have done that. Even though I am usually a person of action, I did not expect him to be so ready to respond. When I told him I wanted to help some of the most desperate people, he replied, "Early in the morning I will show you the place I want you to work."

Mr. Ahmed said that he would drive by our house at six o'clock in the morning and take me to a nearby village and show me the places where many houses of Hindus had been destroyed. Remember that this man was Muslim and he was to take me to a Hindu area so that I could help those people.

I got to our house just before darkness. Sultan was there soon after my arrival. He had not been there in the meantime, but the house, for some reason, looked brighter than it had on my last visit. Maybe it was not the house that looked better but that my attitude was much better. The alarm seemed to go off early the next morning, but I noted that it hadn't. I had not planned breakfast, but wanted to be standing on the side of the road by six o'clock. Mr. Ahmed arrived on time.

He rode up in a jeep with a driver. I climbed in and you would have thought we were two long-lost friends. We turned down a familiar road. We picked up a local man whom I knew but did not say much to him. We went to a village that was well known to me but I didn't mention that to my new friend. Mr. Ahmed quickly announced to a group of those Hindu people that Mr. McKinley would be helping them rebuild their houses.

They looked at me with smiles and I signaled to them by putting my fingers over my mouth. I did not, for some reason, want Mr. Ahmed to know that I knew many of those people very well. We walked around the area and then departed. I got down at our house and gave my new friend a salaam and off he went.

Soon, I got a rickshaw and was back in the same village going over what I wanted them to do while I would be busy trying to locate money to do the building of little houses which were so badly needed.

Though I told them I might have difficulty getting money, I knew they heard none of that. Those people only wanted to know, "When will you begin work?" I ignored the question and told them to kindly prepare the earthen foundations and what size to do each one. The houses were to be twenty feet long and ten feet wide. I left by saying, "I will do what I can to help."

I went back to Dhaka feeling great. In fact, rather than taking a back road out of Feni, I drove the main streets. I kept the vehicle loaded with passengers since there were so few buses and even fewer rickshaws. It was almost beyond belief but even many of the rickshaws had been destroyed. I felt that if you want to help people, then help everyone you can even as you help some in more formal ways such as building houses.

The best help anyone could possibly be for such a task as that before me was having a friend like James Halder to assist. I knew he was trustworthy and he had a massive amount of common sense. He might be threatened in many different ways in the job before us, but he knew I would always be available for any kind of need which might come his way.

We reviewed everything we could think of which we didn't understand very well. We even walked among houses that had survived the war and our purpose was to see how different houses had been constructed. I knew the size but we needed to know every detail. We did not hesitate to let all know that we had support of the "government" officer in our area.

We took ten days to build the first house. We bought materials for all the houses and hence, received a better price for those materials. We were determined, for example, to buy tin for the roofing of the houses at the price that tin sold for before the war. That may have been severe on our part, but we knew that tin had been in storage and hence, we got that price. We knew that the more we saved as we made purchases, the more little houses we could build.

News was spreading in many different directions about our work. How had we been able to respond so quickly? That led some people, who didn't understand James and me, to think that we freely used money. So late one afternoon I drove back to our Feni house and several young men were waiting for me.

They demanded money which they said they were going to use for former freedom fighters. I also knew enough to understand well that this group certainly had not been true freedom fighters. They made several threats and even declared they would destroy our Feni house. Eventually, they departed.

A few days later, I filled the vehicle gas tank at a Feni station. I got in the vehicle and suddenly another group leader came making demands and doing that in a public place. I knew that this group and the previous group which threatened me were enemies. Without too much fear, I told this leader that we gave cash to no one. Others perhaps did that, but we did not. His reply was that the next thing to go into the gasoline tank would be a match while I was still sitting in the vehicle.

I had told the previous group leader to go ahead with the destruction of our house and then to tell people about it. I think that shook him into reality. Those were the only two threats I received during the next six months.

Had those days been normal days, I guess I would have gone directly to the police and demanded they do something immediately.

But these were not normal days by any means. The government needed time to function again. Many people involved before March 25 of the previous year surely would not be involved again, for they had proved themselves as traitors.

If I seem to make it sound like I knew much about what was happening in the new nation of Bangladesh, that is not my intention. All I wanted to do was to function quickly so that I could help people and to me that gives hope and courage for a believer in the Eternal One. My experience a few days later moved my attitude into reality.

The next time I left my family and drove toward Feni I stopped at the first river to wait for the ferry. I had hardly stopped when a most gracious young Muslim came to me and shook my hands with almost overwhelming delight. My colleague, R.T. and I had first met him when we visited his area of Noakhali where the tidal wave had struck. This young man had been a faithful freedom fighter. Now, we met again.

His first words to me were, "If you ever need me, let me know and I will come immediately." I knew that he was well aware of the feelings some had of all Americans. I gave him a serious thanks and left it there. He then said, "Have you heard about our friend Rab?" I had no idea what he was talking about. He ran and in a few minutes was back with a newspaper and among the other front page news was that Rab Chaudhury had been chosen by the Prime Minister to be the Coordinator of Non-government Assistance. I was thrilled for more than one reason.

A few nights before I had been invited to have dinner with Rab. When I arrived at his house, I discovered that there were several others there. All were his dear friends from different areas of Noakali. Here I was a conservative Christian missionary with all of these powerful political leaders from the part of Bangladesh to which I had been and was closely attached in word and in deed.

One of those men was Alam Chasi who had been designated by the Prime Minister as Secretary of Rural Development and Cooperatives. One of the group was soon to be the leader of the National Assembly. One was a newspaper editor of one of Dhaka's largest dailies. We had dinner that night and talked and talked. I assumed this was just a friendly get-together.

However, the next day that group ate every meal together in various places. Many questions were asked me. Everyone in this group, except Rab, had gone into India and worked with the rebel government of Bangladesh. I became a little irritated at their talking so much about those who had chosen India as their place of refuge while Rab had stayed with his family and suffered the deep agony of what might happen to him and a fear of being killed with his family. I felt deeply that I had to respond so I clearly said in English, "I go on record as saying it took more courage and faithfulness to remain here than it did to depart and go to India." At least, I said something like that.

Mr. Alam responded by asking, "Jim, are you saying those of us who departed had less courage?"

I didn't want to give any ground to any statement in my reply, so I said, "I can assuredly tell you that it took great courage for Rab to remain here." Not the next morning, but soon, I was at that river waiting for the ferry when the young man brought me the newspaper telling of Rab's all important appointment.

Rab and I were both busy, but on occasions he called me. One time he asked that I come to his office and talk with him and to come immediately if that was possible. I went. That morning he had been told by the Prime Minister to inform the foreigners living in the big hotel and doing nothing to leave Bangladesh. He showed me a list and I spoke strongly to him about one organization, the Mennonite Central Committee. I knew those people well. Their leader had been evacuated during the war but now was back. However, I don't think he lived in a hotel. I believe he was staying in our guest house.

Anyway, I think I was right to say, "Please keep this organization. They will do wonderful work once they understand what they need to do."

Rab had an answer for me, "Then you take him to Noakhali and show him what to do." In a few days a well trained assistant of the Mennonites went with me and I showed him a vast area along the India-Bangladesh border where hundreds of houses needed to be rebuilt. Almost six months later, they were still building houses in that area and those houses were better than the ones James and I were building.

Except for local politicians and close friends who called on me, I stayed away from government as much as possible. I knew that the formal government was having great difficulty in many areas and I assumed it would take years for some of the problems to be healed. For that reason I refused an opportunity to meet with the Prime Minister. Rab wanted to take me and I certainly would not accept without Tom Thurman being present so I just decided to forget that opportunity. Rab fussed at me but that was okay. He wanted the Prime Minister to meet his friends, the two foreign families, who had been the only foreign families with children to live in his country during those horrible nine months. Though, here I am writing about those experiences now, at that time, I just wanted to work and help destitute people in Bangladesh.

I also wanted Betty and our children to visit the tidal wave disaster area and after I had gone there and seen some of the last houses we helped to rebuild, I felt that it was proper for me to take them on that long, physically tiring journey. So we went to southwest Noakhali District. We saw some of the many newly constructed houses and many of those had been built during the war. We saw the work which had been done in the model village where both Mr. Alam and Rab had been deeply involved. When the house building was completed, it was good to look back and know that five hundred families now had houses in which they could live and no debts were to trouble them in the days ahead.

But the greatest joy was visiting in the home of Captain Aziz who had been so faithful to his land during the freedom struggle. It had been more then ten months since I had seen him. Certainly I will always remember the way he had organized the distribution of blankets just after the tidal wave. His wife served us a beautiful lunch and we enjoyed every second of our visit except for one thing.

Captain Aziz told me of his rescuing a Pakistani soldier from a group which was torturing him after the war. This had happened in a remote area where there were no Indian military and somehow, much earlier, that man had been separated from his unit. He was now living in that very village.

In fact, the Captain sent for him and in just a few minutes standing before us was a man who looked as natural as anyone of us. He didn't seem like a person who would kill even in war, much less after war. I suggested that he be allowed to ride with us to Dhaka and from there we would turn him over to the now better organized Bangladesh army or to the Indian army. But I sincerely believed Captain Aziz when he said that if a radical group saw that man in our vehicle when we were on the ferry crossing a river, then that could be real trouble for us.

Seeing that Pakistani soldier revealed to me how much I wanted all of the violence related to the war to be gone forever. This soldier was learning the Bangla language as if he were going to remain in that village. But I knew hatred would continue to be harbored in many people and that it was to be impossible for him to live a normal life. I learned later that Captain Aziz had died. When I learned that, I hoped that soldier was back in Pakistan.

My relationships had grown more deep with many Bangladesh Muslims. I never eased off in my Bible witness to all who would give me that privilege. Most, whom I believed felt deeply toward me, said over and over to me, "But, Jim, our Allah is the same as your God." I had to live with that. I could not change the perceptions of my Muslim friends. But I could love them in Jesus the Messiah ,or Isa the Masih. I can never say I was satisfied with such a situation and I could only hope and pray for a different kind of day.

As the Bangladesh government became more organized, I felt we would probably be given a visa so that we could return after leave in the United States. But we had to wait until almost a year passed before we were given regular visas. The morning we were to depart for our home country, everything had been organized by our colleagues for our travel to the airport. But just before departure time, Rab Chaudhury came to the guest house saying I was to ride with him. As we rode to the airport Rab was careful to tell me that we would receive a full visa when we were ready to return.On that day of departure, I acknowledged that war, even war that is not your own, brings about many different kinds of circumstances. But we knew we would receive our visas when the time came and of course, we did.

Betty and the children checking on Dad's work of house building.

High school graduation from Woodstock High School, Mussorie, India, 1977.
Kathy in solid white sari, front row, 2nd from left.

Jill at graduation from Dalat High School, Penang, Malaysia, 1991.

CHAPTER NINETEEN
Tragedy to My Family and to Others

Many dear friends were surprised that we would return to a land of Islam where we had endured so many difficult situations during the previous four years. There were times when even I wondered how Cherie and Kathy would respond to our returning to Bangladesh. But in the early part of our eleven months in the USA, a beautiful thing, at least to Dad Jim, happened.

The experience happened when our entire family drove about forty miles to the church where I had been a seminary student pastor. This church had been very kind to us as a young couple and Cherie, our first child, was born while we were living in the house provided by the church. On that Sunday morning I spoke for the pastor and was scheduled to speak again that night.

However, the pastor of that church, the Mount Moriah Baptist Church, had to travel to Louisville that afternoon to visit some of his members in a hospital. When Cherie and Kathy understood that, they asked if they could ride with the pastor to Louisville so they could be at our church in Louisville that night. The pastor was willing and whenever possible, Betty and I wanted to do anything we could to make life more pleasant for any and all of our children. So they went with the pastor.

The pastor returned about three hours later and expressed great surprise at what our daughters had said to him. The three of them were discussing where they would attend high school when they returned to Bangladesh. Evidently there had been no doubts about their willingness to return. The pastor said to his wife, Betty and me, "I could not believe that your daughters are willing to return after hearing you speak this morning." We never again doubted or discussed whether or not we were to return.

Even before the regular time for our return to Bangladesh, we had what could have been a difficult situation. Betty was expecting our fifth child. If she waited until the other children completed their school year, then no airline would accept her as a passenger. So, we easily managed that.

Betty was able to get permission to travel back to Bangladesh early from our International Mission Board so she did. I waited until the four children completed their year's schooling and then we five made the trip back.

While Dad traveled with the four, I decided number five would be the last one. I never knew how many little things had to be done when traveling with four young children while traveling half way around the world. I learned how much Mom was needed. Betty may have had an easier journey than I had; after her arrival, with the help of others, she found a house in which we could live.

Soon after my arrival in Dhaka, Mr. Alam called and asked me to please visit him in his office. Now I put in that word "please" because through the years he could not have been more polite to me in every way. With me, he was always a perfect gentleman.

I went to his office and we talked about a special project involving sheep and chickens. Remember, he was the Secretary of Rural Development and Cooperatives for the national government of Bangladesh.

I was not too interested in either of his suggestions. I knew that goats were a much hardier animal than sheep and that ducks were hardier than chickens.

But we talked at length and then he went back to about fifteen months earlier and made sure he had adequately thanked me for a special project that I had conducted for him. That project had been researching an area south and east of Feni along the India border where he had been told many houses had been destroyed. He wanted me to travel into the area and give him a written report on my findings.

I had made that special study for him and maybe I should not write why he had asked me to make the study inquiry. He had said, "I trust you and this is no time for our country to be involved unless it is absolutely necessary."

He went on to say, "We do have a small amount of money for rebuilding houses in rural areas but I must be absolutely careful that we do the work in the neediest places." I had convinced Mr. Alam that I could take the time to study the area even though I had an extensive house building project going at that very time.

Then he began to hesitate as if he were asking me to do too much. I had the joy of convincing him that I would hardly be missed in my work since it was well organized. I did the study after walking miles to locate the area.

Then, using the village names Mr. Alam had given me, I searched for those areas and found them, but not one house had been destroyed. I wrote my report carefully even giving details of how I found the villages in my search. He was somewhat embarrassed by the findings but added, "That is just why I wanted you to go and see if they really needed help."

During the next four years, though still serving with the government, he reportedly was involved in politics so I was not very much involved with him. I later learned that he was traveling by car with a group of Bangladeshi men. They were traveling to Mecca, the holy city of Islam. The report indicated they had tired of driving and had stopped for some sleep and rest. There my friend of those many years and his group were found dead in their car. Though some news sources claimed they died of gasoline fumes from the engine which they had left running while they slept, I am not sure how my good friend died.

Our fifth child, Jill, was born in July of 1973 without any difficulty, and we as a family rejoiced in her birth. Cherie and Kathy went to Woodstock High School in Mussourie, India, and that was, in a sense, a real blow to us as a family. We missed them so much. Having baby Jill with us helped Betty, the boys, and me, but we wanted the two big sisters who had been like little moms to their younger brothers.

My attention began to turn toward ways that I might be more deeply involved in winning people to Jesus. We knew that we lived in a "new day" in Bangladesh. There was more religious freedom and we sincerely appreciated that generosity of Muslims. But down deeply, I wanted all of my friends to know Jesus the Messiah, the Lord, not just Jesus a prophet.

Several new missionaries from different missionary organizations came to Bangladesh but many of them did not remain long enough to really know the people of that land who had suffered so much.

Bangladesh continued to struggle with so many political parties that wanted to "run" the country. I sometimes thought of most of those parties as wanting to "ruin" the country. However, I had to acknowledge this was often the way of new countries attempting to establish a democracy.

In late 1973 and early 1974, I traveled to northwestern Bangladesh on behalf of another missionary group. I had been told that the area where they wanted me to go had several Hindu families who were interested in Jesus. If they were interested, I thought, I am very much interested in going.

A person whom I did not know too well volunteered to go with me but his first trip was his last trip. He may have been a son of that soil, but the living conditions for him were too difficult. I made five more trips and on none of those did I have another friend with me except a young volunteer on one trip and above all, the Lord Jesus who was the Messiah. That was more than enough for me.

After those six journeys I reported to my friends in the other organization all that had happened. There were two groups ready to become churches and they were waiting for baptisms. I wanted the ones who would be close to them through the years to do the baptizing. I reported there were two other groups who had declared that they too, were ready to receive Jesus as Savior and Lord. I was ready for other such journeys but something happened in our family that prevented that.

In March, when Jill was a little more than nine months of age, the lady who often cared for her took her for a walk in the yard. Our boys and two friends were playing in that yard. But unknown to us, they had a flimsy little bow and arrow which was usually hidden from them, but they were attempting to see how to work it.

As the lady walked by with Jill in her arms, a little arrow flipped up and landed, in all of the space in God's world, in Jill's eye. Betty and I heard only one muffled cry and that was followed by complete silence.

As the lady walked into the screened-in front porch, I noted a small trickle of blood easing down Jill's little face. An eye had burst.

Jill was lifeless. Betty came quickly. I took Jill from the heart-broken lady and said to Betty, "Let's go!" I didn't know where to go but knew somewhere there was someone who could help and we had to find that exact person quickly. Maybe Jill could live.

Be assured, before we departed we loved Jill's two big brothers and assured them and their friends they had done nothing wrong. It was, for sure, at times like this that parents love their children and all children. As parents of five, we surely were not accusers of children who had been playing.

As we drove, I remembered there was a Lutheran missionary doctor at an orthopedic hospital and I knew he could at least advise us. In a short time, we were at that hospital. Only the nursing staff and the administrator were present. This hospital, we learned, was only for doing scheduled surgery on young men who had been injured during the war. Most of the staff was gone for the day.

That hospital administrator was a medical doctor so he was ready to help in any way possible. He advised us about a highly qualified ophthalmologist, Dr. Matin, whose medical office was several miles away. He gave the directions and though I hardly knew what I was doing, I drove directly to that office.

I took Jill from Betty and walked into Dr. Matin's office. He looked surprised and maybe even shocked when he saw that lifeless little light skinned baby in her father's arms.

I said to Dr. Matin, "I have been told that you can care for our baby."

He pointed to his small office and replied something like, "What can I do in a place like this?"

I had an answer ready and said, "I can assist you. You just tell me what to do and I can do it." Then, I mentioned the administrator's name and the hospital, and said, "They will welcome you to use their operating room." In a short time, Betty and I were on our way back to the hospital and we knew that Dr. Matin would be there immediately and he was.

In the meantime, Troy, one of our colleagues and others had remembered there were two Australian doctors at a local hotel. Troy went to the hotel and almost by the time we had arrived at the hospital again, Troy was there with those two doctors. One of the doctors was a plastic surgeon and the other, believe it or not, was a pediatrician with a specialty in anesthesia.

I asked Dr. Matin if he needed the help of those two doctors and I suppose he thought I was dumb to ask such a question. I must add that the hospital administrator was a near perfect Muslim gentleman in all of the arrangements. He had the nursing staff ready and they were led by a British nurse. He did all he could to help a Christian missionary family. I salute him.

This is not a contest but take a quick look—a nine month old American baby with Christian missionary parents; a Bangladeshi Muslim hospital administrator; a highly trained Bangladeshi doctor going far beyond his place of work or duty; a British nurse; a staff of Bangladeshi nurses and two off- duty Australian visiting doctors—with a force of Christian friends from Bangladesh and from many countries of the world, sitting or standing in different places in that hospital, praying for that little baby girl. About one hour later, kind, graceful Dr. Matin said to Betty and me, "Your baby is fine. Some of the nurses will remain with her over-night and she can go home in the morning." I quickly left to care for our boys and Betty spent the night with Jill.

As had always been a way of missionary life, to your colleagues your family is like their own family. The Youngs had stayed with Keith and Wade while we were away. Two days later, I flew to New Delhi, India, with Betty and Jill so Cherie and Kathy could come down from their school and see Betty and Jill before they flew on to the United States for Jill to be fitted with an artificial eye.

The day after the accident, Rab Chaudhury came by to express his concern for us as a family. Others, many others, did the same. Even the Muslim man who owned the house in which we lived came by to express his sorrow.

Perhaps the most beautiful expression offered without a word being spoken was when Pastor Simon came to see Jill while I was away with colleague James Young trying to arrange a flight to the States for Betty and Jill. Betty later told me the beautiful story that Pastor Simon, our pastor and colleague came to the door, seized the door facing with his two hands, cried, and then turned and departed.

Dr. Matin saw Jill the next morning after the accident. When we told him we were going to take her to the States, he fully agreed. The two Australian doctors agreed. Our colleagues agreed. So, we soon had their trip arranged. About four months later, Betty and Jill, with her new eye, returned to Dhaka.

But there was never a dull moment. The owner of the house where we lived came by one day for a short visit. He had stored some planks on the top of the house and he was now ready to use those so we welcomed his taking the planks. But we had become better acquainted through Jill's accident so in a conversation, he told me about a relative, a Bangladesh man who was in the Pakistan army but was being kept under house arrest in Pakistan, along with his family. When he told me the name, it was the same person who, years ago, had come by our house in Comilla during a storm asking if we needed help. I had lost track of Brigadier General Khalil Rahman and now I suddenly knew where he was. The war may have been over, but there were many trappings of it remaining, so here I was involved again.

I first went to the International Red Cross Dhaka office and discovered they were so overwhelmed with red-tape, that I lost hope of getting my friend and his family back into Bangladesh through them. Next, I decided to try the Office of the Representative of the United Nations High Commissioner for Refugees. I discovered that I was able to get past one desk but not past the next desk. I had found "another mess."

I had to find a way. I went to a friend from Australia who worked with another branch of the United Nations. Many years earlier, he had escaped from Eastern Europe when his country was under communism, so he had a deep desire to help me.

Probably the important thing he told me was to be persistent, never give up, and return day after day if necessary. It was necessary and I did it. One day I was talking with one of the office receptionists and got quite a bit irritated. I tried to control myself and having done some of that, I got very loud.

All of a sudden, I discovered that my words were doing just what I wanted them to do. I noticed a door open down a long hallway. Then I noticed a man poke his head out and look in my direction. He asked, "What is wrong down there?" I didn't give time for anyone else to answer and said, "I want to see you and these ladies won't permit that." He asked me to come down the hall and we talked for a long time.

Our discussion led to some movement. I got a list of all family members of the Brigadier and a brief description of each. I was surprised at the number. Even Bangladeshi household helpers' names were on the list. There were about fifteen in all. I returned my list to the Representative. He said, "I think we can pull this off."

I replied, "I also think we can pull it off."

A few days later, a Bangladeshi army jeep pulled up in front of our house and there was my friend. It was now 1974 and I had first met him in 1959. He had nothing but thanks.

Then, not long after that, our landlord came to a house next door for some business. He departed in a baby taxi and after a few hours there he stood at our door. He had gotten down from the baby taxi in a hurry and left a large amount of Bangladesh taka rolled up in a newspaper in the taxi. Even in U.S. dollars, it was a large amount. The amount was enough that I would not have ever made such a mistake.

The landlord and I got into my vehicle and drove to the place where he had gotten out of the little taxi. We asked many people about how we might locate that driver. Of course, in a busy city of a few million people, how were we going to locate one taxi driver?

We gave up and I went back to our house. I had hardly arrived home when a baby taxi pulled up, the driver telling me that a passenger of his had left a paper full of money in his taxi and he did not know what to do with it. I told him I knew the owner and would take the money to him. I gave the man a good financial reward and he departed. When I delivered the money, I never told my landlord that I had used my own money to reward the faithful man. Oh, I didn't go through all of that for money, did I? No, I didn't. Now, since I am writing about Muslims, kindly remember that driver was a poor Muslim man and the house owner was a wealthy Muslim man. If you are waiting for more, wait more and read the "Afterword" in this book.

During the summer of 1974, we had our annual meeting of those in our organization. As time came for us to return to our places of work across Bangladesh, we noted the water level was quickly rising in Dhaka and at the same time, higher areas were dusty. That told us that the rising water was coming from at least three sources other than local rainfall. One of those places was the melting snow from the massive Himalayan mountain range not many miles north of the northern border of Bangladesh. Rainfall had contributed to the melting snow in that mountain area. Streams of every size carried that water south. Even the large rivers contributed to the rapidly flowing water.

Another area which produced that flow of water was northeastern India. That water was carried into Bangladesh by two great rivers. One of those was the Brahmaputra which even brought water from China. The other huge flowing river was the Megna which carried water primarily from parts of northeast India. But possibly the greatest source of that rapidly flowing water was that from northwest India. The Ganges River brought most of the water from that area down near the border of Bangladesh. Then the main flow of the Ganges turned directly south and missed Bangladesh, but a part of Ganges split off and continued southeast into Bangladesh with a new name for that river, the Padma.

All of this water was on its way to the Bay of Bengal or the Indian Ocean. The river banks overflowed and in many places south of Dhaka it was difficult to understand where the rivers ended and the ocean began.

Eventually, most news sources seemed to agree that two-thirds of this new nation was covered with floods. Even many streets in the capital city were filled with water and enough to completely stop the flow of traffic. Some rain began to fall and this only added to the destruction.

After a few weeks, the water began receding. One value, if anyone is searching for values in such situation, was the enrichment of the rice fields as the water receded and left many good elements for enriching the soil.

But during the primary time of the flooding, tens of thousands of poor people whose little huts had been washed away began entering the capital city of Dhaka. There was simply no work for day laborers anywhere and in a few weeks, many of those people were without strength because some of them were living on an extremely small amount of food.

Of course, some relief and rehabilitation organizations began helping as best they could and many of those agencies were Christian organizations. I shall never forget a beautiful scene. I had gone to see how feeding was being done by one organization to which my group had given money. I had hardly arrived there when the President also arrived. He walked by where a Christian young Bangladeshi was passing out food. That young man never slowed his pace of getting that food to those desperate people and when the President saluted him, he simply bowed his head a short distance and kept passing out the food.

I loved the direct work which our organization, now the International Mission Board, began. There was a refugee camp just north of Dhaka. I can only say there were thousands of people who had been taken to that camp. The government quickly approved a project of our digging three large ponds or tanks. These were dug in low areas where the rain had left mud holes.

We organized the poor men who were living in that camp and who were able to do heavy labor. They were in teams of twenty. Each team had a leader and we had guards, people known to us, all over the area. Our primary task was to give work so these people could help themselves.

We were digging ponds for growing fish and for bathing facilities. Also, the dirt dug out in the beginning from those mud holes was used to supply foundations for houses and to raise the level of the roads in the camp. I must admit, I felt good about what we were doing.

It was amazing to see little shacks built quickly for businesses. We paid the workers, more than three thousand of them, one-half in money and the other half in wheat. The Bangladesh Secretary of Relief and Rehabilitation, had approved this project himself. We later learned that several times during working hours, he slipped into the camp just to see what was being done.

The camp did not become a perfect place for poor people to live and many died and there were always graves ready for use, but some real help was given. We understood that at least six people were buried in each grave, but we also understood that many were saved from physical death.

As I write I try to remember that as some of you read, you may forget that most of these people with whom we were involved were Muslims. But I also must add that we would have done the same amount and same kind of help had those being helped were Hindus or even Christians.

One afternoon I took leave from the camp and spent the afternoon traveling the streets of Dhaka. I was trying to understand what was happening to people from all across Bangladesh who had come there as desperate people. I have never apologized to anyone for my taking time to see for myself what was happening. That afternoon, I was walking only a short distance from the guest house and noted a particular woman who was living on the sidewalk with hundreds of others.

I noticed this woman as she caressed her baby lying on that sidewalk. Then, I noticed that woman put her face down on her baby's face. She suddenly lifted her head and screamed. A nearby gentleman described to me what had happened.

When that woman touched her baby with her hands she thought the baby felt cold. To better test her baby's situation, she put her face, which was more tender than her rough calloused hands, on that little one's face and that feeling told her that her baby was dead.

That same afternoon, I watched trucks going through the main streets of the city. Two men with large forks walked behind each truck. When a body would be located by the truck driver, he stopped the vehicle. With their pitch forks, the men lifted the body, tossed it into the truck, and moved on to the next body.

This was only about two years following that war that may have left three million people dead in a period of less than one year. Now in order to receive some international aid, the government was forced to give an estimate of the number of people who had died, not during the flood, but following that flood. I read one source which said that six hundred thousand people died during that time, about one year. The primary cause of death was starvation. Speaking only for myself, I say that I never hesitated to use money from our churches in the United States to attempt at least, to help people in such conditions. Of course, we worked and prayed for a better day for the Bangla people. Above all else, we wanted these blessed people to know Jesus, the Messiah, the Lord.

CHAPTER TWENTY
Meeting the Bangladeshi President

Few happenings in history could have been more heart-breaking than that of the many people dying in the streets and suburbs of Dhaka in 1974-1975. Some people, through the years, have asked me, "Do Christians usually die in such circumstances like those of other religions die?" With reference to Bangladesh, I say without apology that most Christians at least learn how to read and write and to do a particular job whether it is a high paying job or not. This helps much in times of disaster.

Then, some ask about government employment of Christians. With Bangladesh and Pakistan only being considered, I say that there are a few Christians who get government jobs. At one time in Pakistan, the Chief Justice of the highest court was a Christian. But anyone who is today familiar with news knows that while the government in Pakistan apparently does not persecute Christians, radical Muslims do. Churches are attacked and people killed.

But in Bangladesh, while the number of Christians is lower than those in Pakistan, very few, if any, have high government jobs. And I do know that in times of natural or man made disasters, Christians do not hesitate to help one another. Their holy book, the Bible, especially the New Testament or Good News, beckons them to help one another and to help all people in need. I hope they learn some of that because of their relationships to Christian missionaries.

However, I admit that I had much rather help train others so they can help themselves than to have them looking to me for help. Sometimes, it is not easy to help. A little later I will tell you about a development center which my group of missionaries began with strong support from our home organization. The purpose of that center was not to give things to people but help them, no matter how poor they were, to help themselves.

But in the greater area of that center's location, we were trying to help by sinking tube wells for all people. We simply marked the areas carefully and then located the wells geographically in fairness to all people regarding distance to, and between, the wells. But in one area where our plans called for the sinking of four wells, we were not permitted to sink even one well. This permission was refused by local Muslim leaders because they were not going to accept help from Christians. All we could do was move on in our quest to help.

In mid 1975, it seemed Dhaka and the country as a whole was doing much better. As a "foreigner," different governments always had my sympathy. We, as missionaries, were in our annual meeting. News reached us that down Mirpur Road, not far from where we were meeting in the guest house, the President of Bangladesh had been killed by Bangladeshi soldiers. When we had lived at the guest house for a time, we often saw him be driven by with only a motorcycle policeman leading his vehicle. In the mornings, we often watched for his car for we knew he would wave at us.

Of course, we loved him because of his suffering so many years in Pakistan jails. He was a person of freedom. We knew how to help—we prayed for his family and for his country and for the next leadership regardless of when that was to happen.

Regarding the Bangladeshi military in those early years, it appeared they were not united and rather than acting like their Hindu neighbor country, they seemed to think the military had some rights, which other citizens did not have. Please remember, I often had friends who were military leaders.

During those days of stress when many people felt insecure due to a lack of a strong national government, a group of Bangladeshi soldiers set up a machine gun just inside the wall of the guest house yard.

At that time, there were ten little children staying with their parents in the guest house and the house next door. Of all the things for a "foreigner" to do, I approached the officer in charge of the destructive looking machine gun and asked him to move it to another place. His reply was something like this, "We would never hurt people like you., but we will move it on down the street." In a few minutes we saw the machine gun being set up about a block further down Mirpur Road. The next day's newspaper told of how that machine gun crew was killed by another fighting group. I could only think of the kindness of that young officer when I had asked him to move the machine gun.

Finally, it seemed that a new leader was bringing the government under control. He appeared to rule well, but remember, I know little or nothing about such things. I did know that I loved Bangladesh almost as much as I loved my home country. Three of our five children were born there, and another arrived there when she was ten months of age and then another when he was twenty-one days old.

As a group of international missionaries, we seemed to be united in at least one area. We all knew we needed to do something that could help many people help themselves in good times and in bad times. So, our minds and our hearts were busy on what we might be able to do.

In May, 1981, we were having one of our missionary meetings. The primary reason for this meeting was to discuss and maybe come to some conclusion regarding our help in meeting both spiritual and physical human needs. That news reminded us of when we received the news that Sheikh Mujibur Rahaman had been killed in July, 1975. Now the news was that President Zia Rahman had been brutally killed by a group of Bangladeshi soldiers.

Years earlier, I had refused an invitation to meet Prime Minister Sheikh Mujib and that may have been my mistake. My friends and I had an appointment to meet with President Zia. That had been a wonderful meeting. However, it was not easy to schedule that meeting.

It happened like this: I knew one cabinet minister who had helped me before and I had been his friend. Well, I knew this minister favored little children, so Jill, who was then about eight years of age, and I went to his home for a visit. In just a few days' time, the appointment with the President had been made. Three of us missionaries were to represent twenty-one missionary organizations. I had always counted the great value of each of those organizations to the people of Bangladesh.

There was an Australian, a German and myself. But the day before our scheduled meeting, we learned the German missionary could not participate with us for some reason. But Geoff Ryall who was Australian and I went to the President's office for the appointment. When the exact time came for us to meet the President, an army major greeted us and told us we had ten minutes with the President. Immediately, I felt pressure because of the time factor.

We were graciously received by this gentleman. After the introductions and the understanding that we represented that number of organizations, I began presenting our matter rapidly. The President stopped me and said, "Why are you in such a big hurry?"

I apologetically said, "But Sir, what we have to discuss with you is a very serious matter to us and we understand we have only ten minutes with you."

With a somewhat serious expression he said, "Who told you that you had only ten minutes with me? I make those decisions."

I felt better with that and maybe a little more relaxed and said, "I think I should not tell you for someone might be in trouble if I did."

He replied, "He just might be in trouble."

Then President Zia looked at me and said, "You like chocolate cake and coffee, don't you?" Of course, that statement got a strong "yes." President Zia had visited the United States and had been treated graciously. He remembered being served chocolate cake and coffee, so Geoff and I were privileged to relax a few minutes.

Two cabinet members sat nearby during our entire visit but they entered the conversation only when the President asked a question. We talked about the missionary situation and it was evident that he had nothing personally against Christian missionaries. In fact, while serving in the army in the days of Pakistan, he had met missionaries on several occasions. We discussed the newly promulgated law which said that visas would be given for only two years and those would not be renewed. Some staff member had undoubtedly brought up this matter but it had not been fully discussed.

Apparently that staff member knew this was one way to rid the country of international missionaries. It was sure that law was going to be changed. The other matter was that of every missionary organization being registered and having a number of missionary positions approved. That was no problem. The other thing was we had to have budget approval each year and then a report to the government. But the primary concern of missionary organizations was the matter of limited time to two years in Bangladesh.

The President strongly said as if he were talking to a large audience, "No missionary has to leave this country." Or at least he said words to that effect. He then turned to one of the present cabinet members, the Minister of Religion and asked him if he could meet with us and representatives of all missionary organizations the next day. The Minister replied that he was fully scheduled for the next day. To our wonder and amazement, the President continued talking with us and then turned again to that Minister and said for him to meet with us and the others in the morning and he even gave the time. We had that meeting the next morning and at the time stated by the President.

I attended the dedication of a hospital where one of the leading medical professors and practicing doctors of the related hospital was a Methodist missionary from the United States. He also was a very dear friend of mine and that is why I had gotten an invitation for the dedication.

The place was filled with dignitaries from many nations. I was standing along a wall and knew very few people present. But as I was looking around the huge room, my eyes met the President's eyes. He motioned for me to come to him and I gladly and quickly did that.

He was busy but he said that he wanted to talk with the missionary who spoke to him in his own language, which Geoff and I had done in our meeting with him. He had also remembered that I had an eight year old daughter and he asked if I would bring her to a children's meeting which was held in a park near his office. I responded that I would be pleased to do that. Finally in the conversation he said, "If you missionaries ever have problems, please let me know."

President Zia was a friend of Christian missionaries. We were all shocked just like we had been when Prime Minister Sheikh Mujib had been killed. I knew many political leaders at that time but promised myself that I was going to keep my distance. I could not bear the thought of a high ranking government officer being killed so brutally. My friendship with civil servants was and had been on most occasions not supposed to be political.

Both Prime Minister Sheikh Mujib and President Zia would have been most pleased to see what we were able to do with the center which was called the Development Service Center. As I have said many times, we had to make sure that service at the Center was the kind that developed the ability of poor people to help themselves and it also helped others. The Center was sold recently but sold to a deeply concerned Christian man who now has as his director the same missionary who was the director when it was operated by our organization, The International Mission Board, SBC.

Though prolific in its production of fish, goats, and ducks, the Center was often the center of disturbances. For example, some local Muslims wanted to name a certain number of employees and at one time, by force, took control of the entire place. However, as they should have known, the Bangladesh Government honored what we had been doing, so their police responded to our call without hesitation. One of the involved men was in hiding for almost a year fearing what the police would do to him.

There were constant problems, probably because of the Center's massive value. The two agriculturalists who had been in charge seemed to constantly find better ways for poor landless people to be able to help themselves.

About four years ago, I visited the center. I was pleased that I had been a part of such a venture. I was shown how a family could live on a plot of land, maybe no more than one-tenth of acre and have a small cow or a goat, four or five ducks, vegetables grown on that plot and more. I also learned that those families could live in a little house on that plot and do everything that was to be done. Hatching a particular fish could been done and then those little fish would grow in a tiny pond of water. A special feed for the animals could also be grown.

Though, at times even now, I know that my physical health and mental health were greatly disturbed by some of the assaults on what we were attempting and doing for the good of humanity. At the same time, we were building self-confidence, often in illiterate poor people. I find myself thanking Lord God Almighty, with whom I can converse in simple language, for His giving me the privilege of being in a land of Islam and yet free to be involved in so much for His glory.

When giving thanks, mostly privately, I always remember that any and every witness for Him is never wasted for He uses all of that for Himself. In my mind, there is no doubt about that. My living, loving and personal God is not like anyone else. He stands alone with all power in Heaven and on earth and is accessible to us as mortal human beings.

In 1985, a lesser tidal wave struck the coast of Noakhali District. Bill Burkhalter and R.T. Buckley responded beautifully in helping to restore the livelihood of many people in that area. They built boats for fishing in the ocean coastal areas and employed local people to make fishing nets.

All of this produced food, but not only food. This project produced work for many people, as it established some of those who had lost most, with a brighter future. Also, ducks were delivered to the people who had lost so much. My dedicated colleagues even rebuilt some small houses for the poorest of people.

They sank tube wells in that ocean area where fresh water was difficult to locate and they found it, which is sometimes not an easy task. It seems that ocean area water, no matter how deep in the soil it is found, likes to absorb more salt. But fresh water is in the greater area. Often, however, nothing but diligence in the search can locate that water.

I had the privilege of helping deliver approximately thirty-nine truck loads of sheep to the area. Richard purchased the sheep at the DS Center and prepared them with good feeding for several days. Then he and his staff loaded six trucks filled with sheep and just at darkness, those trucks were escorted to the main road in front of the house where my family lived.

My job then was to ride most of the time in the lead truck. We journeyed from darkness to the break of day to reach our destination. I had no experience with truck drivers, but through ups and downs over that long nighttime traveling, we managed to reach the final destination. In charge then would be R.T. or Bill and as soon as the distribution was completed we were more than ready for a return to Dhaka.

That kind of delivery covered the first four trips, or twenty-four truck loads of sheep. The fifth trip was a difficult one. Bill and I were together on the final delivery, with the location point being an island several miles from the main coast. We thought we had sufficient space on two large boats, but after we had loaded one boat, workers from different areas began to arrive to cross that body of water and reach their homes. They filled the second boat.

The sheep were hungry and had now been in trucks for about twenty-four hours. Our only choice was to unload the rest of the sheep and surround them with guards, for night was approaching. We had a few guards with us and hired more as one of us was to travel with that first boat and the other one had to work out details to load the remainder of the sheep on another boat early in the morning. We had to work with the tide rising and falling. So, in helping others, we were learning about the land in which we lived.

With his boat load of sheep, Bill had to depart, for soon the tide would begin to lessen and there were little islands just under the ocean water at high tide, but then those islands seemed to rise up as the water level lowered. I waved bye to Bill and watched as his boat moved out of sight.

So, here I was with not a village in sight with three truck loads of sheep. All six trucks had now departed for Dhaka. We organized the sheep as best we could. They were tired so that helped. Guards were to keep the sheep together and one of them was to let me know if problems developed. I eventually found some food which helped. Then I found a place to rest on a wooden cot with no cover. I didn't sleep that night and was called once since apparently some people from a distant village decided they might be able to take the sheep from us, which they couldn't. We were getting tougher in this kind of work so we simply informed those near-by robbers that they had to fight us to get the sheep. In a sense, or maybe without much sense, I was so tired I actually felt like enjoying this struggle. Let me just move along by saying no one took even one sheep from us that long tiring night. As the light began to shine, a boat arrived from the island and we loaded the sheep and we traveled quickly across the body of high tide water.

Bill greeted us upon our arrival. We arranged for a government officer to supervise the distribution according to a list of names. We knew he had to be correct because on a small island everyone knows what everyone else is doing. So, before the tide got too low, Bill and I were on our way back to his house. Since I was driving and because I knew I could not sleep that night, after a wonderful meal served by Joyce, Bill's wife, I moved out toward Dhaka, about a five hour trip. I felt as though I could sleep for days when I reached home just before the third night of that trip ended. I hadn't slept at all during those three nights.

We had one more journey to make before ending this all-important project. This time we had nine trucks loaded with more than one thousand sheep. We had never traveled "through the fields and dirt roads" before, but we would make it somehow. Bill and I again had my van for making traveling easier. We arrived just before noon at what seemed to be the end of our truck's advance. It had rained and the dirt roads and fields were muddy.

So, we had many suggestions—one person suggested that we distribute the sheep in the area where the trucks had to turn back toward a better road. The area where we were had been hit by that cyclonic tidal wave and many houses had been destroyed as well as most animals. However, it was our assignment to get these nine truck loads of sheep to another island like the one on the previous trip. We were determined to do what we had begun for this journey. Our purpose was to deliver the sheep to the boat which would take those sheep to the island.

Our determination to get the sheep to the boat was helped by a government officer who lived on that island. He had been part of the original plan as to where each trip's sheep were to be delivered. So, when he understood we were ready to walk the sheep for about ten miles, he joined us. As we hired local extra guards, that government officer became more courageous.

So, when sheep were cut out of the group by those who were attempting to take them from us, the government man always joined the pursuit of lost sheep and brought them back to our mud road. I admit people like him gave me added strength even though I was driving my van along that mud road and that wasn't too great a strain on me. Though often the vehicle had to be pushed to get it through the extremely muddy areas, I could only think how much we were to need the vehicle after the sheep were loaded on the boat.

After about four and one-half hours of driving those sheep, we arrived at the coast where the boat was to dock. We unloaded those weaker sheep which had been in my van and then I moved back to the end of the line splashing mud as I went. Several trips like that first one had given me courage and hope. We were doing what some would call "the impossible." Just before night the last of the sheep were loaded on the boat. I had given my word that when the boat arrived, the dock person was to tell the captain of the boat to wait until I reached there with the last of the sheep.

One of the proudest men I have ever seen in action was that government man as he walked up the gang plank and waved goodbye to us as the boat began to move out into the ocean. It was as if he had won life's greatest prize. I later learned that he had told the people from his home island that he would be coming with the sheep and they were depending on him. Most of my passengers were asleep as we started toward Bill's house in the vehicle which again splashed mud everywhere. The job was done and since I had only gone two nights without sleep on that trip, I had no complaints.

CHAPTER TWENTY-ONE
Driving in Bangladesh

Since retiring from the International Mission Board in 1992, I have returned to Bangladesh on four occasions. But I have not driven a vehicle in Dhaka, the capital of Bangladesh, nor have I desired to drive there. In our later years in Dhaka, driving there became very difficult because of the different kinds of vehicles going through the streets. Often some of the persons in charge of the different kinds of conveyances did not ever consider others but they seemed to be only attempting to get to their destination as quickly as possible.

An example of the traffic difficulty is the bullock drawn cart. I think it is an amazing feat to understand how that vehicle gets through the streets. The bullocks, of course, are not necessarily in any hurry and from what I have experienced, it is not an easy task to speed them up even one iota. Then, along comes an elite government officer in his vehicle and his driver seems to think he has a priority wherever he drives. However, neither the bullocks nor their driver are impressed so their pace remains the same—steady but sure.

While changes are happening rapidly in traffic regulations, it is an almost impossible task to improve the flow of that traffic. For years, Dhaka was known as the city with the world's largest number of cycle rickshaws. Though many main streets no longer permit the rickshaws, they are in the city on other streets so traffic moving on to the main streets is naturally congested.

I was traveling with a group of Bangladeshi Christians and we were entering the congested area of the city. We came upon an accident in which many people had been injured. There were no ambulances. All of my friends asked me to take as many wounded people my vehicle could manage. We literally filled the van with those injured people. One man, who seemed to know several of the injured ones, rode with me to the hospital. I did very well, I thought, in managing the traffic in getting to the main hospital of the city.

The uninjured passenger quickly called for help in getting the injured people into the emergency area of the hospital. Then we began unloading them. I watched as the procedure seemed to be moving very well. But all of a sudden, a Muslim woman began cursing me in her language and telling everyone why Allah would surely punish me for injuring all of those people. I often have wondered about that woman...was she expecting me to give her money to stop her flow of ugly language? Had she been practicing this when other accidents had happened? Maybe or maybe not.

The kind gentleman who had ridden with me had been so gracious and he didn't lose his graciousness. He did his best to tell the woman that I was only helping those people and that I had nothing to do with the horrible accident. Anyway, in some situations, you just can't win.

While I was using the water hose to clean the blood from the van, I thought, "If you don't get involved, you can't help in most situations." So, the next time I came upon a similar situation, I made at least one different choice and it was more pleasant if events relating to such incidents can be pleasant.

This accident happened west of the city about fifteen miles from the congested area. At first, when the traffic slowed, I could not detect what was happening. Then I began to see civilians directing traffic.

As my vehicle moved up closer where I could be seen by one of the helping men; he screamed to his friends in his language by saying, "This one will not help us."

I moved my vehicle forward and yelled to that man, "This one will help." With that he began apologizing. They began loading my vehicle with badly injured people. This situation was very difficult, for a passenger bus had gone off the road and down a high embankment and turned over.

It was a sad situation and I didn't have an uninjured man to ride with me. But I knew I wasn't going to the same hospital but to one nearer and better able to care for these people. It was an orthopedic hospital. It was in its early years of work and I had friends, doctors and others who worked there. I had hardly stopped the van when someone cried out, "It's Mr. McKinley. He has been in an accident."

Well, we got that part corrected but the response was so different. Medical people seemed to come from every direction to help. Muslim friends, one after another and some of them were those who cleaned the floors said, "Oh, Sir, we are glad you were not hurt in the accident."

A Muslim staff member of that hospital said, "Sir, we expect you to help others." There certainly was no abusive cursing that day. We also win some, don't we?

Betty and I heard the noise even though we were in our living room. There had been an accident on the road about two hundred feet from where we were sitting. I ran to the door and then crossed the road. At about the same time I arrived, a Muslim motorcycle policeman had arrived.

What I quickly understood was that a large truck approached two motorcycles from the rear and had run over them. The bodies of those two drivers were mangled. Much of the blood began to dry but more blood made its way out of the two bodies. I felt deeply for the policeman. He was so horrified that he seemed to hardly know what to do.

The policeman asked if someone would help him load the two bodies into a baby-taxi. No one replied so I said, "Sir, I am willing to help you."

He looked at me and said only one word, "You?" and I replied with one word, "Yes." We placed the two mangled bodies into the little baby taxi and as we did blood seemed to squirt everywhere. Then the policeman said to me, "I will take the bodies to the nearest hospital but I fear they will not take them."

So I asked the policeman, "Do you want me to help you?" I think his fear about the entire matter was that the two dead men were foreigners of some kind. That might complicate things, especially since the truck driver had disappeared and all of the people around the scene affirmed that he was a Bangladeshi. Why he had run over those two as he did, no one knew.

I got my mini van out quickly and followed the baby-taxi and the motorcycle policeman. Sure enough, the hospital attendant said that the bodies must be taken to the Medical College Hospital. The policeman turned to me and said, "How can I get the bodies to that hospital? They can't be taken such a long distance in this baby-taxi."

I had a ready answer which I think startled the policeman for I said, "We can take them in my vehicle." He didn't reply with a verbal answer but the soft slight smile on his face told me thanks, but I didn't need thanks.

He again asked for volunteers to help him lift the bodies into my van but no one responded so I walked up and took hold of the top body and he immediately began lifting along with my slight help.

In a few minutes we were ready to move on to the other hospital. As the policeman rode his motorcycle and led the way for me, I realized I was covered with blood. My hands seemed like they had been butchered and blood was all over my clothing. I looked closely at the policeman riding a short distance in front of me and he looked just as bloody.

As soon as we arrived at the hospital I asked the policeman for his permission to search the bodies for some kind of identification. Immediately I found a telephone number written in English. However, when I noted some other papers I realized that even though I did not know that language, I had seen enough to know that it was Thai. With the permission of the policeman, I called that number and the reply came from the Thailand Embassy. The Embassy promised to have someone at the hospital within thirty minutes and they did.

After the phone call, I told the policeman that I was going to return to my home but he asked that I wait and explain to the Embassy people what had happened. I did that—how could anyone do less for such a kind, considerate, and faithful policeman?

The Thai Embassy person arrived. We talked briefly and he understood the nervousness of the policeman. He took my telephone number. Then he seemed to be unable to say "thanks" enough. I wanted to go. I had done my thing. So I said good bye to my two new friends, the policeman and the Thai, and departed.

It was a hot day and the sun was bearing down forcefully. I thought there is no way I can tolerate this odor all the way back to our house but I did. As soon as possible, I had the water hose going full blast and sprayed the inside of the van as if it were the outside. Red water had flowed, but the vehicle was somewhat clean.

The following day a telephone call came from the Thai Embassy. It was their staff member again on the phone. The two young men with families back in Thailand were in Bangladesh working with an aluminum company and the Embassy was preparing to send the bodies back to Thailand, possibly even that day.

All of this was a difficult situation for an evangelical missionary. I did not like to be involved so closely to the death of any person whether from Bangladesh or Thailand or any other place in my God's great world, if those persons died without "knowing" my Lord Jesus the Messiah. As I worked, I offered a prayer for the kind policeman and for the families of those two young men who had died in that accident in front of my home.

While our children were familiar with Muslim weddings in Bangladesh, they had not been to a wedding which was western. An Australian woman worked in our organization's office as a secretary and of course our colleagues had given us the information about her wedding which was to be in Dhaka. Though we were not able to do everything we wanted to do for our children, at least most of the time we attempted to do those special things which someday would help them in preparation for their return to their home-land. So, Betty and I agreed we should take them on that one hundred mile, or five hour, journey and return the same day. That way they would miss only one day of their home-schooling.

By six o'clock in the morning we were on our way. At the first ferry stop, we had a perfect breakfast. The hot chocolate which Betty had prepared before our departure was still hot.

The children loved the hot chocolate and I have no doubt that they loved their mother more because of the extra trouble she often took to do the better things for them. Betty and I drank hot coffee.

With an over-abundant supply of food, we feasted. If the children tired of eating, we knew they could complete the task later, for we had two more ferries before reaching Dhaka.

The wedding was in the early afternoon and after the informal reception, we were on our way home. We crossed the last of the ferries as darkness fell. The darkness that night was deep but that only made the headlights of the van seem more forceful as they broke through that darkness and gave us good light for driving on the slightly more than one lane highway.

Betty and Wade were in the front seat with me and Wade was sleeping in his mother's lap with his face turned upward. The other three had sufficient space in the back two seats. The headlights showed me a large herd of cattle in the distance. I slowed down somewhat and noticed that the cattlemen were herding the cattle to the side of the road. So it appeared that we could move on without hesitating. But I was wrong. We were probably doing about forty miles per hour.

All of a sudden, I saw a man plunging across the road. Apparently, he was not related to the cattle herd and for some reason, we later learned, he saw the headlights of the approaching vehicle and the cattle on the opposite side of the road. He felt he needed to cross the road in front of the vehicle because there was no room for him between the cattle and the vehicle.

We soon learned that young man had literally jumped in the air in front of our vehicle and we had struck him. The front windshield scattered into Wade's face and Betty's lap, but they were uninjured. The headlights were gone. I stopped the vehicle only to call out, "I will return." In the middle of the night with your family present in a vehicle, I knew better than to hesitate knowing that we could be attacked and maybe seriously injured or worse by a mob of men.

In the darkness of the night and all of the confusion, no one probably heard my words and had they heard those words, they would not have depended upon them. Men were screaming and trying to regroup their cattle. We later learned they had no relationship to the injured man.

We moved on to a police station about ten miles away and how blessed we were in such a situation. The moon began to show us the road. We reached the police station and I had everything planned—I asked Betty to bring the children into the station. I was talking to the officer-in-charge when Betty and the children walked in. That policeman was trying to convince me that I had struck a cow and not a man, but I knew better. Since I was speaking in his language and not mine, he had to take me seriously. I asked for four policemen to accompany me back to the scene of the accident.

Betty and the children remained at the station as we five drove back to the scene. When we got there, we saw no cattle, no injured man, and no body. The four policemen assured me that I had struck a cow and that cow moved on with the herd which was now probably in a nearby village. I did not accept that. We drove slowly, watching for anyone who might have some information.

All of a sudden, a rickshaw pulled on to the main road. The top of the rickshaw was turned down so I could see two men in the seat with one lying with his head in the lap of the other one. We stopped. We had found the man we had hit. A village doctor had bandaged his head and other parts of his body and his friend in the rickshaw was taking him to his home some miles away.

We soon had the two of them in the vehicle with the four policemen and me. We were back at the station in about another one-half hour. As we arrived at the station, the kind man accompanying his friend kept saying he did not want to go into the station but I convinced him the police would not do any harm to his friend or to him. I also convinced him that in just a few minutes, we would be on our way to the hospital in Comilla. It was interesting to watch the men at the Chandina police station as we walked in with the four policemen and the friend of the injured man.

The police seemed to be dumb-struck for they never replied to anything I said. Neither did they hinder us. We reloaded and moved on toward Comilla about twelve miles away. As we drove, we were able to talk with the friend.

He said the man had seen the cattle, the lights of the van and felt he could cross the road before we reached the spot. So he blamed no one but himself.

If the police had been shocked, the hospital attendants seemed just as shocked. Betty and the children entered the hospital with the injured man and his friend and while a doctor was being called, I did what I could to make the victim more comfortable. The doctor looked at the injured man, at Betty and the children and my interpretation of this silent question was, "What on earth is happening, it is past midnight?"

In a few minutes the doctor gave his report. There was no serious injury., but they were willing to keep the man and release him in the morning, which meant to me he was willing to release him when daylight came. I had only one statement to the doctor, "Please keep him until I return early in the morning from Feni, our home." He agreed to that.

We drove on toward Feni which was about forty miles or maybe one and one-half hour away. We arrived at Feni around two o'clock. We had attended a beautiful informal wedding and had crossed six rivers on six ferries to get home. We had injured a man and even feared that we had killed him, but we hadn't. We had driven about eighty miles in the middle of the night without headlights, and we had reached home safely. That journey had taken about twenty hours. We could only give thanks again to our God who manages well in our different situations.

After about four hours, I was on the road again returning to the hospital in Comilla. The same doctor was on duty and informed me that he was ready to dismiss the patient. During the night the patient's friend had told him about our family. He was sorry that he had caused us so much trouble. Then I decided to ask him a question as to why he ran in front of our vehicle.

This man's reply was that he had seen the vehicle lights and he saw that mass of cattle. He said that he didn't know where to go since he was approaching the side of the road where the cattle were. Then he decided that the best thing to do was to run fast and cross before our vehicle reached his crossing. He was surely sorry for all that had happened.

I knew he would not be able to work for several days or maybe even several weeks so I asked him if I could give him money to help him. He refused by saying all that happened was his fault so he could not take money from me. I understood his thinking but was able to convince him to take money for lunch and some for a few days. As he and his friend walked away, I climbed into the van and began driving back to Feni. As I drove home I knew we had done right by taking our children to the wedding. God would work everything else out.

CHAPTER TWENTY- TWO
Peace-Time Difficult Days
A Messy Situation but Good Results

My camera was ready but what I saw was not what I wanted. I wanted this picture to show smiles on the faces of the two Christian women. I knew that according to their tradition that they should not smile, but down deep I knew I wanted smiles to indicate the joy in their lives which they had found in Jesus.

But the story behind my knowing these two women was not an everyday story that most people ever experience. I had known these women and their families for about ten years and they had been followers of Jesus for most of that time. Now, as I was taking more pictures than usual, I knew that within a few months, Betty and I were returning to the United States for retirement from our organization.

These two were of the best examples of people who had truly found a new life through Jesus the Savior. In the years before I had the privilege of making their acquaintance, they had been badly abused sexually. They were what are often called "low-caste Hindus."

I had learned over the years that some wealthy, educated Muslim men from the big city had learned about these Hindu women, especially after they became Christians. Most of these men had families and maybe some of them had influence in politics and other areas in the life of elite people.

Rather than use and abuse the "street women" in the city who might carry some of the worst kinds of sexual disease, these sorry men began to look elsewhere. I learned that such men have connections and that for a small amount of money they can often get what and whom they want. The more I learned, the angrier I became. I asked a few Muslim friends whom I knew I could trust about my getting involved in this situation. Most of them gave me the go-ahead, so I went ahead.

I knew there was only a remote possibility that I might lose my right to remain in Bangladesh but I had been warned of that happening. I knew without a doubt that some of my good Muslim friends would never betray me, so I moved into an unknown area of international mission work. I had no training in such situations.

So, these "big city" men learned how to find clean women and apparently made the most of that opportunity. There were times in which I wondered about my involvement but most of the time I was determined to clean up the situation. First, let me tell you about how I learned of the fear of these women of those big city "boys."

You can tell, of course, as you have read the earlier part of this chapter that this entire thing made me deeply angry. The first time I traveled to this area was a most difficult experience. I was traveling with a Christian co-worker. This was a total journey of about six miles and we had walked that distance and you can understand that both of us were tired.

My friend was much more nicely dressed than I was. I usually dressed down when going into an area where primarily poor people lived. So I can only guess how we appeared. My Christian friend was dressed more like the rascal men who came from the big city. I was dressed more like the casual "Hollywood" type. Hollywood? How would poor village people, primarily Hindu, who had never been to a movie, know anything about Hollywood? Somewhere along the way they would have heard story after story that would have begun with a young man who had gone to the big city and seen a sexually explicit American movie. So I was like one of the movie's casually dressed men who maybe appeared one or two times in such a film. But those kinds of stories travel rapidly.

The two women friends, along with about ten more of their friends, were gathering wood for cooking in that area where trees were located. Suddenly, my friend and I appeared. Those women saw us, screamed, and ran toward their houses. I felt horrible. My colleague told me something of what they may have thought when they saw us. He knew about stories being circulated in many rural areas that I did not know. Now I knew and I didn't like what I had heard.

At my suggestion the two of us turned around and began walking that six mile journey to our vehicle. As we walked, I thought of all the disruption we had caused to those twelve women. I felt bad about the entire situation.

I worked through this and my help came from my colleague as we walked and then from Betty. I determined my God would override all of that ugly incident and somehow that He would make it possible for my friend and me to share His love with those who wanted a better way of life.

When I prepared to take that photo of the two women about ten years later, there was an all-together different situation. You see, the two were now my sisters in Jesus the Christ. My colleague and I had walked into that area dozens of times and shared God's kind of love with those women and their husbands. There were about a dozen little churches, and all of them were from the same group.

Much had happened between that first day and the day nearing my retirement. First, as I stated earlier in this chapter, I consulted some of my good Muslim friends whom I knew would stand with me in the event I got into difficulty when confronting some of the so called big city men. But before that, I learned that one local wealthy village Muslim man had been involved and without him the city men would not even been to able to enter that area.

I had a challenge. I was learning about some other ugly incident nearly every time I went into that area. I succeeded to spread the word and I did that by simply saying it to any and all whom I met in that area. Some of those men from the city and the local rascal, I knew, would hear what I began to say to anyone who would listen to me. In that area, word began to come to me that some of the local Muslim wives were pleased to hear what I was attempting.

Could you imagine such a thing happening? Absolutely! As I talked, or some might say run off at the mouth, I began to hear stories about Muslim wives I would never be able to meet face to face, who were commending me for my efforts at cleaning up some of the bad things which were happening. One story of one brave Muslim woman describes this.

One day I decided to walk by myself into a village area where only Muslims lived. I had been told the exact house of the local Muslim who was the agent of the city men. I knew the husband was not at home. I did not go to the door of that house but called out from one side where there was no door or window of the house. The wife in that house answered. She said something like this, "Oh yes, Mr. McKinley, we know who you are and we are pleased with what you are doing. We Muslim wives talk much about the good this will do us. So, we have determined that we will do all we can while you are doing what you can do."

I could have shouted. My God had been working in all of this mess so I would take care that He be given the glory for all that was happening. That women said more and it was something like this, "Mr. McKinley, you know that inside the walls of our houses, we Muslim women have much authority. We can make it unbearable for our husbands if it becomes necessary." I knew it had become necessary.

But how could this happen? How could a western Christian man talk with a very conservative Muslim woman and not worry about the results? So how could I not care who knew about the conversation? Openness, not face to face, but through the walls of a nice bamboo house, was the way to do it. But there is much more to the story.

One day I suggested to Betty that we load two bicycles into the van which was assigned to me. We could travel on a main road and if there was no rainfall in the area, we could probably ride in the vehicle to a point within two or three miles of the village destination.

As we began driving on the dirt road, we discovered it had rained in that area. That meant trouble for the bikes. We moved forward but not for long. The road was simply too slick for the vehicle. So we unloaded the bikes and I placed a long screw driver in my back pocket. About every one-half mile we stopped to clean the mud out from under the little metal parts covering the upper area of the tires. It grew tiresome, but the screw driver was helpful in cleaning out some of the mud which was hindering the movement of the bike tires.

When we turned off the main road on to a village road, the situation was better. A few minutes after we entered that village road, we arrived at our destination. It was apparent that the news was traveling rapidly as to how we had arrived in their village.

Of course, these kind people saw their first ever Caucasian woman and that woman, of all the unheard of things, had ridden into their village on a bike. You would have thought Betty was queen of that area. They rubbed her arms and shoulders. She received a perfect welcome.

My purpose worked. I had proof I was a married man and my wife did not hesitate to travel a most difficult journey to arrive at their village with her husband. Through all of that mess, I had no doubt that those women had cleared me of any bad thoughts they may have had in the past.

For months, every time I entered their village they wanted to know when Betty was coming again to be with them. The Muslim women, especially some of the rascal group's wives, got to meet Betty that day. They talked freely about common things and left the messy stuff for Betty's husband.

Though many Hindu people in that area continued coming to know Jesus as Savior, I also continued with that effort against the Muslim rascal group. Betty did not have the opportunity to meet the wife of the big trouble maker on her historical visit, but on other visits, I again talked with that woman through the bamboo walls of her house.

Looking back over the years, I remember so well listening to the conversation Betty had with one of the Muslim women. That woman was cooking food on an open fire in the yard. You would have thought that was the most important thing for a once in a lifetime conversation. As Betty's husband, I can only say that their conversation was on a very high level. The proof came during a later visit when I met that woman's husband for the first time. I did not hesitate to tell him unless he corrected his life-style and stopped troubling other women, I would have the police come and arrest him.

Now I know that what I said to that man was big talk, and I do not know how the police would have responded to my threat to the man, but it is possible they might have done exactly what I asked them to do. However, the police would have to walk at least six miles in and six miles out to fulfill my request. How could I have pulled that off? I would have talked with one of my highly ranked police friends in the capital city and if he did not respond, I would have gone to another friend and tried the same.

I knew God expects the best from all of us and if He wanted to use me in a messy situation like this one, then I was ready and had been ready for months. In many of my private times, I find myself talking with my God about people like these mentioned in this chapter, only a part of whose story I have been telling. In anything as moral as this is, I had a sufficient number of Muslim leaders whom I have no doubt, would stand with me in what I did. Some might even say, "Jim did what I might not do but he did what we believe is right."

Oh, I almost forgot. My camera was ready. I asked a simple question of my two "sisters." "Do you remember the first time you saw me?" Smiles moved over their faces and I got a beautiful picture.

CHAPTER TWENTY-THREE
The Good and the Bad

I was sitting on a very small cane mat on a dirt floor. There were about fifteen men who had become believers in Jesus the Messiah sitting on a large mat facing me. Most of those men I had not met until we began a study on the responsibility of the local church.

Speaking of being pleased...I was more than pleased, if such is possible, to have a responsible opportunity like this. These men, formerly Hindus, had a tremendous responsibility. Though they had come to know Jesus through the witness of other former Hindus, they now had the tremendous obligation or joy of sharing their new life with others in their ethnic group or people group. I was sitting there with my Bangla Bible in my lap doing my best to give them some help in their new role as ministers of Jesus the Christ.

All of a sudden, a very nicely dressed man with a long flowing beard walked in and without any introduction began calling out for one person who was considered the leader of that group of about fifteen men. Those fifteen men never made any movement nor did they speak even one word to the man. Those fifteen respected that I was their teacher and people like them highly respect teachers of most kinds. Hence, they did not know how to respond to such an abrupt disturbance of this teaching situation.

Of course, since I was in my thirty-third year of living in that culture, I knew it was my responsibility to respond to the man who had disturbed our process of teaching and learning. I spoke to the man with words like this, "Would you kindly move away for we are doing a very sacred thing? We are studying the Bible." I used language I thought he would understand as a Muslim.

Also I knew that we probably had big trouble, but I had no idea what procedure that man was going to follow. But he did depart. I was probably at least fifteen years older than he was and I knew that gave me some advantage in such an ugly situation.

As I continued teaching, my mind was troubled by what he possibly might do against those kind men I was attempting to teach. I was also thinking that those fifteen were no longer able to concentrate.

We stopped our lesson and had a cup of hot tea. I always counted a cup of hot tea as one of my God's great blessings. It just seemed to clear the throat and help relax the body as it moved through your mouth and down into your stomach. At least, for me, that hot tea did help. I began asking the leader of the group who the man was who had done a very improper thing by disturbing our teaching and learning. The group knew him well.

He was a Hindu convert to Islam and I learned that he was greatly disturbed because many Hindus in his area were not becoming Muslims but were becoming followers of Jesus the Messiah. This had disturbed him, I learned because primarily it was a huge embarrassment to him. Though I had not the fortune of being involved in telling those fifteen about the Jesus the Christ of the cross, I was pleased to be associated with them.

That day and most of the time when I went into an area like this, especially where there were new followers of Jesus, I had someone with me with both spiritual power and a good amount of physical power. My fellow believer that day was extremely nervous. He had enough understanding that in a situation like this, there possibly could be some violent behavior.

Later, I learned in conversation with him that he was sure the Muslim man and his friends were going to physically attack the two of us. I was not sure his feelings were correct but he had good understanding of such situations since he had experienced such activity before.

Nevertheless, after drinking a second cup of hot tea, I was ready to return to my teaching role. All of the fifteen seemed ready to continue, at least until something else happened. Nothing else happened and after a long teaching session, we shared a good lunch and then my friend and I prepared to depart.

We had two fears as we began walking. The first was that we had to walk down a dirt path which ran in front of a large mosque. The second fear was this man, the former Hindu, now a Muslim leader, might lead others to attack those new followers of Jesus.

We talked as we walked. After walking maybe one-quarter of a mile, we not only noted the mosque on the right side of our path but probably about fifty feet from the path, we also saw that man and a group standing on the path with no possibility for us to proceed if we remained on the path. I would not claim that I had been in such a situation before but I had been in similar situations.

Immediately I knew what I was going to do. My fellow-path walker was younger and much stronger physically than I, but I said to him as we walked, "When I give the signal, you quickly step into the ditch on the left side and continue walking but walk even faster." Then as my colleague stepped into the ditch, I followed him but remained between him and the mob. I knew they would probably hesitate to strike me first so I had to attempt to protect my friend.

We continued walking in the ditch. With a half smile on his face, my friend said, "We do funny things, don't we?" I looked back as we stepped back on the path and it was apparent that we had startled the mob.

I said to my friend, "Are you ready to run?" I knew he was able to run faster and much farther than I but I also was ready to run, so off we went. Our boat was no more than a mile away. The boatman was ready and off we went. We knew we were physically safe, for the time at least.

As we had been running I had heard the leader of that group scream out loudly, "We will take your friends to the mosque on Sunday and make Muslims out of them. Don't you ever return to this area." Near where we had parked our van there was a police station. The officer-in-charge was not present but we did tell some of his officers what had happened. The only reply from them was something like, "We know about him. He is half-crazy."

That was Friday afternoon. We arrived back at our homes later but I could not seem to get my mind on anything except what had happened that day. In thinking about what had happened, I realized what could happen to the fifteen, their families and other friends in that area who were new believers in Jesus the Messiah.

The next day I talked at length with local Baptist leaders. Then I talked with international missionaries of other groups seeking their counsel about what I should do. The agreement definitely was that I must not forsake those local new believers. So what do I do? I began preparing a letter addressed to the local police station which my friend and I had visited for a few minutes. I also made copies of that letter for many police who had very high ranks. I knew this would help the local station near the mosque to take action to protect our believer friends.

I got in touch with my colleague who had gone through the Friday experience with me and he agreed to travel with me to that area where big trouble might be in the making. By nine o'clock Sunday morning we had arrived at the police station.

The officer-in-charge was present. He had already sent a few of his policemen to the area of trouble. However, he assured us he would quickly arrange for additional police to be sent. Then I told him that my friend and I would go with those police. He gave a solid no to our going.

The more I talked with that officer, the more I understood about the mosque leader and his local involvement. There was little doubt that the police were wishing that man had never become a Muslim or as one said, "He really hasn't become a true Muslim." Well, I never responded to statements like that, but left their thoughts entirely to them.

I returned to that area several times and was always greeted at the police station. Later it was reported that the man with whom we had been so deeply involved had moved on to another area. That experience had definitely involved both the good and the bad.

Even today, I emotionally tire as I re-experience some of those days. But way down in my soul, I can only thank my God for so many wonderful days, weeks, months, and years spent in living with Muslims and getting to know many of them well. I continue to remember my deep feeling that no positive witness for the Living God is ever wasted.

As best as I can remember, the following experience happened in my thirty-third year in Bangla land. It may have been my deepest involvement where I could have or as some might say, should have, lost my right to remain in that land that I came to love so much.

A gracious pastor came to me early one morning. He knew that if he came early enough, we could talk before I departed for rural areas. I was needed more in those rural areas than at home or even in studying the things of God.

Near the church building were several houses of Christians and Hindus which had been bulldozed as if they were trash. They had been bulldozed by an Imam, or leader of a mosque, although I'm not sure he deserves that title.

This man who lived in his own six story building with his private mosque located on the top wanted to make the area into a park. I am sure that he did not have permission in writing from any government officer, but he had hired the bulldozer and supervised the destruction of about one hundred little houses which may have been built on government land.

So when this pastor asked me to kindly help in this situation, I did ask other local pastors and missionaries from other groups to advise me. The primary answer I received from these friends was, "You may get kicked out of the country if you get too deeply involved."

My reply was something like this, "Helping others might be a good reason for being kicked out." Then I went with my pastor friend to the site of the destruction of those little houses.

I wanted to talk with that Imam. I asked one person who was employed by him to ask if I could talk with him in his office. The man returned and said the Imam was too busy to talk with me. Then I tried what may have been a dumb thing, but at least it was an effort to speak with that man. I had carefully studied the story of Ahab and Jezzebel in the Old Testament and I intended to tell that man he had done a very bad thing against some of the poorest people in Bangladesh.

So I climbed upon a nearby wall with my camera. I tried, but not too successfully, to appear to be an international reporter. However, that didn't have any effect. Finally, I sent a note telling him I was an international missionary and I understood his language ,so if we talked there would be no problem. That didn't work. That Imam wasn't about to "get himself dirty" talking with a "little person" like me.

I turned to my pastor friend and apologized for my failure. Then a beautiful thing happened. The pastor asked me to walk to his near-by house. He gave me a wonderful cup of hot tea that quieted my spirit a little at least. This helped me not to feel so sad when I left the destruction of those houses which had included many of the earthly possessions of some in Bangladesh who were among the poorest people in this land.

A beautiful thing happened as I walked away. The pastor rubbed my arms and my shoulders as did many of his people and dozens of the poor Hindus. With that rubbing, I felt that they were telling me thanks for trying and that somehow they would find another place and build little houses to live in for a time, at least. Some people know how to encourage others. Those people did. I didn't worry about being kicked out of the country. Perhaps hundreds of Muslim people would have been ready to stand with me against that violent man who was crude, mean, and had an almost impossible way of life. You lose some but I had not lost that one. Good, in time, always wins. Evil is blessed by the devil. Good is blessed by Almighty God. We wait for His time.

A man from a village that I had never visited knocked at our door. He was one of several new believers in Jesus in his village. They were a growing church with hopefully a bright future for their Lord.

This man told me that I needed to go quickly to that village. The problem was these new church people were former Hindus. On the property where they were building a little building to serve as their worship center, they had cut down a tulsi tree. That kind of tree is sacred to many Hindus.

But the trouble had really blossomed when a Hindu soldier serving in the Bangladesh army came home for a visit. It is my understanding that there are not many Hindus serving in this army so maybe this one was particularly proud of his achievement and now had found an opportunity to express his authority.

He had warned these Christians who had cut down the tulsi tree that he was going to have their houses destroyed. A soldier in a small village like this carries a good amount of clout, or maybe he was just testing those new Christians.

Anyway, I was immediately on my way with this man who had come for me. As we drove, then rode a boat and then walked, we had time to talk so he gave me a full description of what was happening. We lost no time as we traveled. We reached the village just before darkness. The last part of the boat ride had been across fields where the water was about two feet deep. Several times as we made the long journey, the boat would drag on the earth which would hinder our progress for a short time.

When we arrived in the village, all of the people understood who I was though only a few of them had seen me in other places during the past few months. But the soldier was present. I wasn't sure, but I thought that he possibly was looking for some big money as a bribe. If so, he had a losing cause. His threats went beyond himself. He threatened to bring other soldiers into that village for doing what he wanted done. I wasn't impressed.

The primary thing I did was to say publicly that these people were no longer Hindus and that they had the right to cut down a tree on their own property. The soldier's reply was that the tree was sacred and that no one had any right to destroy it. Darkness was rapidly approaching. We had to do something quickly. I surely did not want to be walking and then riding in that little boat after dark. But what to do?

As He usually does, my God gave us an answer through a group of three or four Muslim men from a nearby village. Their reply was that these Christians had the right to cut down the tree because it was not sacred to them any longer. The Muslim leader said that they supported the Christians in what they had done.

There was a lot of rumbling among all who were present. I was nearing the end of a longtime missionary career but never expected I would be caught in such circumstances. I had to be or at least to appear, relaxed as if I had all of the time in the world to work on this problem.

So after the Muslims had spoken, I said to the soldier, "You can be assured that if you destroy any property of these church people, then I will go to your army base and explain in detail anything and everything you have done." I meant just exactly that. The soldier departed, but the Muslim group told him before his departure that if he harmed anyone or destroyed anything, they would give their support to the Christians.

I was soon free to depart for that long journey home by walking in the darkness, with no light for I had forgotten to take a light of some kind when I had left our house quickly, early that afternoon. With the beautiful moon shining and brightening our way through the water, we eventually reached my vehicle. That mini van ride let me know how physically and emotionally tired I really was. Through the years of living in East Pakistan and now Bangladesh, I had heard many times that Muslims felt if Hindus were not going to become Muslims, then they wanted them to become Christians. Perhaps for some Muslims, that was true.

Now, in this twenty-third chapter, I am ready to write my final story about LIVING WITH MUSLIMS. You have surely noted as you have read this story that often I depended on highly responsible Muslim government officers when I really needed help. You have also noted the times that many Muslim government officers have depended on me for things they might not be able to do but that I could do.

That is why I saved this story to be the last in this book. I guess, down deep, this will make me feel better, but not older by any means.

It happened during the Gulf War. Although Bangladesh had many of her soldiers serving with the allies at that time, many Muslim leaders were opposed to any USA presence on Islamic soil. You read earlier a story about the attempted attack on our house and how our God so beautifully intervened.

Well, this was in January, 1991. Twenty young boys, some of them not even teenagers, along with one man who was probably about fifty years of age, were taken on a long journey. They were taken by a "broker," who had promised their families he would find jobs for them on the other side of India in Pakistan.

These were very poor families but they got money together for the broker and the journey began. According to the story given to me by a very high ranking government official, who was involved deeply in the security of Bangladesh, the man did take those twenty-one job seekers all the way across India and entered Pakistan. Most of this first part of the story came from that government officer whom I will call Mr. S. P.

On entering Pakistan, the broker deserted those job-hunters. They were helpless. They had no money. The broker had all of the money and he was gone. They were arrested as illegal aliens and jailed. After some time and I understand lots of pressure from different groups, the Pakistani government sent those young men back to Bangladesh by plane.

Now another arrest was carried out in Bangladesh upon their arrival at the airport in Dhaka. The reason for the arrest—somebody had to pay for those plane tickets.

They were taken to the police station nearest the international airport. Then they were transferred to the central or primary jail of that entire country. Though their personal bags were left at the airport police station, for reasons beyond me, they were forgotten in that massive jail.

My friend, Mr. S. P. went to visit the jail as part of his responsibilities. He was checking on the security of the jail for there was a very high former government official in the jail and there had been reports that certain political groups were going to attempt to break into the jail and rescue that person.

With the Gulf War and with this highly recognized former government official in the jail, it was a tough time for my friend. At that time, the Chief Justice of the Supreme Court in Bangladesh was Acting President.

My involvement began when this Mr. S. P. called and requested me to come to his office. I went immediately. He had gone to the jail to inspect it for security and discovered those twenty boys and the older man. He was shocked and then he began telling me the story.

He had a problem and that problem was the amount of money owed. That debt, if I understood correctly, was with one government department. Anyway, the money had to be deposited with the federal security or some such part of the government and then the person with the receipt could take that group from the central jail.

What a mess! He said that if we could find the money from some source, we could get them out of jail. I said without hesitating, "I can find the money." Of course, I did not know where I would find three thousand US dollars, but I went to work and found it.

I returned to the office of Mr. S. P the next day with the receipt in my hands and passed it on to him. My colleague James Young went with me at my request. James and I spent a long time in Mr. S. P.'s office. We were especially interested in his answering the phones.

There were eight phones and each was a different color with a little light on top which was how he knew which of the phones was ringing. We were amazed to sit there and hear him give all kinds of instructions. A phone rang. He answered it and listened for a short time and then began giving orders. The more of that James and I heard the more we knew we needed to get out of that office.

Suddenly, we knew for sure that the time for our departure had arrived. The phone rang. Mr. S. P. answered and he didn't talk but the person calling did all of the talking except for the "Yes Sir" which we heard over and over. Neither of us doubted who was making that call. It was the Acting President.

When he finally completed that call I said to him, "Mr. S. P., we must get out of this office right now. We have no right to hear national secrets."

We received a clear response, "If I need someone to be in my office at such times, I am pleased to have the two of you." I thought, but we are foreigners. He continued speaking to us, "If there is anybody whom I can trust, it is the two of you." We remained until he gave us permission to depart.

Meanwhile, I had another problem since he had told me how to get the young men or at least fourteen of them and the older man out of the jail. There was some complication about the others which I did not understand. I was not about to ask James to go with me the next day so I thought of what else I needed to do before we departed.

I knew this much. I needed a few police vehicles to travel to that jail in the old part of the city, for any American at that Gulf War time was in danger. I asked for police vehicles to accompany me the next morning. Mr. S.P. replied immediately, "No it is better for you to go alone. If there are police accompanying you they will only draw attention and they are much more likely to be attacked than you are." Okay. That was it.

It was interesting that Betty never objected to my doing such things. Maybe she felt as much a part of what I did as if she were doing it. I accepted that without question. Early the next morning I was ready for making that journey to the jail.

It could not have been more disturbing for there were constantly groups marching, opposing the USA participation in the Gulf, the land of the Muslims. But as I drove early in the morning, there was little traffic, for most people wanted to avoid the mobs in the streets. I saw none of the mobs and apparently none of them saw me.

There was a mass of people waiting at the front door as if they were waiting for an opportunity to enter the jail. I parked some distance away and I made sure the space in front of my van was open. Of course, I turned the vehicle toward the main road from the jail. Then I began walking toward that mass of people knowing that was my only way into that place.

I gave my entrance permission card to the first guard and he departed. In the meantime, everyone seemed to want to know why I was there and their questions were not friendly. When I told them why I was there their mood changed and you would have thought we were long-lost friends. Many of them were there to find a way to get friends or family members out of that jail.

The guard returned with a high ranking officer, the deputy inspector of jails. I had no choice but to drink tea with him. The moment that was over, I asked for the prisoners. I told him I was to take fifteen people. He agreed that was correct. We walked a short distance and there before me were the fifteen and all of them were squatting. I quickly explained to them what we were going to do.

I was very careful to tell them about the large group of people outside the jail. I told them to remain near me and even what color the vehicle was and exactly where it was parked. I was fearful we would be parted by that mass of people and then I would not be able to relocate all of them.

Actually, I discovered that there was absolutely no possibility of our being separated. They surrounded me so closely I could hardly walk. I opened the large sliding door of the van and the only way I know to say it is they all leaped into the vehicle at the same time. When I counted and knew that I had the entire group, I quickly got into the driver's seat and we got out of that place.

From the jail we went to the near-by police station and collected their personal belongings which had been there for several weeks. Now we didn't try to move so fast, I told them I had money for them to buy their bus tickets and a little extra money for food in route to their home areas. They listened to every word I spoke.

As we made our way to the main bus station, I explained who I was and where in Bangladesh some of my colleagues lived. I encouraged them to meet one or any of my colleagues if they ever had that opportunity. I only knew the general areas to which they were going but did my best by passing other information on to them.

During my last months I met occasionally with Mr. S. P. One day in his office he asked me a very hard question. "Why would any Muslim ever want to leave Islam and become a Christian?" Of course, I was startled because immediately the question tore into my mind—why is he asking me that question? Has he been warned to find out from an old missionary the answer or at least his version of the answer?

Before I could begin my answer, he began answering the question himself. I was startled at the way he had done the questioning. Then I thought, he has been asked to do this, and he can give a report at the top level as if he had gotten an answer from a missionary.

June, 1991, arrived. Our colleagues and others did many beautiful things for Betty and me. One gentleman who was an active cabinet secretary had us in his home with many of his friends present. He was not ashamed in any way to let people know that this Christian missionary couple were friends of his and his wonderful wife. That night when most of the crowd had departed and Betty had gotten into the vehicle with others of our colleagues, the host and his wife came to the door next to the driver's seat.

The two were standing near to me. I looked at his wife and said, "You know I like your husband very much."

Her response was beautiful to a man who knows his wife loves him. As she tugged on his arm, her reply was, "I like him too." And away we went.

Within just a few days, we were ready to depart for the airport and up drove a very nice car and the passenger got out and walked toward me, saying, "Jim, you please ride with me." I did. I rode with him as I went back in 1972 about six months after Bangladesh had become an independent nation. Abdur Rab Chaudhury and I sat in the back seat. He was Secretary of Agriculture for Bangladesh and much of his interest in agriculture had come through our participation in trying to help his country through our Development Service Center.

Our days of Living With Muslims may have come to an end. Though we would hear about many of them and other Muslims as time passed on, we had to now experience the results of September 11, 2001. We could pray for a better day and for greater opportunity to share God's love which has been so beautifully revealed in Jesus the Messiah.

Kindly, patiently read the AFTERWORD.

The "Five" in 1973.

The "Five" in 1974.

Watching the sunrise on Mt. Everest
(after a four hour drive to this perfect location).

AFTERWORD
Part One

To my Christian brothers and sisters wherever they are located:

It is my deep belief that our Muslim friends across our God's massive world need our Jesus the Messiah. So that leaves us with a deep responsibility. No excuse, for any reason, will erase this all important task.

In light of that deep feeling and all-important responsibility, I am making several statements where I think we can become more involved.

First of all, hate must be obliterated from all of our inward feelings or outward expressions of those feelings. For example, rather than hate Osama bin Laden, we should love him in Jesus and for Jesus' sake. Hatred, which I hear expressed so often, must not be part of whom we are as God's people. That leaves us deeply committed to pray for people like bin Laden.

Second, we must be friends with whomever, wherever there is opportunity. If there is no opportunity for friendship, then we need to begin the search and find at least some opportunity for a relationship with Muslim people who are around us.

Some Muslims who fear we are trying to make Christians out of them will probably not want any kind of relationship with us. So, be kind to them in whatever relationships you may be able to establish. Begin by inviting them to your home for dinner. One thing which can be done at that time is to ask one of them to get something out of your refrigerator to help you with serving dinner or simple light refreshments. Remember that many, or maybe even most, have heard from childhood that Christians drink alcoholic beverages. Of course, they will see there are no such drinks in your refrigerator.

Included in friendships is the responsibility to share a New Testament and if done with kindness, anytime is acceptable for sharing God's Word with them so they can read it when they have opportunity. On one occasion, as I was moving the last of our family belongings out of our house in Feni, my beloved "Farmer Friend,"

Alam Chasi, asked me for a copy of a New Testament as he was watching me pack those priceless copies into a box. I gave him a copy and he replied quietly but so that I could hear him, "Maybe this will help me understand why you seem to want to help us so much." Without uttering my reply, I thought, "That book will help you understand me."

Many months ago here in Louisville, Kentucky, we invited a Muslim family into our home for dinner. They accepted the invitation but before our actual time together, this family asked us to visit them for dinner in the apartment where they were living temporarily. This family certainly was a distinguished couple and their son, and we had beautiful times together during their short visit in the United States.

After this family returned to their home country, I received an e-mail from the father asking me that if I ever visited their home country, to please stay with them and that they would not have any other guests during the time I was with them. To you, as a reader of *Living With Muslims,* I say that if I have opportunity to visit the country of this family, I certainly will spend some of my time with them.

One of the best things which can happen to a Christian family is to have time with a Muslim family. You will remember reading the brief account of the young college student in Feni who walked with me from downtown to our residence. Remember that he asked me if I had a picture of a naked American woman which I would give him. It is for sure, this young man thought of Christians as being heathen to the core and his request revealed that he had heard this through the years. But for sure, my family was the first western Christian family he had ever known anything about. So, maybe he didn't consider that he thought badly about us but this was just the way of western Christians in general. This event happened early in our eight years in Feni and I never heard any more about the subject which he had presented that day. For sure, during the early days of the war for the independence of Bangladesh, if many local people had believed we were that kind of people, we would have been in great difficulty.

I wish I could remember where I had been at that time, but at least I remember that I was flying with my family into Dhaka, which was my home at that time. One of my most interesting conversations ever was with a gentleman from the country of The Sudan. As we landed at the airport, he said to me, "I wish I did not have to go the hotel because I would like to stay with you during my time in Dhaka." He, an African Muslim and I, an American international missionary, had experienced a beautiful time on that flight and I wished I could spend days talking with him. He understood little about the Christian faith. He also spoke little about Islam for I could tell he knew practically nothing about his religion. He had never read the Quran in his own language though he said he had known Arabic well from the time of his childhood. That gentleman was serving with the United Nations.

On one occasion I was invited to a dinner by the United States Ambassador. The dinner was given to honor the Director of the Agency for International Development of the United States. I had ridden a boat out of the stairway of our house to a road location which was not under water due to a massive flood. From that point I had ridden a baby taxi to the place of the dinner. Of course being invited to such an occasion was surely an honor for me but I wasn't able to do very much with that honor that evening.

However, one of the people whom I met was a high court lawyer of Bangladesh. He was not impressed with me when he understood I was just an international missionary. That was okay since I was not too impressed with him. Undoubtedly the reason I had received an invitation was because of the number two person in our embassy who had told me one day about his awareness of what we were doing with our Development Service Center. He had said something like this, "You folks are doing more with your thousands of dollars than our government is doing with our millions of dollars." So, you can understand why I wasn't too much troubled by the opinion of the high court lawyer.

In the course of the evening, I had a great conversation with a man whom I counted to be one of, if not the most helpful citizen of Bangladesh, when it came to helping the poor "helping themselves." This gentleman was a Ph.D. graduate of Vanderbilt University. He usually addressed me as Colonel Jim because I was a Kentucky Colonel like tens of thousands of others. The few times I talked with this gentleman were most helpful. Near the end of our conversation that night he asked, "But Colonel Jim, how did you get here tonight?" He knew our area of the city was under water as parts of the area where he lived were also. I told him how I had made the journey and I was wearing a dress suit. How did I get home that night? That gentleman drove me to the point where the road boats were available and from there, our stairway wasn't but a short distance.

Of course the point is that I wanted you as a reader to hear the above stories but also as a committed Christian, that you never fear "put downs," but know that your God will honor you more than you even need to be honored in every effort you make for Him.

The most important thing for us as believers in Jesus, who has done everything that could ever be needed, is to live out our faith wherever we are.

Third, we must be proper in our relationships with our Muslim friends. Proper dress, especially for women, is a must. Our friends must be able to understand that we are not the "Hollywood type," and we as men do not need to be western even by shaking hands with a Muslim woman. Christian women should not extend their hands for a handshake with a Muslim man. I will list books which I think might be of help to you in learning from others who understand. These scholars who have written of their expertise in different areas can help us. When our first two daughters went to India for high school study, a family friend had a son who was going to the same school to begin his high school study. I traveled with our daughters and the mother traveled with her son. All of these details were known by that woman's husband. On our return trip from the school in route back to Bangladesh, we rode by taxi for about one hundred and fifty miles. We stayed overnight at a YMCA hotel in New Delhi, India.

Let me say that I know of no woman who has ever acted more properly to me than that Muslim woman on that trip to and from the school of our children. We, as two families, had known each other for years before this trip happened and we are friends until this very day. Some people might have called what we did as being questionable, but I do not think so. But care must be taken because some people base what they know on news and some news travels rapidly. In a Muslim country that news may get additions as it goes from one person to another. You know how that also happens to us and our kind too often.

Fourth, we must be willing to give special attention to learning about Islam, the religion of Muslim people. I have stated earlier that I am going to mention some books about Islam which have been written by both Christians and Muslims. Some of the Muslim writers will be the philosophical types. The books written by Christians will be of the more conservative type, at least in my opinion.

Fifth, we must be willing to act in every area of life with our best possible understanding of God's Holy Word, the Bible. Many of us will probably look for more answers from the New Testament than from the Old Testament. But we must never overlook the Ten Commandments of the Old Testament in Exodus 20:3-17. However, we will, along with that, remember the beautiful summary of the Commandments as Jesus gave them in Matthew 22:37-39. One translation says of those three verses, And He (Jesus) said to them, "You shall love the Lord, your God with all your heart, and with all your soul, and with all your mind. This is the great and foremost commandment. The second is like it, you shall love your neighbor as yourself."

Part Two
To Muslim People Across The World
I Kindly Write The Following:

Please remember that my family and I lived with Muslim people for over three decades.

First, some of my dearest friends were those with whom I had the deepest of relationships. Remember the Secretary of Agriculture, the S.P., and Alam Chasi, my dear friend, who loved his missionary friend enough to do anything to help him. Also remember the elderly man whose son I pulled out of a filthy ditch and took home. He was so drunk that I hate alcohol to this day. Also remember the kind treatment to my family in 1971 when there was no law in East Pakistan, or at least in Feni, or Noakhali. You have read about all of these people earlier in this book.

I mention the above so that maybe you will not be too angry at me for what I write about Muslims or about your religion, Islam.

Please, if there is ever opportunity, read the Bible carefully. Kindly remember that in history there have been attempts to destroy that Book but all of those attempts have failed because it is God's Word and not man's word. So, today, after these many years, we have that Book in hundreds of languages and we want that Book to be in every language so that all people can read for themselves or listen as others read it in their mother language.

Second, since September 11, 2001, when the attack was made on America as a nation, many people here in the United States have decided that Islam is a violent religion. We all know of ugly behavior on the part of many leaders in religion and those in national governments who have been guilty of the most wicked behavior through the years. However, I believe that many Muslims along with many Christians believe that we are now living in a civilized time. So, let's get away from heathen behavior, which brings the death of many people, friends of yours and maybe mine.

Third, the current situation in our world where there is so much violence seems to be one of the darker ages of history. Consider the places where there is an attempt to destroy people based on religion.

We are living with killings based on religion. Is there not a special relationship with Almighty God for His human creation? How will others have opportunity for a turning to The God if they are killed before that opportunity comes to them?

Fourth, you know, or you would not be reading a book written by a Christian missionary, that we must know each other better and if we do know each other better, then we will not attempt to destroy one another. Destroying others is what the heathen people would do.

Fifth, I do the following growing out of my experience of living with one country's people for almost thirty-four years and many Americans asking me. Since September 11. 2001, I have found myself thinking about the people of Bangladesh where by far the largest percentage of the people are Muslims and most of them are not a violent people. I have considered, without any statistical help because such is absolutely not available about any country, that most of the Muslims I knew in Bangladesh would never have thought of killing me or my family. In fact, they did just the opposite. I sometimes think that at least ninety percent of these people are of that kind. Then, there are others, whom I call "philosophers," who would claim that they have all of the answers; most are not very much involved in the daily life of the common people. Among those who write books, some seem to be cowards and are afraid to write what they really believe.

But then according to news sources in more recent months, there are those who certainly call themselves "terrorists," and they claim the Muslim's Holy Quran as their source for action. I probably knew some of them during the Pakistan independence movement but I spent most of my time with those of the ninety percent group mentioned above. Surely, in Bangladesh, there are less than five percent of the Muslim people who would be called terrorists.

In all of the confusion and killing currently, I find myself praying more than ever before, not only for myself, my family and my committed Christian friends, but for others in Almighty God's world. I am not ashamed to say that I pray for Osama bin Laden. I do not think I am simply dreaming when I say I would like to be able to talk with him in his language or in my language. I believe I would tell him that I would pray for him to find a life other than that of attempting to kill other human beings, because we are all God's creation. He gave everyone the breath of life when they came into this world or else we would not be.

Let me also ask you to understand that all western people are not Christians. You know that all Americans are not even Christians and are insulted if they are even considered Christians. Christian women are not the Hollywood movie type which you see in movie theaters. I fear that much of the Islamic world thinks of Christian women when they view a filthy western movie. That is far from the truth. How I wish that all the world could understand what a true Christian woman is like such as what the people of Feni, East Pakistan/ Bangladesh, understood about my wife, Betty.

I think it is only right that the philosophical Muslims who are true scholars would speak out more loudly and clearly if they have something about the Quran which all Muslims should know. But I fear that those scholars are fearful of speaking how they truly feel and understand. If what you know or understand is truth, then why fear speaking that truth?

Part Three
To The Western World:

I say wake up before it is too late. The God of righteousness tolerates much but He may cease His tolerance at His choosing. He will not ask you or us as His true believers, when He will make a change.

There are many things which cause great disruption in our world. One of those is certainly sexual relationships which are outside of God's teaching given in the Bible. An example of what I am talking about is a woman whose beauty is judged by the shape of her breast or at least by the part of her breast which she seems to delightfully show. I grew up with my dad, one brother, my mother and five sisters. Though the house in which we lived was small, I never thought that I should try to get to see the differences in my dad, my brother and me as opposed to my mother and my sisters. If you truly love someone of the opposite sex, then surely it is not because of the particular shape of parts of the human body. What about those who are crippled from birth? I am truly amazed at some of those who spend their lives together with someone of the opposite sex whose body is what we ordinarily called dysfunctional or at least shaped unusually. True love is more than the body.

In some circles, you may see a person and say something like, "Isn't she beautiful?" Or maybe, though less likely, "Isn't he hand-some?" Someone else might say, "I hadn't noticed." Then, as you and others continue to watch, all may agree, "Yes, her behavior is almost perfect." Or "His behavior is surely something, isn't it?"

What I have attempted to say in the above two paragraphs is that we truly must judge others primarily by their behavior, not on parts of their physical bodies. Have you ever noted a former movie star and say, "She surely has lost her beauty." I have noted, and I am sure you have noted some older people and said something like, "It is amazing how good they look."

Don't feel too bad toward me for the above, please. Of the nine or ten largest Muslim countries or groups of Muslims, in the world, I have spent considerable time in four of those and those four have the four largest groups of Muslims in the world. In being in those countries often and many times with Betty and our children, I never thought of being afraid. I am not sure, however, that I would feel that way today. I love Muslim people just as much now as I did when I was with them, but things in our world have changed. September 11 may be the cause of most of those changes. The radical groups in Islam have caused some of us in the free world to take a different look. Most of us probably blame some Muslims and some of us totally blame all Muslims.

But all of us as Americans and citizens of other western countries must watch our arrogance. It is not our responsibility to express arrogance by speaking or writing about all of our accomplishments. At times I think our friends, the friends of America, in the world today are primarily those whom we are at this particular time in history helping. If we were not helping them is it not possible that they would hate us? Maybe there is such hatred and jealousy but they choose not to express that for they want the help to continue. We do not need to boast every time we help someone else or even help another nation. In recent years, when the Berlin Wall fell, some of us began to think of an all together different time for our world. Some of us, with maybe not much understanding of such, thought we were moving toward years of peace and working together across the world. But now, China and North Korea have become more assertive in today's world. No less assertive is Iran. Either they have, or will have if things continue as they are, the most volatile of weapons, possibly with no restrictions on where they use them.

What I have just said means to me that we need Almighty God. At the same time, we must admit that we do not necessarily have a special arrangement with Him as Westerners. The point is that we must honor Him and live as He has beckoned us to live—that is, according to His Word.

We, as a nation must clean up or better said, be cleaned up. I have seen only one movie by going to a movie theater since retirement in 1992. I have seen probably hundreds of movies on television. So, today we have it all, but possibly the most dangerous for our children and grandchildren and for all of us is the Internet. While we might guard against the movie house and even television, the use of the computer is so enticing and so readily available, partly because the Internet can be so helpful for the young and the old. We must find ways to guard our children from some areas of the Internet.

For thirty four years my family and I were a part of the East or more particularly, South Asia. I believe the stories told in this book have indicated that we lived through some tough times. Most of that time, we did not live in fear. Again, at times, we may have been afraid, but that fear usually passed before it harmed our attitude.

Part Four
So, Where Does All Of This Leave Us?

Where does it leave the western part of the world? Where does it leave those of us who are believers and are not, according to God's Word, supposed to be selfish?

Though our country may be powerful enough to blast some small countries off the face of the earth, we are not powerful enough to find the terrorists scattered across God's massive world in the mountains, in the valleys, in the towns, in the cities, on the ocean and other smaller areas of water, and even in the rural areas and such seemingly safe places, again out across the world.

SO, WHERE DOES THAT LEAVE US? Hopefully, we are willing to live for our God. We know how to live for Him by looking at how Jesus the Christ or the Messiah (Isa Masih) lived and died and lived again. May we learn from Him and for His glory.

BOOKS ON ISLAM OR ABOUT MUSLIMS

1. A *History of The Arab Peoples,* by Albert Hourani, Warner Books, 1991.

2. *The Life of Muhammad,* by A. Guillaume, A translation of Ibn Ishaq's Sirat Rasul Allah, Oxford University Press, 1978. Do your best to locate this book.

The Life and Times of Muhammad, by Sir John Glubb, Cooper Square Press, 1998.

The Life and Work of Muhammad, by Yahiya Emerick, Alpha, A Pearson Education Company, 2002.

Muhammad, A Biography of The Prophet, Karen Armstrong, Harper, 1992.

3. *Islam,* by Caesar E. Farah, Barron's, 2000.

Islam Under Siege, by Akbar S. Ahmed, Polity Press, 2003.

What's Right With Islam, by Imam Feisal Abdul Rauf, J Harper, 2004.

4. *Miniskirts, Mothers & Muslims, A Christian Woman in a Muslim Land,* by Christine A. Mallpuhi, Monarch Books, 2004.

Voices Behind the Veil, Ergun Mehmet Caner, General Editor, Kregel Publications, 2003. (All of the writers are women.)

The Trouble With Islam Today, A Muslim's Call for Reform in Her Faith, by Irshad Manji, St. Martins Griffin, 2003.

(McKinley thinks of her as a far-out radical Muslim woman.)

5. *Islam, A Popular Dictionary of,* by Ian Richard Netton, NTC Publishing Group, 1997. (There are many such dictionaries).

6. Books by Christian Authors:

Islam and America, by George Braswell, Broadman & Holman, 2005.

What You Need To Know About Islam & Muslims, by George Braswell, Broadman & Holman, 2000.

Unveiling Islam, by Ergun Caner and Emir Coner, Kregel Publications, 2002.

Is The Father of Jesus The God Of Muhammad? by Timothy George, Zondervan, 2002,

Islam, An Introduction For Christians, edited by Paul Varo Martinson, Augsburg, 1994.

The Unseen Face of Islam, by Bill Musk, Mark, 1989.

The Cross and The Crescent, by Phil Parshall, Tyndale, 1989.

Understanding Muslims Teachings and Traditions, by Phil Parshall, Baker Books, 1994.

Reasoning From The Scriptures With Muslims, by Ron Rhodes, Harvest House Publishers, 2002.

7. *Why The Rest Hates The West,* by Meic Pearse, Inter Varsity Press, 2004.

Christians, Muslims, And Islamic Rage, by Christopher Catherwood, Zondervan, 2003.

8. *Saddam King of Terror,* by Con Coughlin, Harper Collins Publishers Inc., 2002

Taliban, by Ahmed Rashid, Yale University Press, 2001.

In The Name Of Osama bin Laden, by Roland Jacquard, Duke University Press, 2002.

Bin Laden, The Man Who Declared War On America, by Yossef Bodansky, Prima Publishing, 2001.

The Osama bin Laden I Know, by Peter L. Bergen, Free Press, 2006.

A usual load of Bangladesh passengers.

The boy mourning the death of his father.

This well, in our front yard, giving water to thousands during a flood.